The Forbi
Zone 1940

CONTENTS

The Forbidden Zone 1940

Anne Angelo

To order additional copies of this book, contact:
Xlibris
AU TFN: 1 800 844 927 (Toll Free inside Australia)
AU Local: (02) 8310 8187 (+61 2 8310 8187 from outside Australia)
www.Xlibris.com.au
Orders@Xlibris.com.au
838783

NOTE FROM THE AUTHOR

This is a continuation of my story in 'A Sprig of White Heather and a Scottish Lass' Very soon after Britain declared war on Germany, I returned to France, crossing the Channel in a fishing boat.

My hotel was used to billet French military personnel initially, and later, the British Expeditionary Forces, the BEF. Sometimes this resulted in me fighting for my honour, as these men, or boys as many of them still were, tried to fill a personal void in their lives.

One day as I was out driving, I collided with a British Army car. This was my meeting with Gerald, and the start of a relationship which was to grow beyond my wildest dreams.

For a time I joined the ambulance drivers, but this proved to be fraught with danger, and after two brushes with death I resigned.

Then in mid-1940, the German Army thrust down into the north of France, where Lille is situated. Gerald had to move on. Destiny was taking him from me with agonising uncertainty, but I knew I must survive and find him again, somewhere.

I had left my departure too late, and I found myself in amongst the swarms of refugees. After four days of being under air attack, being diverted, and driving through razed towns strewn with the bodies of the civilian population, I finally reached the comparative tranquility of Paris. But this in turn fell, and once again I found myself fleeing, this time to Brittany. I tried desperately to get a ship to England, but I was in the wrong place at the wrong time, and despaired as I saw my last chance disappearing out to sea.

With the German occupation established, civilian life in France was initially encouraged to return to normal. I could not get back to England, I saw no point in staying in Brittany, so I returned to my home in Lille.

Lille was in the Forbidden Zone, an area in the north of France which Hitler had decreed was to be cordoned off—his springboard for the invasion of Britain. Life was difficult through lack of food, heating, and medicine—made worse by the oppressive Germans who often took delight in worsening our plight. A few days in jail became a frequent occurrence for me, and I was labelled as a 'British hostage', under threat of punishment for any assistance given by the French to any escaping British servicemen.

Before long, I became involved in the Resistance, helping those very same British servicemen to escape.

As their easy first victories began to falter, the Germans increased their cruelty towards the civilian population. Life became desperate.

To make matters worse for me, a member of our organisation gave information to the Germans. I found myself with a price on my head, and I had to assume a false identity until I could escape. Firstly, I tried to take a fishing boat across the Channel, and had actually started out to sea before I was forced to hastily retreat to avoid detection. After a short stay in Lille, I once again set off, this time hidden in an orange crate on the back of a lorry to cross the Somme, and then on to Paris. From there it was across the demarcation line into unoccupied France and to neutral Monte Carlo. After consolidating my position, I set off through the South of France, through Spain, to Portugal, where I hoped to get passage through the U-boat gauntlet to England. As it turned out, I had to take a coastal collier to Gibraltar, and then travel by convoy to Scotland.

After a short stay at home, I was off to London. I took employment managing a restaurant, and continued to enquire after Gerald. Where could I find him? I need not have worried, though, for it was he who found me. And with that reunion, the whole war seemed to have ended.

CHAPTER 1

Reflections

GERALD CAME AND went; life dragged on. We all wondered what Hitler was planning for us. Gerald told us nothing. I had finished with ambulances and whatever they were carrying. The young men from the BEF came and went and helped to drink my cellar dry, but I didn't care, I felt that I would not be able to hang on to this house once the Germans arrived in France. From what I'd heard about their behaviour in Poland, I had no illusions about us. I suddenly became afraid for Gerald. We'd had such wonderful moments in the past few months that I'd come to idolize him. We loved each other so dearly it seemed almost impossible to imagine both of us in our own separate corners surviving what was to come; and seeing the skies black with planes all day, I knew it was going to be sheer murder.

He'd arrived in the night, red eyed and looking so exhausted. I was sure he hadn't slept for quite a long time. He'd told me to leave as the Germans were butchering everybody in their paths. I said I would, but as I gazed down on the streaming masses of refugees who kept passing in an unbroken line, I could not bear the thought of joining them, even though I knew I must.

I turned away from the window and gazed around my room, and my mind went back to the day I arrived in this beautiful house in Lille. I knew I would lose everything I'd come to love and cherish if I were not here to protect it; but when I looked down at the screaming refugees, I knew deep down I could never save it.

I could remember vividly the day I arrived. Not so many years ago, but so much had happened in that time that it seemed like another life. Going through those plate glass doors was breathtaking. It was like entering a cathedral. A huge foyer went up the full three stories to the roof, which was stained glass. The sunlight coming through bathed everything in rosy pink. A grand staircase curved up from left to right around the far wall. The walls all the way up were cream tiles. Hanging from the ceiling a magnificent chandelier sparkled and shimmered like a huge diamond. There must have been a thousand crystal droplets. Against the wall, in the curve of the staircase, a huge gilt mirror reflected the mass of flowers in front of it. 'Breathtaking' was the only word. My room was like stepping into French history. Like a vision in rose and silver, it was so utterly feminine it simply breathed romance. It could have been a room for Marie Antoinette or Josephine. Cream table curtains in a crossover style gave it a personal and intimate air. Heavy drapes in blush rose brocade held back during the day would hang loose at night and guarantee a restful sleep. A rose satin eiderdown gleamed softly through the lace bedspread on the luxurious bed. Elegant with silk cushions, a hand-carved chaise-longue stretched invitingly. The exquisite Louis IV writing desk was romance itself, as was the perfectly matched dressing table with its delicately carved legs and fragile wing mirrors, and near it, a huge door which opened into an exquisite bathroom.

What a contrast to the stark life in Scotland where I'd been brought up. Some people think we ourselves are responsible for what we become, but it's not so. What we are is almost completely due to things beyond our control. We make some decisions—yes, of course, but they're really only relatively small ones. Even they are made in the light of what's happened to us in the past. Shakespeare makes Cassius in Julius Caesar say, 'The fault, dear Brutus, is not in our stars but in ourselves that we are underlings.' But he is wrong. What we are is basically in our stars and not in ourselves. 'Stars' is nothing to do with it. It plans the circumstances and environment into which we are born. Primarily, we are the result of the genes we inherit from our parents. After we're born, the lives our parents have lived have their effect on us. We are further shaped by the place we live, the climate, and what happens to us in our formative years. Everybody we meet has an influence on us, either for good or bad. I'd tolerated my father's harsh treatment while growing up, not because I wanted to, but because I had no choice. I hoped I had not inherited his heartlessness and selfishness. Looking back, I wondered how my brother, Peter, who was two years younger than me, and I could possibly have survived the punishments meted out to us at the tender age of eleven and thirteen.

I recalled the time when Peter learnt to ride motorbikes and drive cars. Father had about a dozen little Standards, Morrises, Cowleys, and Oxfords, a De Dion Bouton which I hated, and a Lancia which was so big I could hardly reach the pedals. These and more were hired out to the officers of the Royal Navy when they came to Scotland in spring and autumn for manoeuvres in the North Sea. How I loved to see them steaming in!

We used to wait till Father went out somewhere and then find out which way the one and only constable was going, then take one of the cars out and go off in a different direction. But after we successfully evaded everybody for quite some time, Father found out. He didn't let on, but he fixed the brakes on the Morris Cowley so that they wouldn't work and I would probably be killed on the hills. I was on a lovely bit of straight road when, suddenly, I came to a humped stone bridge with a sharp bend. The brakes didn't work, and I hit the bridge. I went out over the top and hit the river, or burn as the Scots call them. When I woke up, I was in water up to my chin, with an awful headache and a twisted ankle. When I crawled up the rocks and got out, I could see the Morris some distance away in a field. There were some aeroplanes there too. I was crawling to it when two airmen found me, carried me to their shed, and gave me some tea laced with brandy. According to them, the crumpled mudguard had acted as a brake and saved me. We never found the dickie seat from the back. It had probably ended up in the river. They had a look at the brakes and found that someone had taken the split pin out of the rod. They seemed to think it was deliberate. From what Father had said, Mother guessed he'd done it on purpose.

The annual Highland games were coming up, and Father said I could drive the bus. He said if I wanted driving, then he'd give me all the driving in the future. I was terrified. I thought he'd fix things again and this time I would be killed. Mother tried to argue with him, but it was useless. He could see I was on the verge of hysterics when the day arrived, but he calmly tied a money pouch round my waist and placed a two-gallon benzene tin behind my back, started the bus up, and told me to get on with it. I wished it would backfire and break his arm, but it didn't. It started straight off, and I was on my way, with only about a foot to spare on either side of the narrow road till I got to the fountain in High Street. I couldn't see to reverse, so I had to go round the fountain to turn. Somehow, I managed, and Father counted the money I brought home and found it correct, but I had kept two shillings and sixpence in tips which I split up three ways—Mother, Peter, and me—and it gave us a brilliant idea for making money for ourselves.

When the fleet came in, Peter and I had to be around the garage all day at the weekends hiring out the cars, motorbikes, and bicycles. We had to fill the cars with benzene. One day one of the stewards asked us if we knew where they could get some flowers. We said we'd get them from the nursery. And so we launched our first business venture, selling flowers which we kept in a bucket of water. We took it in turns to stand at the top of the pier with them. We doubled our money each time.

Soon Father had me driving the naval officers to the lakes to fish or to the hills to shoot. They were wonderful days. I found some wonderful places—places where no one had ever been before. The mist would be lifting, and it would be all clean and new. As the clouds lightened, it would get clearer, and all the colours would come up out of the ground. There would be pale mauves and greys and blues and greens all mixing together like in a dream.

I didn't want to remember Father's cruelty when he wanted me to leave school, but between Dr McKay and the headmaster, I managed to stay on till I had my leaving certificate. I had to work even harder than before to compensate for staying on in school, or the academy as it's known in Scotland; but I didn't mind as Peter and I had started selling whisky which we bought at the distillery next door to the nursery. I sometimes wondered what they thought at that distillery, probably that we were buying it for Father and his cronies. The Special Review week was marvellous for us. We got through four cases. I was beginning to get nervous, but Peter only laughed.

ANNE ANGELO

The base was full of ships, and our whisky was going like hotcakes. I'd just taken two more bottles to Peter down along the pier. There were only two left. Then we'd have to go and get some more. I was working out how many gallons we were going to get through and how much we were going to make if it kept up like this. Standing by the garage door was Lord Louis Mountbatten. His photo had been in the papers a lot. He was in full dress uniform, all white and gold. He had his hands on his hips and looked annoyed.

'Come on, young miss,' he said. 'Get a move on. I'd like ten gallons please.'

I nearly burst out laughing. I thought 'Ten gallons! Golly, what a party someone's going to have. The whole fleet will be tiddly. Ten gallons in one pop. Wait till Peter hears about that. We'll have to go and get it for them.'

I walked on air.

'Yes, sir,' I said as I got closer. 'That'll be all right. We can do that for you. More if you want. The only thing is though, you'll have to wait a wee while. We'll have to go out and get it for you first.'

'You'll have to what?' His eyes narrowed, and he looked at me intently. 'What do you mean you'll have to go out and get it for me? Go where? Haven't you got any in the pump?'

And then I saw the big black Bentley standing there. I felt myself going red.

'Oh, you mean benzene?'

'Well, what else do you think I meant? Whisky or something? What else do you sell by the gallon up here?'

It was his 'whisky' that did it. Why would he mention whisky if he didn't know? He must have known and he'd come to catch us. It was only a trap. They were probably down there now grabbing Peter. They'd take us off to prison. I wished I'd never done the flowers. I thought of what it was going to do to Mother. And how Father would crow. He'd love it.

I looked at him, and he was altogether different. He was like the figure of doom standing there. I thought, 'As soon as I've filled him up, he'll make me get in and take me away. I'll probably never even see Mother or Peter again.' I felt so miserable I could have howled.

'Hey hey,' he said. 'Watch what you're doing. I want it in the tank, not all over the ground.'

I hadn't put it in properly, and it was squirting back. When it rang up 10, I stopped and put the hose back in its rest and waited for him to tell me to get in. When he didn't, I looked at him and said, 'Well, there's your ten gallons, sir.'

'Not according to my gauge it's not,' he said sharply. 'Have a look for yourself. It says only 9, and there was a bit in there before you started. You didn't put that much on the ground. I want ten, not nine, miss. I'd like my other gallon please.'

It was too much. Now he'd get me for selling him short. I burst into tears. I hadn't meant to cheat him. I'd forgotten to prime the pump. It was a hand pump. It had to be primed before each sale. It took a gallon to prime. I'd been so flustered I'd forgotten.

'I'm sorry,' I sobbed. 'Please, I didn't want to do it. But it's for Peter. So he can be an engineer.'

'What on earth?' Oh, come on, young miss,' he said. 'It's not as bad as all that. I'm not going to cart you off to prison or make you walk the plank or anything. Just give me my other gallon. There's a good girl. I want to get along.'

As soon as he'd gone, I raced down the pier looking for Peter. He was still there on the edge coaming with his jars of flowers. I told him to throw the whisky over the side. They'd be here any minute.

'Can't,' he said, grinning like mad. 'I've already sold 'em. I'm having a field day. Whiz back up and get the other two bottles. But what's wrong, Slinks? You've been crying. Your face is all tear-stained. Here, bend down.'

I had to wet his hanky with spit. He wiped my face while I told him what had happened.

'You're a big dope, Slinks,' he said. 'We're not doing anything wrong. It's only your guilty conscience. I bet they've known all along. They'd have to. Someone would tell 'em. I'll bet His Nibs is sitting in a mess room somewhere right now enjoying a good snifter of our whisky.'

ANNE ANGELO

Father thought I would work in the garage once I got my leaving, but he was wrong. Dr McKay and the local chemist came to see him and insisted I serve an apprenticeship as a chemist. After much arguing and scowling, he agreed on the condition I gave him 2/6 weekly. Dr McKay lent me books on anatomy and physiology and helped me with my problems. We still sold flowers and whisky when the fleet was in, and used the money to buy engineering books for Peter, who wanted to study by correspondence. Three years passed, and I was walking on air. I'd done it and was ready to face anything. But I hadn't reckoned with Father, who flatly refused to give me the money to go to Edinburgh to sit my exams. I thought I would lose my mind, especially when I looked at my mother's stricken face. There was no way I could outwit him.

I was down at the docks brooding. The fleet wasn't in. Cromarty Firth was rough and grey. It was generally like that just before a storm. It came, tearing in as if it were going to smash up the piers and toss them up on the shore. Great green mountains came rushing in, their glassy sides getting higher and higher. As they got up speed, the tops slid off into white froth. The wind sliced it off and threw it into my face so I couldn't see, and my lips stung with salt. My mind was in such a turmoil it made me feel that the Cromarty Firth and I were kindred spirits. I walked slowly home.

It seems strange how destiny plays a part in our lives. This time it was again through our friend and good Samaritan, Dr McKay. (Years later, when I thought about him, I was almost sure he was in love with Mother without ever saying a word.) A few days later, he handed Peter a copy of *The London Times*, and said we might be interested in looking through the 'Situations Vacant' as it was now too late to sit for the pharmacy examinations. Mother took it and opened the pages. It was a few days old, but one never knew. Suddenly she cried out excitedly, 'Listen to this! "Governess wanted, French family. Must have good French, English and Latin. Apply with recent photograph and copies of two references, to advertiser 241 rue Nationale Lille, France."' If only it hadn't gone, it was made for me. I had a photo taken which I sent on with references from Dr McKay and Mr McPhee, the schoolmaster.

A few days later, a telegram arrived. I'd got the job. Father walked in while we were celebrating. He wouldn't give me money for the fare. 'First you wanted Edinburgh, now you want France. What's the matter with you? You'll stay here where you belong!' he bellowed and then stormed out of the kitchen.

Our faces weren't down for long before Peter returned, almost airborne with joy. He handed Mother quite a large sum of money. 'It was Dr McKay,' he said, grinning with glee. 'I bumped into him, and he asked if Anne had got the job in France. When I said yes but we couldn't get money for her fare, he told me to wait and he'd come back in a few minutes. He did, with Father's account for repairs, and asked me to receipt it as it would save him a trip to the garage, and to give the money to mother—she would know what to do with it. He was as pleased as punch.'

Mother agreed and remarked, 'He's just the loveliest man ever. Oh, but doesn't the Lord work in wonderful ways.' She crossed herself. 'Come on, quickly,' she said. 'There's packing to be done, and you will be on that train tonight for France, to start your new job as governess to that nice Monsieur Le Blanc.'

To me it was like the gates of heaven opening.

I would not be home when Father found out about the money. I pitied the others I was leaving behind. His fury would know no bounds.

Monsieur Le Blanc was a charming man, and his children were adorable—two girls and one boy who went to boarding school—and the youngest, Gilbert, usually had a governess. From our conversation, I gathered that Monsieur Le Blanc spent most of his time away on business, and his wife had died three years previously. He needed somebody reliable to take care of Gilbert and also the house and staff during his absences. A door had closed, and a door had opened; and Father—with his punishments of porridge three times a day, his daily salt herrings, his cruelty and selfishness to Mother—was in the past. The blizzards had been replaced by the sunshine. It was heavenly.

Six months later, I was completely in command of the situation, thanks to Bonne-maman, who taught me so much. Paul's wife was her daughter. There had been a succession of governesses who enjoyed life to the fullest when Monsieur Le Blanc was away, leaving Gilbert alone with the servants who slept two floors above him. This had made her very angry.

She'd taken a great liking to me, so we took holidays all over Europe, and somehow Monsieur Le Blanc did not object as long as I was with Gilbert. They were wonderful years of happiness. I even had the use of a car, a beautiful black Buick. He said I would need it when I was on my own for running the house or taking the children out whenever necessary. Everything I could possibly want was provided for me. I had no potatoes to dig, no flowers and whisky to sell to get myself pocket money, no father demanding nearly all my wages. I banked half and sent the other half home to Mother. I knew she got it. I sent it through Dr McKay.

I'd realised what a horror her life must be. I'd been reared in that life. I'd never known any better. Suddenly I'd been released and found this Paradise. For her it was the opposite. This was the life she'd known. Suddenly she'd been snatched away and taken into that. In place of this lovely warm climate, wealth, and affection, she had freezing blizzards, deprivation, and hatred. For her, there'd be no release, no reprieve. Her letters showed her utter hopelessness. Dr McKay could do no more for her. Her diabetes was getting steadily worse. He said it was as much the misery and isolation as the poor food. The cure was in her own hands. But we knew she would never take it.

The morning we set out for Switzerland is as fresh in my mind as yesterday. It was clear, fresh, and bracing. Autumn was well on its way. Bonne-maman's big opulent Packard was packed and ready to go. They had trouble getting all our suitcases into the boot. Mother's, with its Stewart rug strapped to its side, wasn't among them. It was put away in the back of my wardrobe, along with my Stewart costume and Glengarry. The Scottish tawpie who'd been so proud of them was gone. Bonne-maman had got me everything new. I didn't know it then, but I was the picture of the modern young French female. My ski instructor told me. He taught me lots of things.

The three of us sat together in the back seat: Bonne-maman looking every inch the wealthy aristocrat, Gilbert in the middle looking the perfect golden-haired cherub, and me in the other corner. Gustave, her dignified Swedish chauffeur, firmly closed the door, and with his shiny peaked cap at precisely the correct angle and his blue uniform spotless, climbed into the front and started up. They all waved and wished us 'Bon voyage' and 'Bon chance'. We rolled round the drive, out, and away.

We stopped at Cambrai for lunch. It was at Cambrai I saw my first real parasols. They were in the window of the little boutique next door. They were so dainty and feminine they instantly reminded me of the one Mother had made for me years ago and which Father had torn up.

*   *   *

CHAPTER 2

The Depression Hits

O N RETURNING FROM Switzerland, we went to St Lunaire for the yearly get-together with the grandchildren. It was the last day, and m'sieu came to pick up his three kids. And my world suddenly crumbled and fell to pieces. The depression had caught up with him.

He said he'd had to make changes. He wouldn't be at 241 anymore. Things were too uncertain. He'd shifted to Paris. He'd bought a house. It was smaller, and there was only room for the cook and one maid. He'd have to let the rest of us go. He'd pay me three months in advance, and it would give me time to look for something else. If I wanted to, I could stay on at 241 until the time was up. He was going to sell or let it. If he couldn't in that time, he'd close it up. And he gave me the Buick. He said I'd looked after it so well I deserved it. Then he took his children and left us.

Its utter unexpectedness gave us a shock. Bonne-maman and I didn't go for our usual lovely wander up along the coast. We came straight home. Home? It was no longer my home. It was a house I was living in on borrowed time.

They were all gone. Except Marie-Louise, the housekeeper, who was left in charge with one maid to help her. M'sieu had taken all his personal things but left the furniture and furnishings. Marie-Louise had brought in her old uncle Jacques to do the gardening and her nephew young Jacques for the odd jobs. He was a radical who'd dropped out from the university.

It was impossible to get another place. I tried everywhere. I supposed it was because I was older. They preferred younger ones. And everyone was getting nervous about Germany. Lots of the wealthier families were getting out of the north of France. I wrote everywhere to people I'd met but no one knew of anything. Bonne-maman tried all her friends, but it was no good. I put an advertisement in the local papers.

Governess seeks engagement. Refined Scottish lady, 23, with English, French and Latin, last position 3 years, will go anywhere, very fond of children.

My heart was breaking to see the havoc wrought by this depression. Hundreds of thousands of people thrown out of work, factories closed down, and soup kitchens being set up everywhere. Bonne-maman had not yet left, so I made my way to rue Vauban to see her. How I was going to miss this wonderful old lady. She'd lost both her daughter and her husband in the same year, and now she showered all her love and devotion on Gilbert, some of which rubbed off on me. I ceased to be a governess and had become her protégé and travelled wherever the whim took her, but her favourite spot was the coast of Brittany, where she owned a villa on the cliff of St Lunaire overlooking the sea. I imagined she'd be going there and not to Monaco where she owned an apartment. She didn't use it much but preferred it to hotels on her trips to Italy or Switzerland, as she always travelled by road with her faithful Gustave driving her gleaming black Packard.

When I arrived, she was arranging for the house to be locked up, leaving only the gardener in charge. She suggested I should go with her and Gilbert to St Lunaire, but as much as I loved her, I could not bear the thought of abandoning the home in Lille. She said she had an idea and would ring Monsieur Le Blanc in Paris.

The next day, she arrived, but she didn't look happy. 'So', she said, leaning with both hands on the top of her walking stick and looking from me to Marie-Louise and young Jacques, 'this is what you do all day, is it?' I tried to explain to her how impossible it was to keep it looking as it used to be without enough staff, how hopeless it was.

'Nothing's hopeless at all,' she snapped. 'How do any of you know what the future holds? But that's not the point. You're all still being paid, and you should still be working. Off you go.' She glared at Jacques. 'There's plenty of the day left yet, and you, Anne, come to the study with me. There's no need for any of you to think it's hopeless. You never know what might turn up.'

She waited until Marie-Louise had gone and the door was shut and asked me if I had any money. I told her I had. Not much, but a little. 'Yes', she said with a twinkle in her eye, 'I rather fancy you have. You're a good manager, and you don't waste anything. Well now, I think you could stay on here and run the place as a private hotel. It would be better to have you here than to have it shut up. What do you say to that for an idea?'

It was a fantastic idea, but I couldn't see it had any sense for me. My little bit of money wouldn't last long trying to run a place as big as this—the rent, the food, the bills. 'I wouldn't know how to start,' I said.

'No, of course you wouldn't,' she answered quite sharply. 'And you'll never learn, will you, until you try? Yes, it would be a gamble, but we could send you clients. Everybody isn't bankrupt, you know. There are still Government people, heads of state, important people who will be running around frantically trying to put the country back on its feet. Actually, you should do very well, unless I'm very much mistaken, so give it a try. M'sieu won't charge you any rent. He doesn't really love this house as you do. He's only keeping it for the children, and they can come to me during the holidays. It's a gamble, but I think it will pay off. It needs a competent and trustworthy person to make it a success. You're the most likely person, my dear. Marie-Louise hasn't got the ability. I think he'd be very pleased if he knew you were interested. Well? Will you give it a try?'

I got up and went round behind her and hugged her. I felt I had to do something, and it seemed the most natural. It was a thing I'd often wanted to do. I pressed a kiss into her hair and told her if she could do this for me, I'd be grateful for the rest of my life. And she liked it, although she made out she didn't.

'Now, now', she murmured, gently freeing herself, 'there's no need for any of that, my dear. It's as much for him as it is for you. And you deserve it. You've been a good girl and never let us down. All right, then. I'll see what I can do. But I wouldn't mention it to the others, though. Just in case things go wrong.'

And I didn't. Although they kept asking about my packing. When was I going to get on with it?

It was Thursday afternoon. We had to be out by the Friday. Bonne-maman rang and said it was all settled. The rent would be a nominal one franc a month. I could have it as long as things continued as they were and as long as I looked after the furniture and kept the place in good repair. It could be terminated by six months' notice in writing by either of us. He wished me good luck with it and said he'd send me people if he could.

That was a heady moment. I had the maddest urge to rush round and do crazy things. But I knew I couldn't. Not anymore. Things would have to be different. I think that was when I really grew up. It was like when I'd first walked down those stairs in my new French clothes. I'd put aside everything Scottish and become a new person. Here it was again. I'd put off being a governess and become the mistress. The whole house was mine to do as I pleased. They were my staff. It was a marvellous feeling.

I went and told them. When they all said they'd stay on with me, I got some champagne for them. I thought it was a day to celebrate.

*   *   *

ANNE ANGELO

CHAPTER 3

The Threat Approaches

I T WAS A marvellous success right from the start. I was amazed how easy it was. Everything fell into place as if it had all been there just waiting for me.

The first thing I did was to shift into m'sieu's bureau. It was the master suite. And from it I'd be better able to know what was going on. The small landing where its few steps met the main staircase let me see down into the foyer and out through the portico down to the footpath. The windows at the rear gave me a clear view over the whole garden to the back gates. And the rooms were better. The bathroom was the best in the house. It was a dream. Not only were the tiles and the colour scheme better, but the towel rails were actually chromed hot-water pipes so the towels were always warm and snuggly. There were polished-copper hot-water pipes in the cupboards to keep pyjamas and things heavenly to get into.

It took Heloise and me a full day to do the shifting. It was then I found out how much stuff I had. I'd never have got it all packed. She thought it was silly, me having so much. She thought my parasols especially were crazy.

'But, madame', she said, 'what's the good of them? You can't use them. They'd think you were silly going out with a parasol these days. I don't believe in keeping a lot of junk.'

But they weren't junk. Not to me. Apart from being the most exquisitely feminine things I had, each one was memento. A souvenir of someplace I'd been. Mostly with Bonne-maman. Each one had a story. They represented steps in my development. I hung them along the rail on my wardrobe doors in the order I got them, and they looked lovely.

Then Marie-Louise got me the staff I wanted. I didn't get them all. Only enough to get the place all cleaned up again. Bonne-maman gave us a month and then came and looked us over. She was pleased.

'Yes, my dear,' she said as we came back down the main staircase. 'That's more like it. I knew you could do it. That's much better than the way it was going. He'll be very pleased. Well now, I suppose you're nearly ready for some guests, aren't you? Have you had any response to your advertisements yet?'

I hadn't, and I told her so. She didn't mention it again. But a fortnight later, I had a phone call from Paris asking if I could accommodate a family of four overnight in three days' time. Could I? It sent everybody scurrying like beavers to get ready in time.

I got the rest of the staff. I didn't take Albert the butler. He was a good one, and everybody knew him, but he couldn't see there'd been a change. I was no longer the children's governess to be treated with scorn and condescension. And that was a pity, because I'd had all I wanted of that. So I got a new one. A six-foot ex-Army sergeant major named Alphonse. He was most impressive. I kept old Jacques on as an undergardener and young Jacques as odd jobs. I did that for Marie-Louise although she didn't ask me to. I wanted her to be happy. And it was a good thing I did. The three of them saved my bacon lots of times when the war came.

Those first guests turned out to be the Villeneuves from Morez in the Franche-Comte. We'd called on them when we got back into France after taking the shortcut up the mountain zigzag coming home from the Winter Sports at Lausanne. There were the four of them—the parents and two grown-up daughters. They were holidaying, going through to Norway and Sweden. When I found out that Bon-maman had written them about me and 241, I set out to make their stay as enjoyable as I could. And I must've succeeded. They booked for one night and stayed a week.

The girls were eighteen and twenty-one and about as romantic as I'd been when I first came to Lille. So I put them in my Louis XIV. I thought it would appeal to them. And it did. They were in ecstasy over it. I put the parents in the Gold Room next door, and they thought it

ANNE ANGELO

was perfect. They spent hours out on the balcony looking down over the traffic in the rue Nationale.

The weather was good, so I took them out everywhere I could think of. I tried to show them things they wouldn't see at home. I drove them out to Neuville-en-Ferrain to have a look at the Maginot line. I took them to the Citadelle. It's a huge massive fortress built in the 1670s by Vauban and Simon Vollant. It's still regarded as one of the great marvels of military architecture. I packed an al fresco lunch so we could make a day of it.

I took them and showed them how Lille got its name where the Basilique Notre Dame de la Treille now stands. In the tenth century, the Comtes de Flandre built an important chateau there. It was then an island in the Basse-Deule. It's from that island—l'ile—that the name 'Lille' was formed. The Basilique was begun in 1854. Our oldest building, though, is the Chapelle Notre Dame de Reconciliation. It was built in the thirteenth century. I took them to so many churches and places and told them so much about them that they were quite convinced Lille was my hometown. I didn't see any reason to tell them otherwise. But it did show me how completely French I'd become.

I filled their evenings by taking them to the opera, the ballet, and the theatre. They were all musical. The girls could play quite well. So I arranged musical evenings. I had a full grand piano in the main salon and a boudoir grand in the small one. The girls played for me and the staff in the small salon. And I brought in singers and musicians so they could play in concert with professionals in the big salon. And they were well able to hold their own. The parents were as proud as punch. When it came time to go, they all said they'd never had such an enjoyable stay. They'd come again for their next holidays. And they'd certainly tell their friends about me. And that was all I wanted. It'd been hectic, and I was considerably out of pocket, but it turned out a good investment.

From then on, the world beat a path to my doors. And it was the sort of world I wanted. Wealthy people, influential people, society figures—they came from all over France. I had Government ministers and members of the House of Representatives; prominent people in the arts, the opera and the ballet; notables from show business and radio.

I made sure the society columnists knew what was going on at 241 rue Nationale. The parties in my dining room and salons, the brilliant crowds of elegant people chatting over their champagne in my foyer became news. I'd arrived.

And I learned about tact and discretion and the odd little quirks people had. For instance, one very high official in the Department of Finance came with his wife so often that we became good friends. He would quietly drop me the hint that this country or that country was about to de-value or re-value its currency. In the strictest confidence, of course. I was able to do very well for myself. On the other hand, this same gentleman had a thing against flowers. I had flowers everywhere. Particularly at the foot of the main staircase in front of the big mirror. Poor Alphonse my butler would come to me in great distress. 'Madame! Please! You really must speak to him. He is impossible. Come and see. And they are only freshly arranged.'

And there, heaped on the heart of a rose or filling the trumpet of a lily or hibiscus would be a pile of cigar ash. And I had plenty of ashtrays everywhere. He took a delight in it. But what could I do? Could I go and remonstrate with him when he'd just put me in the way of making enough to buy every flower in the market ten times over? And how could I explain to Alphonse why I couldn't? I had to just get fresh flowers and let Alphonse think what he liked. I know I lost face in his eyes.

Some of the men gave me problems in other ways too. Ways that didn't endear them to me in the least. I suppose I was an attractive proposition to them. I was on my own and obviously doing very well. But some of them had their wives with them. I wasn't interested in any affairs like that. If they'd do that to their wives, what would they do to me when they met someone new and my time was finished? I was looking for someone, yes, of course I was. If an Aquinas or someone like my brother Peter had come along, my life would have been complete. It was hard work on my own. But I'd find him someday. In the meantime, I was making good hay and wanted to keep on doing it while I could. I was well aware that, that 'can be terminated by six months' notice in writing' could be applied at any time. I wanted to get as much behind me as I could.

It was about this time, as I mingled and I thought on more than an even footing with these people, that I began to wonder how it had all come about. How it was me here doing this.

When I first came to this house, I must have been as gauche as gauche.

We had three bad scares. One was in June 1938, one in September the same year, and one in June 1939. Each time, my guests fled, and I was left with an empty house. On the last one, in June 1939, I followed them. I packed what I could into the Oldsmobile and fled to Paris. At that time, I had the original Buick, a 1937 Buick and a new Olds I'd got from America through Cherbourg. Alphonse looked after the cars. He was good. He'd been in Transport in the Army. I felt so foolish when nothing happened and I had to come back to 241 that I didn't do that again although there was always the worry.

For a long time, I'd been wanting to go home to see my mother. Her health worried me. I also wanted to see how Father was towards me. I'd had no word from him. It seemed to me that if things got much worse with Germany, I might be wise to get out. And the only place I had was Scotland. But it would depend on him. Whether he'd let me or not.

So when we heard on 20 August that Germany and Russia had signed a Non-Aggression Pact, I decided to go. I'd go for a fortnight. If things were all right, I'd send for the rest of my things and stay. The house was going smoothly. Alphonse could look after the guests, and Marie-Louise could handle the rest. I left on the twenty-sixth. But it was a mistake. I should never have done it. Things were never the same afterwards. But maybe it wasn't a mistake: it was just something I had to do.

*　　*　　*

CHAPTER 4

War

I SHOULD HAVE TURNED back when I got to Calais. It was bedlam. Half of Europe was there, frantically trying to get away. It was as if the devil himself was after them. I'd never have dreamed it would be anything like that.

It was even worse at Folkstone. It was a rough crossing, and we were all a bit edgy. It was push or be pushed. I nearly got arrested. It was at Customs and Immigration. We'd shuffled along and stood, shuffled along and stood for what must have been hours. I'd got to where I was next. Some great oaf with a black walrus moustache tried to push in ahead of me. I didn't stand for it. He said he was from some consulate or other and had to get to London in a hurry. I said that was too bad. I was from rue Nationale, Lille, and I had to get to Scotland in a hurry. He'd have to wait his turn. It brewed up quite nicely. He was about forty-five and fat, with an accent. His wife went and fetched a policeman.

I don't know what she'd said to him, but he was against me from the start. He could have been a countryman of theirs. He had the same sort of accent. He told me to stand back and wait my turn. I said it was my turn. It was them who'd pushed in, not me. He said if I didn't stand back and keep quiet, he'd arrest me for creating a disturbance in a public place. He'd just asked for my papers and pulled out his notebook when the chief customs man came to see what was going on.

He was a Scotsman. As soon as I heard him speak, I came out with my braw'st Invergordon, using every 'Och' and 'Ye ken' I could. The storm vanished, and we were Scots wha ha'e in no time. He checked with the ones behind me and found I was right. Then he sent the g.o. and his wife back to the end of the queue and attended to me himself.

Another Scot from down the queue came along and patted me on the shoulder.

'Aye, an' guid fer ye, lassie,' he said. 'That's the way tae fix 'em. Ye're a sonsie wee thing. We're a' proud o' ye!'

When the customs man had finished, he wished me good luck and said to let him know if I had any more trouble. He was from Inverness, not more than thirty miles from Invergordon. And I did look him up again. It was on the way back. He was a tower of strength.

Invergordon was a mistake from the moment I got there. It all seemed changed. It was smaller, and different. And it was cold. It was only late summer, but I froze. I didn't get warm the whole time I was there. I stayed only eight days. I left the day the War was declared. Maybe my blood had got thinner, or maybe I hadn't got the right clothes. I'd taken a suitcase full of all my best things. I didn't want to risk losing them if they had to be sent. Maybe that was a mistake.

There were hardly any of my friends left. And those I did find were too busy to talk. I was like a fish out of water. They were the loneliest, coldest, most miserable eight days of my life.

Father was impossible. He hadn't changed towards me. He still had the old idea that it was his job to find a husband for me. He sat and listened while I was telling them what I'd been doing. And I think he was pleased I'd done so well. But when I told him I wasn't interested in getting married, I knew he was thinking up some scheme for me. I'd never know when he'd spring it. But it was Mother's insulin injections that really brought things to a head.

He was giving them to her himself. He wouldn't pay for the doctor or a nurse. I thought he might be giving her too much. She thought so too. She often got bad spells just after having one. But he wouldn't tell me. And he wouldn't let me see. So I went to the doctor and asked what he'd prescribed. But he wouldn't tell me. We didn't get on too well. It wasn't Dr McKay. It was a new man. So I went to the chemist to find out how much Father was buying. It was too much. So I asked Father about it.

I wasn't nasty. I only tried to show him that he could do her more harm than good by overdosing her. He went into a rage. He said it was none of my business. I had no right to go round asking questions. Someone had rung him from the doctor's. If I thought there was something wrong, I should go to the police and not go round trying to stir up trouble. It was his house, and she was his wife. If I didn't like anything, I could get out and go back where I'd come from. They'd got on all right without me, and they'd get on all right without me again.

The next morning was that fateful third of September when Mr. Chamberlain told us we were at war with Germany. We'd been warned the previous night that he'd be making an announcement, and we were all in the kitchen waiting. Father still only allowed the wireless to be on for an hour each night, but this was special. It decided me.

I knew I had to go straightaway, or there'd be restrictions, and I wouldn't be able to go at all. There was nothing for me in Invergordon. I'd never be safe from Father and his schemes. The only real home I had was in Lille. And the sooner I got back to it, the better. I caught the first train.

But restrictions were already on. All foreigners had been warned to leave England or be interned. There were hundreds of Germans, Poles, and all sorts there. I couldn't get a clearance. They said it would be too dangerous. A single girl on her own wouldn't have a chance. They told me to go back home. I didn't. Instead I battled my way on to a train to Folkstone. I thought of the helpful customs man saying to let him know if I had any more trouble. So I asked for him, and he fixed it in no time. There were fishing boats taking people across. All the ferries were booked out for weeks ahead. He even gave me a note to his opposite number so I'd have no trouble there.

And I didn't. No trouble with my clearance, I mean. The only trouble I had was getting a boat. Actually, one got me. I got kidnapped, or shanghaied, or whatever it is.

It was chaos. There was no one to tell you where to go or what to do. I got onto a jetty. There were small fishing boats along each side, loading up. People were rushing about. Everybody had luggage. They'd bang you with it and not even care if they knocked you over. There were family groups standing around saying their farewells. There were suitcases and children everywhere. My case was heavy. I put it down for a moment to have a spell and look around. Suddenly this Corsican pirate appeared from nowhere in front of me.

What he lacked in age and size, he made up for in fierceness. He was about twenty-two and not as tall as me, but I was scared for a moment. He had a black beanie on his head, a black roll-neck pullover, and black trousers tucked into black knee boots and held up by a wide black leather belt with a ferocious-looking sheath-knife at the hip. His features were concealed behind a mass of black whiskers, but the eyes reassured me. They were sharp and alert, but friendly, even cheeky.

'Is it zat mam'selle is going to France? Yes?' he said.

'Yes, I am.'

'And is it zat you are alone? Yes?'

'Yes.'

'Ah! C'est bien! Alors, now we can go!' He swung my suitcase up onto his shoulder and turned to go. 'You come,' he said. 'We only waiting for one more. Now we go. I show you. Please, you hurry.' And away he went.

It was so quick he was gone before I could stop him. Shouting did no good. There was nothing for me to do but go after him. But I didn't have a hope of catching him. His sea boots were better than my high heels. And he had a flying start. The suitcase made them open up and let him through. But when I got there, they'd closed up again and resented me. I had to go round. And there was everything in the world to trip over. I had to keep my eyes on my suitcase. Once I lost it, I'd never have found it again. He went down onto one of the boats, turned and came back towards the stern, and vanished down a hatchway.

I had to be careful down the gangway. It had big cleats across it and only a rope for a handrail. I'd reached the deck when he came up again, but without my bag. There were two others just like himself, and he stopped and talked to them. I went on past and down to get my bag.

It was a steep ladder with handrails on both sides. I went down backwards. It was a dim little cabin with people sitting round a table. My bag was in a corner with some others. I'd just got it and turned to come up when I felt we were moving. There was the vibration from an engine. I dropped it and ran back up, but it was too late. We were already clear of the jetty and picking up speed. I asked them down below where we were going, and they said Calais. They seemed surprised I'd asked. There were nine of them, and they seemed happy about it, so I sat down with them and relaxed. We talked.

They were all middle-aged. There were nine of them: three French couples, one Hungarian couple, and a Dutchman by himself. He said his wife and family were waiting for him in Boulogne. They asked me where my man was but didn't seem to believe me when I said I didn't have one. I saw the Hungarians whisper to each other and knew it was about me. They weren't very sociable, so I didn't stay. Anyway, it got too stuffy. As the engine got hotter, the smell of stale fish and fuel oil was overpowering. The men made it worse by smoking.

That was a problem I had with my guests. The smoking. They'd puff great clouds of it from their pipes and cigars with never a thought as to where it was going. I'd get most of it up in my bureau. In the mornings, after the house had been shut up all night, it smelled horrible. It's partly why I had so many flowers everywhere. They helped freshen it.

Anyway, it was better up on deck. She was only a little thing but she chugged along well. The wheelhouse in the middle was hardly wider than his shoulders. He had a klaxon in there, and whenever any of the others even thought of coming our way, he'd let loose a rude 'Ah-OOO-ah!' at them with it. Hanging on the side of the wheelhouse was a round, flat lifebuoy, one of those with the big hole in the centre, had *La Crevette Effronte*—the *Saucy Shrimp*—on it in bold black letters. The deck wasn't very high out of the water. It was a bit higher at the bows. The front was all taken up by a low hatch with a tarpaulin cover on it. In the middle of it was our gangway with its rope handrail. A wooden railing about a metre high went all round the deck so you didn't fall overboard. I went up and sat on the front of the hatch so I could look out and see where we were going. The sea was flat.

We were a fair way out before they came for my fare. It was the one who'd taken my suitcase. He was the captain. But I think they were brothers and he was the oldest. He wanted nearly twice what I'd paid going over, and I wouldn't pay it. I said I'd pay what I'd paid before. It had only been about a week ago, and it couldn't have gone up that much. I stuck to English. It put him at a disadvantage. It had worked all right at Ventimiglia. He called out, 'Etienne!' When he came, they talked it over in French, and then they both came at me.

'Why you be like zis?' they said. 'You want to go to France, yes? Zen what is wrong? We take you, yes. But we cannot take you for zat much. We have to eat. Yes? How we eat if you not pay? Ze ozzers, zey all pay. Why not you?'

I said I didn't care what the others had paid. I wasn't going to. They had to eat, yes. But not caviar and champagne at my expense. The other boat had managed all right. And it'd been bigger with more expenses.

'Yes, but it is different. And now is war, non? We have ze risk. If ze Boche he catch us, we lose everysing.'

I stuck to my guns. I said if the Germans caught us, I wouldn't get to France anyway, so why should I pay anything at all?

They went off a bit and talked it over in French. I heard them say, 'She is not really a bad one. It is just that she is English. They are all crazy. We will give her the treatment. I think it will fix her.'

They came back to me.

'All right,' they said. 'You want to be like zat, you be like zat. No trouble. We take you ovair but you no get off. We bring you back. You get anozzair boat. You see what you pay him. You will be sorry.' And they went away.

Then we ran into fog. It was thick and heavy. It closed round and wrapped us in white cotton wool. There was only the soft slap, slap of the water under our forefoot and the vibrations from the engine. It breathed cold and damp in my face. It condensed and ran down my nose. The wheelhouse peered at me through it like the ghost on the battlements in *Hamlet*. The 'La Crevette Effronte' round its top gleamed blackly. I knew I was being watched and talked about behind that window.

I couldn't imagine what their 'treatment' was going to be. I really couldn't see there was much they could do. The others knew I was here. I didn't think they'd stand for any nonsense. But it niggled.

He came and asked if I was going to stay there. I said I was if it was all right. I didn't like it in the cabin. It was too stuffy and they were smoking.

I was well wrapped up. I had a good coat and gloves. My toque fitted snugly. I'd let my hair grow long again and did it up at the back. The toque covered it. The fog didn't worry me in that way.

'Ah!' he said. 'So you do not smoke, eh? Zat is good.' I thought he sounded more friendly. 'Yes, it is all right, you can stay zere. And you can do somesing for us. For everyone. Yes? You watch for ze submarines. Ze Boche, he have zem everywhere. He see us first, and pouff! We all fini. You watch. Yes?'

I said I would. I asked him what I should look for. He thought I was silly to ask.

'What you look for? Sacre vache, les Anglais!' He poked a forefinger up stiffly and moved it slowly along the level like a periscope. 'Zere! You look for somesing like zat. You see him and you call us. Tout de suite! We do ze rest.' He went away muttering to himself something about imbeciles.

And I did see something. Under the fog the sea was flat and had an oily sort of film on it. I saw something sticking up in the water straight ahead. I waited until I was sure and then stood up and shouted to them and pointed. The engine stopped, and they came a-running.

By that time, though, I was feeling such a fool. I could see it was only an empty bottle. He reached over and got it as it came past. He brought it and held it under my nose.

'Zere!' he said disgustedly. 'Zere is your submarine! A whisky bottle! Mon Dieu, what is ze mattair wis you?' He flung it over the side, and they went back into their wheelhouse. The engine resumed its quiet chug-a-lug.

It was the last straw. He didn't have to be so nasty. The tears came, and I couldn't stop them. The only good thing was that no one could see. But sitting there, crying alone in the fog, did me good. It made me face up to how lonely I was.

I did need someone. I needed someone to be with me. To put an arm round me and comfort me. Bonne-maman had been right. And so had Father, in his own way. Everybody needed someone. Two could stand where one would fall. I'd never have been on the wretched little boat if I'd had someone with me. And I wouldn't have been treated like this either.

I tried to imagine the man I'd look for. He'd have to be something like my brother Peter. Or Dr McKay. Or even Aquinas. They were all much alike. Tall and clean and nice. Peter had always been fun. I remembered the drives. And selling our whisky to the sailors. The time Lord Louis had nearly caught us with the ten gallons. And suddenly I had to laugh.

That whisky bottle in the water had been a finger, pointing at me. Accusing me. I wondered how far it had travelled and how long it'd been in the water to get where it was. Peter and I had charged twice what we paid for our whisky. We'd had to, to get money for Peter's studies. These pirates—they were only boys, really—were doing this for their living. And they were risking their lives. I went and paid them what they'd asked.

It was remarkable. I came out, and the fog was gone. Calais was straight ahead of us. We were in and tied up within half an hour. It was the eighth of September.

There was a fine drizzle. When the captain brought my suitcase up, he put it and me into the wheelhouse and told me to wait a moment. He went down and came back with a leather overcoat and a sou'wester. He said they weren't much good, but they were better than nothing. I could have them. If I came back this way sometime, I could bring them back. If I didn't, it wouldn't matter. Nobody ever used them. They'd been left a long time ago by a passenger. He tied the strings of the sou'wester under my chin. 'Zere,' he said. 'Now you will not get wet. Bon chance!'

As I went up the gangway, someone called out in French, 'Hey, Etienne! Take a look! Not bad, eh? Ooo-la-la! I wonder if she's got anyone.' The other one answered, 'What's the matter with you? You chicken or something? Why don't you ask her? She won't bite.'

It was lovely. It made my day. I knew there was nothing wrong with my ankles, but it was nice to hear. I gave them a wave and a smile. They were nice boys, really. Them and their *Saucy Shrimp*. But they were nothing like I had in mind. So I kept going. It was raining, and I was worried about the hotel. I must have looked like something from *The Shoes of the Fisherman* as I went along.

*   *   *

ANNE ANGELO

CHAPTER 5

Return To Lille

THAT HAPPINESS CARRIED me until I got out at Lille station. I was riding the wave. I'd had my trip and was back safely. That was out of my system. I had a lovely warm feeling of contentment and anticipation. But at the station, it died. The life I'd known was gone.

It was almost deserted. There wasn't a taxi. I rang for Alphonse to come and get me but got no answer. I rang and rang, but it did no good. The trams weren't running. There was nothing for it but walk. It was raining. I put on the leather coat and sou'wester again and picked up my suitcase. I managed forty steps bashing it against my leg before I put it down and changed hands. By the time I got there, I was hot, wet, and sticky; and I'd had enough.

The doors were shut, bolted on the inside. I had to plod on through the rain round and in the back way.

When I got there, there wasn't a soul anywhere. The place was empty. No guests. No staff. Nobody.

I went up and all through. They'd all taken their things and gone—butler, cook, maids, and gardeners. Except Marie-Louise and old Jacques. Their things were still in their rooms, but there was no sign of either of them. My bureau was still locked, and everything was all right inside. There were dirty dishes in the kitchen. The cars were all still in the garage. But nothing to show what had happened.

I was making myself a cup of coffee when the two old faithfuls walked in. I always thought of them as that afterwards. They'd been shopping. Deliveries had stopped. The stores had nothing to deliver.

Panic-buying had cleaned them out. They'd found only some bread and liverwurst. The trust they had in me made me ashamed.

'We didn't worry, madame. We knew you'd come back. We told them, but they wouldn't listen. They said you'd looked after yourself and got out while you could. They were going too. When Alphonse got his call-up, they asked for their money and left. The guests all went the first day. Oh, madame, what's going to happen? Will the Germans really come?'

I'd have liked to have known that myself. The only thing to do was sit tight and find out. Food was going to be the thing. It was good that the others had left when they had. There was that much more for us.

A month had passed, during which I fought desperately to prevent my home from being requisitioned, but finally I gave in. I had not wanted to, not because of any selfishness or unwillingness to help in the war, far from it, but because most of my friends had gladly opened their homes to the troops, and had watched those homes of which they were so proud being slowly and systematically reduced to shambles. I had picked out a liaison officer with a few of his colleagues and their batmen who had sworn not to harm even the most insignificant of my belongings. On the contrary, they would keep everything in perfect order during their stay. Captain Verley, who was to be in charge, promised to see to it personally. It seemed all right to me. I would be paid for the rooms they used, they would look after the heating and cleaning, and all I had to do was to look on.

I kept my bureau and a room each for Marie-Louise and old Jacques on the top floor. The telephone switchboard went into the small salon. They made that their offices. They took control of the kitchens. Our food came up to us on trays. Food we could never have got otherwise. And I got paid. But I certainly wasn't safer. I was taught things about Army officers I'd much sooner not have been taught. I'd always had the highest regard for them. Higher even than for Navy ones. Probably because I'd never met any.

In the first place, they were rough. They had hard boots with steel plates and nails. It wasn't only officers. They brought cooks and batmen and drivers. Mud got tramped into the deep pile of the stair treads. And into the carpets. The tiles in the foyer and down the front steps were cut and defaced. None of them ever thought to clean their boots, and they were in and out all the time. Some of the rooms had three and four camp beds in them. They kept the best suites—the ones on the first floor, overlooking the street—for the top-ranking officers. But it was the beginning of the end for my fine hotel. I tried to ring m'sieu in Paris about it, but there was no one there.

There was no consideration for anything. Things got marked with cigars and cigarettes and wet glasses. Chairs and furniture got damaged and broken by rough usage. Glasses and crockery got smashed unnecessarily. At their parties, it was a great thing to get up on the grand piano with a glass of beer and do a dance. Or tip a glass into the works 'to make it play better'. Very few of them could really play. They'd just sit there and bash. They'd egg their women on to get up and can-can on the dining-room table. There was no thought of what it was doing to the table. They'd beat time on it with the handles of the knives and forks in their fists. They generally invited us, but we didn't go very often. They always wanted us to drink too much.

It seemed to me that when men got into uniform and got away with other men, they completely changed. They became a race apart. I didn't know if the Navy and the Air Force were the same. All the nice, good things they were taught when they were growing up got thrown out. They became utterly irresponsible. Civilians and civilian things weren't important. They were only there to be used and then discarded. British officers came and organised darts competitions. They used valuable pictures and door panels for their targets and thought nothing of it.

Enid Hunter, a friend and fellow British resident, called on me the following week. We had become closer since the start of the War, as if clinging together for comfort.

'How are you getting on with your bodyguard?' she asked.

'Oh. Not so badly, but I wonder if I'll ever see those white tiles on the kitchen floor again. There must be at least four inches of mud on them. I sometimes wonder if they intend to dig trenches down there when they have enough mud.'

'Serves you right for having them there, and Frenchies at that,' retorted Enid.

'Don't be so silly. I had no choice. We're not in the right district for the BEF. Haven't you anyone billeted on you?'

'Good heavens no. Our rooms are all full up—on paper at any rate.'

'You might have given me the tip. On second thought, I'm not so badly off. They do cover expenses.'

'If you ever get paid by the requisitioning people,' laughed Enid. 'Still, you have kept the first and second floors to yourself, haven't you? You never know, business might pick up one day.'

'If only it would,' I said. 'But I'll give it a month or two yet. If nothing happens, I'll get myself a job to keep me from going crazy. This eternal waiting for something to happen is wearing me down. Do you think the Hun will get over the Maginot line?'

'I don't know anything about the Germans. I don't think I've ever met one in my life. If it were the Irish now, they would walk over it in a couple of hours.'

'I hope you are right, Enid, because from what I hear, we have quite a lot of Irish coming over here. Do you think they could walk into Germany overnight, end the war on the spot, and put us all out of our misery?'

'Why not? All you want is enough of them,' replied Enid proudly. 'And there had better be enough Germans there to keep them busy, otherwise they'll start on wiping out all the Scots and English in their own regiments.'

'You are a bloodthirsty lot, aren't you? But tell me what I can do to pass the time and be useful.'

'Well,' said Enid calmly, 'what about keeping the troops happy? I can't imagine you doing anything else.'

'Don't be such a beast,' I retorted, trying hard to keep from slapping Enid's face. 'There must be lots of war work somewhere around.'

'Is there, how interesting. I wonder where?'

My blood was boiling. 'Stop being such a sarcastic beast. What's biting you anyway? I suppose my old friend Eddie, whom I see once a year or less, is being called up or something. Is he?'

'Of course not. He's an American, but he did say something the other day about America being bound to come into the war sooner or later now that Britain was in it, and that he might as well go home while he had the chance. I couldn't very well tell him that he had plenty of time. After all, the war was almost over before they came over last time. Not that I blame them, of course. I don't. Why should they? Just because Britain can't keep out of wars, it doesn't mean that America must come in and help out.'

'Oh, don't let's talk politics, Enid, for heaven's sake. They are corrupt. Haven't you made any headway with Eddie at all? Personally, I don't know what you see in him.'

'You wouldn't. He's much too safe and secure for you. You want something dangerous all the time. The more complicated a man's nature or affairs, the more you fall for them. You want adventure all the way. Well, why don't you join the ambulance corps? You'll get plenty of excitement with them. I've seen some of the ambulances when they returned, riddles like sieves. You'd love it, you'd wallow in it, but it's not amusing.'

'What a brilliant idea, Enid.' I was beginning to sit up and take notice. 'How do I get in touch with them?'

'You're crazy, my dear. I was only pulling your leg. That particular branch won't last. They've lost too many drivers. It's crazy to have women for it, but it is an American outfit.'

'Oh, be a sport and give me the address of their headquarters. What exactly does one have to do?'

'I'm a bit vague about it. Madame Crecy told me that women drove these ambulances in the direction of the Maginot line but kept in the safety zone. So much for the safety area. They've been shot up and blown up wholesale.'

'What about the wounded?' I asked, perplexed.

'Funny you should mention that. I have never heard anybody mention the wounded. Supposing there aren't any. Supposing they carry other things. Butchers as they are, I don't think the Jerries would blow up ambulances, unless, of course, they were not legitimate ambulances' she said meaningfully.

'You've got me intrigued. I must join up. Get the address from Madame Crecy, there's a dear,' I pleaded.

'I'm damned sorry I mentioned it. Where on earth do you find the virtue in being brave over something which is quite unnecessary?' asked Enid.

'How would you like to come out to dinner tonight?' I asked sweetly, changing the subject. 'We could go to the Paridis. You might meet some of your countrymen.'

'All right. Will you call for me? I suppose you still have your car.'

'Of course I have, till death do us part. Not even a Jerry will take it away from me, except over my dead body.'

'From what I hear of the atrocities in other countries, my dear young lady, that won't be difficult,' retorted Enid.

As we entered the Paradis, a considerable disturbance made me nudge my friend. 'Oh, oh', I said, 'what about doing a spot of rescuing?'

'Oh, for heaven's sake, let's mind our own business. This place is in an uproar as it is tonight without anything else.'

'But surely you can't stand here and see those poor Scots boys over there have any more of their uniforms torn off by Renee and her cronies?'

'Well, they shouldn't drink so much. Anyway, they're not my countrymen, they're yours,' she said flatly.

'That settles it. I'll go over alone, you can pick up the pieces.' So saying, I marched over to where the disturbance was in progress.

'Hallo Renee,' I said sweetly, 'Since when have you gone in for cradle snatching? What's happened to your wife-weary businessmen? Surely they haven't gone to the front without you. They couldn't do such a thing. Not to the sweetest girl in the world.' Renee glared at me, her arm half raised, threatening to strike me with her bag. The three young men stared at us with their mouths gaping.

I looked at them and in my broadest Scottish accent said quickly, 'You got me inta this, noo get me oot o' it.' There was a yell of 'Scotland forever!' The youngest of them grabbed Renee round the waist and went off dancing at a spot a safe distance from the others, while Renee shouted 'Chameau' across at me.

'What's she calling you?' asked the least tipsy of the remaining two. 'A camel,' I replied. 'But I don't see the connection.'

He looked me up and down, his head wobbling on his neck, trying hard to keep his eyes open. 'Neither do I,' he blurted finally. 'Have a drink?'

Enid had reappeared on the scene by this time, and we stood back and looked at the two boys. They couldn't have been more than twenty, but they had three pips on their shoulders. They were so tight; they just sat there on their red chromium stools and stared, not saying a word. One of them had already lost four buttons plus pieces of material from his tunic but it didn't seem to worry him.

'You've lost some buttons,' I said, trying to break the spell.

'I know, the girls—souvenirs.'

'What are your names anyway?'

'This is Tony Stewart, he's going to be a lawyer. I'm Johnny Kirkwood, I'm in insurance, and that martyr over there still dancing I'm sure, though I can't see him, is Neil Graham. His father's a parson. Now you know all about us, so you can call us the three musketeers.'

'Well, I can call you that, but are you as good as they were?'

'I don't know,' said Johnny. 'All I know is that I am bloody afraid. I can't help it, but I am. We all are, only Neil never shows it. He'll be a parson too someday, if he survives.'

'Why don't you go out and have something to eat. You'll feel better after a good meal, and don't drink so much champagne. You're not used to it. Don't think because the others here can sink gallons of it that you can too. They were brought up on it.'

'Okay. We will on one condition. That you come with us. And thanks for the lecture, Mother. I know we're all sorts of fools, but we're so bloody browned off doing nothing. There's nothing to do except get blither, and then we don't think of what's coming to us.'

Neil came up to them, mopping his brow. 'Phew, who was she anyway?' he asked.

'Oh, just a very notorious tart. Why do you have to get mixed up with her kind? They won't be content with your buttons next time,' replied Enid, taking part in all this for the first time.

'Now, what about this dinner we're going to have?' She went on, 'Anybody got any suggestions?'

'Don't know this ruddy town,' said Tony.

'You decide, Anne,' said Enid. 'You know all the dives in this town, famous and infamous.'

'All right. Let's go to the chicken place. It's not expensive, and you can watch your chicken being roasted over a spit before you get it. They are delicious.'

It was a merry evening, the boys sobered up quite a lot, and I drove them all home to their billets about six kilometres out. They were very grateful and promised to ring me next day, but I didn't expect them to. Strangely enough, they did.

Within a few weeks, we were all great friends. The only snag was the weather. It was now bitterly cold, and snow had started to fall, but I had driven them home every evening in spite of the weather and the slippery roads. It seemed to the others quite a normal procedure to keep on doing it.

I stuck it out as long as I could, but in the end, I had to tell them flatly that it would have to stop. So I didn't see so much of them. My last return journey had been a nightmare. Although previously I'd managed to keep clear of the tram lines, this time I had driven right into them. It was impossible to get off them again. The snow was banked up on either side, and I had to go to the depot. This was about three kilometres beyond my home. To make matters worse, on arriving there, the old car had spluttered and stopped dead, as if rebelling against such treatment, and had refused to start up again. On investigation, I found that there was not a drop of petrol in the tank. There was nothing to do but lock the doors, leave the car, and walk home. I was frozen stiff, my feet were killing me, and my dancing sandals were ruined, but I trudged on through the snow. The roads were completely deserted, and it wasn't until I had reached home, worn out and furious, that the first signs of life came clanging along the road. It was a tramcar from the same depot from which I'd started off nearly an hour earlier. I could have committed a murder.

From then onwards, I allowed the three boys to sleep the night at the house if they were unable to find a taxi. I gave little supper parties to avoid going out in the cold.

'Will anybody know where to find you if the offensive starts tonight?' I asked them one evening.

'I doubt it,' said Johnny, quite unconcerned. 'But we won't be the only ones they won't find. I doubt if any of us go home at night. None of the other blokes we know do, so they can't court-martial all of us. But there won't be an offensive, so don't start worrying about it. I'm more worried about my knowing what to do if ever it does start. You probably won't believe me, but I have never even seen a grenade. I don't know if I am brave or a coward. How can we know? All I know is that I am afraid of this war starting.'

'How silly to make kids like you captains. Whose bright idea was that anyway? What's happened to the good old regulars, the soldiers of experience, the born soldiers?'

'Oh, they're much too old. They're all around forty or so. They wouldn't be much good in a war like this. They need youth and speed,' said Tony, trying to look a superman.

'Maybe you're right', I replied, 'but don't be offended if I say what I think of the whole thing. There's one thing you youngsters will be able to do better than the old soldiers, and that is run. I don't mean towards the enemy either.'

'Oh, I say, that's not fair,' Johnny broke in. 'You're making us all out to be young cowards. We might be very brave and noble soldiers. We can't know till this thing starts. But you can't call us cowards because we're only twenty years old.'

'I'm not saying you are cowards. It's your inexperience I have against you. Then you are all conscripts. The old regular soldiers made the Army their careers, their futures, and they know the meaning of war, and yet some of them will have to take orders from you kids. It's all wrong. We'll never win the war without them in the lead,' I went on sadly.

'Oh, forget about the war,' said Johnny. 'What interests me most at the moment is whether I'll get my major's crown before my twenty first birthday. I've only two months to go.'

'I wonder what you want it for,' I murmured.

'Two things,' was his reply. 'To be able to say that I was a major at twenty, and of course, the extra money.' I watched them with an expression of pity mingled with contempt for youth. Here it was, blatant unconcern about the future of people and their countries. To them the only important thing was the extra pay, and for what? To fritter away on enjoying themselves.

One night, it was late and raining, they had to be on early in the morning, I said they could sleep on my bureau floor. We got them pillows and blankets. I went off up to my room. I shut my door and went to bed. I didn't lock it. It didn't occur to me.

I'd just got off to sleep when I was awakened by one of them getting into bed with me. I put on my bed light—it had a cord switch that I kept under the pillows—and saw it was the younger one, in only his singlet.

'What on earth do you think you're doing?' I said. 'Get out of here and stop this nonsense. Or I'll scream.'

'Oh, don't be like that,' he said. 'I'm not going to hurt you. It's too cold out there. I can't sleep. I thought you wouldn't mind if I came in here with you. No one'll be any the wiser. He's asleep, and I've shut the door. We can keep each other warm and be as snug as bugs in a rug.'

'Oh, you did, didn't you? Well, I do mind, and you're not going to. You're not coming into my bed. Do you think I'm silly? Why would I want you? You're not such a marvellous specimen as all that. You've got a wife. You go back to England and see her, if that's what you want. Now please get out of my bed. I want to get some sleep.'

'But why? What's wrong? You do with the Frogs, why not with me? You like me. I know you do. You wouldn't have done what you have if you didn't. Oh, come on, I won't tell anyone.'

'I did like you, yes. I thought you were rather a nice boy, but now you've shown me otherwise. I should never've been friendly to you. I suppose you'll both be the same. I'm very sorry, there'll be no more of it. But let me tell you, I don't do what you think I do with the Frogs, as you call them, and I don't like you saying I do. But that's your affair. Now will you please get out of my bedroom before I pick up that phone and get somebody up here? If I have to, I assure you, your commanding officer will hear about it. Now, are you going or not?'

ANNE ANGELO

He went. He looked like a sheepish, naughty little boy, but he went. 'And please shut the door behind you.'

He shut it. But it didn't latch. I got up to shut and lock it, but just as I got there, I heard, 'So you muffed it, did you? I might've known you would. I should've gone myself. Now neither of us'll get her. You're a clot. She was a damn pushover.'

I left the door and went to the wardrobe and got a dressing gown. I put it on and went out to them.

'I'd like you two to get dressed, please, and find somewhere else to pass the night. I'll give you five minutes, and then I'll do something about it.' Neither of them said a word.

I never spoke to either of them again. It ruined everything. I never knew, when I was talking to any of the others, what they were thinking. I didn't know if they really thought of me like that, or if he'd only made it up. There was no way I could find out.

I thought locking my doors would be safe enough, my windows were too high, but I was wrong. Mother had told me that locks were for good men, bad ones would get in; but I hadn't understood her. I was taught.

One evening we went down, I was opposite an artillery major. He was French, but I'd never seen him before. He was about fifty, big, but far too fat. He had little sharp eyes and kept looking at me all through dinner. I think he tried to play feet, but I pulled mine back so he couldn't. He made such a pest of himself that I left early and went up to bed.

But I had a nightmare. I was in a bed back in that dirty old house in Ventimiglia. The fat hairy brother came in and shut the door. He had nothing on and looked horrible. He came and got into bed with me. I couldn't stop him; I couldn't move. I tried to scream but couldn't. I could feel his hairy body on me. I could hear him grunting. I felt his hands pawing at me. It was so ghastly I woke up.

And it was real! There was somebody! Instinctively, I wrenched myself sideways. I got a hand under the pillows for the light switch. It was the French artillery major. I got round and hooked my heels over the side and wriggled from under him, fighting him off with my hands.

I got my bottom to the edge but couldn't go any farther. He had hold of my nightie, trying to drag me back. There was nothing for it but let him have it. I slipped my arms and shoulders free and dropped to the floor. I got up and ran.

I got the door open and went out into the bureau. The outside door was shut, so I went to the desk and pressed the bell for Marie-Louise, shouting at the top of my voice, 'M'aidez! Marie-Louise! M'aidez! M'aidez!' Her window was just above mine, round the corner. I kept going round the desk because of the bell. But he pulled out the chair and blocked me. So I scooted round the chaise-longue and back into the bedroom. I managed to get the door shut but couldn't hold it. The key was gone.

The wardrobe door was open. As I ran, I knocked one of the parasols off the rail. It gave me an idea. I got back again and got it. I used it like a sword, to poke him off with. It was beauty. I grabbed a handful and got three. They were terrific. When he snatched one from me, I used another. I tried to get him in his belly. I thought it would do the most good there and discourage him. I'd never seen a man in that condition. I'd never even seen a man with no clothes on. I suppose me being nude only aroused him all the more. He said some awful things.

It was the craziest few minutes. I thought of Peter and me in the garden at home playing the Three Musketeers with that first parasol Mother had made us. Prancing around and jabbing at him and yelling my head off, I felt like D'Artagnan. When I could, I got some more ammunition. There were bits of parasol, like great broken butterflies, all over the bedroom and bureau. I'd go round the bed a couple of times, and then up and over it and out to the bureau to have a go at the bell. I got to the telephone, but he was on to me before anyone answered.

I got down to my last parasol. It was a beauty, with a steel shaft and a straight, carved handle like the one Mother had made us. It had a thong to loop round your wrist. But I knew it wouldn't last long. I was going to need something else if help didn't come. Once he got hold of them, I had to let them go. I thought of getting a coat or frock to throw over his head, but it would take both hands and time to get one off a hanger. I had a big box of powder on my dressing table. I thought if I could get hold of it and throw it in his eyes, I might be able to get away. I worked my way near it. But the silly loop trapped me. When he grabbed my sword, I couldn't get away. I got the powder with my left hand and flung it, but it didn't go in his eyes. He kept hold of the shaft and pulled me to him and grabbed my wrist. And then he stopped, staring over at the doorway. I turned to see what he was looking at, and it was Marie-Louise. She was there with one hand on the doorknob, and her face a picture of utter disbelief. She was in a nightie and a dressing gown with an apron over the top and pink fluffy slippers on her feet. Her hair was in curlers.

'M'aidez, Marie-Louise!' I managed to croak. 'M'aidez! Vite, vite!'

'Oh, Mon Dieu!' she gasped. 'Ma pauvre petite!' She put her head down, threw her apron up over it, and ran at him. Her head hit him full on his great bulging hairy stomach. He let out a huge 'Whoof!' and went down. It was exactly the same as when old Mrs Ross, back in their kitchen in Invergordon had run at Geordie's father—the time he died. Except this major wasn't dead. He was only knocked out.

We quickly got some of my stockings and tied his hands and feet. Then we dragged him out onto the small landing outside my bureau door and left him there. He looked grotesque. There were patches of my powder all over him. She wanted to get a towel to throw over him to cover his nudity, but I said no. Naked he came, naked let them find him. She hurried off back up to her room. I locked my doors and went back to bed.

But he must have moved during the night. They found him in the morning on the tiles down in the foyer at the bottom of the main staircase with a broken hip and collarbone. We never saw him again.

It was inevitable that what had happened with the British captains and the French major would affect me. Combined with what I'd seen and heard, and the way they regarded the women who came to their dinners and parties, it showed me quite plainly that Army officers were not the same as the Navy ones I'd had such wonderful times with in Invergordon. They'd been like uncles and brothers to me. I realised that with these men, I'd have to be on my guard the whole time.

They were all very different to me after the major incident. It was in their eyes and the way they spoke to me. I don't know whether they thought I'd done that to him all by myself. Likely they thought I had. He'd unmistakably rolled down from my door, and equally, they were my stockings, and it was my powder. Nobody asked me about it, and so I didn't tell them. Their commanding officer was the only one who made any reference to it whatsoever.

He rang me the next morning and asked if I could spare him a few minutes. There were two of them there. It all seemed very casual. Was everything going all right with me? Was I well? Was I happy having them in my hotel? Did I have any complaint? He understood that one of his officers had had too much to drink last night and behaved foolishly. He hoped he hadn't been too much of a nuisance. He was normally a very fine fellow.

I told them everything was fine with me, and I was quite well, thank you very much. No, I had no complaint, and I was happy having them in my hotel. 'Ah, there! Do you hear that?' he said. 'Ma'mselle is quite well and has no complaint. Excellent. Make a note of that. Well, Ma'mselle, I think that is all. Thank you very much for giving us your time. If you do ever have any complaint, I trust you will come directly to me.'

His putting it down to a drunken spree didn't make it any better at all. It only showed me how much sympathy and redress I'd have got if things had gone the other way. I'd have been an object of scorn and derision. I could never have raised my head again.

We found how he'd got into my bedroom. He'd slid a sheet of newspaper under the bureau door. Then he'd poked through the keyhole with a pencil and poked the key out to fall on the paper inside. It had then been simple to ease the paper out with the key resting on it. He'd done the same with the bedroom. The newspaper and pencil were there on the floor. Old Jacques made me loops of string to go through the handles of the keys and round the doorknobs so that if they were poked out, they wouldn't fall. They'd hang from the door handles. He also put bolts on the insides for me.

*   *   *

ANNE ANGELO

HRH the Duke of Gloucester on the back steps
of the hotel around Christmas 1939.

CHAPTER 6

Ambulance Driver

MY FIRST DAY with the ambulance outfit was the most soul-destroying day I had ever spent up till that time. I couldn't understand why, in order to drive an ambulance, I had to undergo such extensive physical training. I and many other women, with more money than sense, were marched round and round the barracks for three solid hours. None of us had expected this and had certainly not come prepared for this. Some wore three-inch heels, and others had beautiful hats perched on their heads. None of us had expected a real live sergeant major to bellow orders to 'form fours and forward march' and all the rest of it, complete with the usual sergeant major's vocabulary. But there he was, storming up and down like a bull in a china shop, calling down curses on the heads of whoever was responsible for sending him such an assortment of imbeciles. One lovely girl got so angry she left the ranks, went up to him, and hit him over the head with her saucy hat, then quietly walked out. We never saw her again.

The afternoon was spent in lectures on maintenance. We inspected workshops with engines and accessories all neatly arranged and started learning how an engine worked from start to finish. I found it very difficult in French. Apart from that, I didn't see the point in learning engineering. We were only going to drive the beastly things, not make them. And all this marching and toughening up didn't make sense. Unless, of course, the job would be to drive the ambulance to their destination and then walk back after each trip. That did make sense, if only because such an idea was preposterous—or so I thought.

A few weeks later, a thaw had set in, the roads were very slushy, but I was glad to be able to drive to and from the ambulance depot with comparative safety. I was speeding home one evening along the main road when something I hadn't seen in the fading light came out of a side road and hit me with the force of a rocket. I jammed on my brakes, skidded, and came to rest on the other side of the road. The first thing I knew was a man's head stuck through the window.

'What happened? Are you hurt?' he asked.

I didn't answer, and after a while, the police came. Some first-aid men were cleaning up my face.

'Poor mademoiselle, but you were very lucky.'

'What happened to the bloke who hit me?'

'He's gone to hospital. He was a French dispatch rider, and he hit you right in the side. You've only a dent in the side of your car, but he was lucky too. His crash helmet saved him, and he's only suffering from shock. I'll give you a lift to your home if you like, and your garage man can come and collect your car.'

I was none the worse for the accident, or so I thought, until that afternoon when the chief of police walked in to make some inquiries. He was a little fat man with small beady black eyes. He certainly didn't look clever enough to be chief of the Surete. I wondered where he kept his qualifications hidden.

'You probably don't know me, but I know you very well. As a matter of fact, I had to vouch for your good behaviour before you were allowed to open up this place as a hotel.'

'Thank you,' I said, not feeling in the least grateful. I loathed policemen, big fry and small fry, too much to make an exception. 'I hadn't realised that policemen in France had such sweeping powers, but surely you would not waste your valuable time in coming here to discuss my good or bad behaviour.' My tone was acid. He was such a repulsive little man, and those small black eyes were so shrewd, so cunning. He seemed to be weighing me up, but for what?

'Well, no,' he said, sitting down without being asked. 'It appears that you had an accident with your car when you collided with a dispatch rider. The Army are taking a very serious view of the matter.'

I glared at him. 'What a nerve. He was in the wrong. I was on the main road, which gave me the right of way. He smashed up my car and myself, and you're trying to tell me that it was my fault.'

'No, I don't say you were in the wrong, but you are a civilian, and you hit the Army. And to make matters worse, you are not even French. As for priority on the roads, the Army has it, so you see, they have a very good case against you.'

'Well, let them get on with it. They have nothing else to do anyway, have they? They can't find any Germans to fight with, so they might as well have a kick at the civilians. From what I have seen of the French Army up till now, it's "Pourri", just like a rotten apple, but I don't care. Thank God I am not French so they can't do much to me.'

'That is where you are wrong,' he said smoothly. 'They can do quite a lot to you, and that is why I'm here. I am responsible for the civilians, so it is us against the Army. They can insist on my putting you in prison, if only to set an example to the rest of the civilians should any more obstruct them in their work.'

'I still don't see the point in your coming here. What do you intend doing? Are you going to lock me up in my own hotel, or are you going to march me off to jail?'

'That depends on you, mademoiselle.' He smiled, got up, and walked towards me. 'I can be a very useful friend, you know, but you'll have to be nice to me.' I could feel his hot breath on my neck, and the smell of garlic was so nauseating I had a vulgar impulse to spit. Fortunately for me, I refrained from carrying out such an undignified act.

'Your wife would object to my being nice to you now, wouldn't she?' I didn't even know if he was married—not that it seemed to make any difference, but I had to play for time.

'My wife wouldn't know. I'm very fond of my wife', he went on, 'and I wouldn't dream of upsetting her by reporting all my little affairs to her. That would be asking for trouble.'

I was thinking fast. If only I could put up with the attentions of this revolting little man, including his repulsive garlic breath, I might have a very useful weapon in my hands should I need help in the future, knowing as I now did that he didn't tell his wife how he behaved outside. But could I? Maybe I could match my wits against his, have somebody there each time he called, unless he called unexpectedly. 'All right,' I suggested, 'come and have dinner with me when you have settled my problem with the Army. You can give me a ring.'

'Thank you. I will,' he replied, reaching out for his hat. He turned to me. 'Shall we seal our agreement with a kiss?'

I did not move.

'My God', I thought, 'he doesn't waste much time.' I let him kiss me, shutting my eyes tight to blot out the ugliness of his face, but I couldn't blot out the garlic. I wanted to be sick, and sickness kept rising into my throat, making me terrified that I would be sick into his mouth. Somehow or other, I choked it back, and eventually, he let me go. I tried to smile at him, but it was the sickliest smile I'd ever attempted. He bowed himself out of the bureau, and I sank down on the floor in a heap. Whenever I had any hard thinking to do, the discomfort of the floor helped me to concentrate. 'Why on earth do I get into so many scrapes? I'm sure that other people don't, yet here I am, playing mother to a bunch of youths on one hand and starting a revolting affair with a policeman on the other to keep out of jail, and yet all I've been trying to do is help with the war. It's very poor thanks, and I get damn all out of it. Anyway, thank goodness my training is almost over, and I'll do my first ambulance trip any day now.'

A few days later, that loathsome policeman rang up. I heard his name for the first time.

'This is Mr Jacques Derval of the Surete,' he announced over the wire.

'Have you any news for me?' I asked.

'I've settled everything. We can discuss it at our meeting tonight,' he replied guardedly.

I wondered if his wife was in the office with him. 'Thank you. I'll expect you at seven thirty.' I spent the rest of the day frantically searching for my three young proteges, but without success. I rang up Enid Hunter, but she had an attack of the flu. There was nobody else I could ask to appear punctually and presumably unexpectedly that evening, so I arranged with old Marie-Louise that she should keep popping in and out of the bureau every fifteen minutes or so.

With the punctuality of policemen, Mr Derval arrived. His eyes followed every line of my body. I felt terrified lest he possessed vision of x-ray quality capable of dissolving clothes. I'd fortified myself with four cocktails, so the dinner went off quite well. Marie-Louise brought in the coffee and liqueurs, and we drew our armchairs round the fire. Mr Derval looked impatiently at Marie-Louise, who was making a labour of the job of clearing away the table. 'Tell her to leave those dishes there,' he said in a desperate voice.

'But, mademoiselle,' replied the old woman, 'if I don't take them down now and wash up, I can't go to bed, and I'm so tired.' I turned my head away from Derval and winked at my servant. Poor Marie-Louise got half the plates on to her tray and walked slowly out of the room, leaving the door open. Mr Derval got up hastily and shut it. He came over and sat on the arm of my chair.

'Ma cherie,' he breathed, putting his arm around my shoulders and pressing me to him. He was bending over in an attempt to kiss me when Marie-Louise entered with her empty tray. He sprang to his feet, cursing under his breath, and stood facing the wall, looking at the picture, while the old servant clumsily cleared the table. When she had gone, he rushed over and sat on my lap. I burst out laughing. A lot of funny things had happened since I'd been in France, but never had a man sat on my lap before. He was no lightweight either. His hands started wandering up and down my body, and I was glad I'd had the foresight to put on a frock which did up at the back. If I hadn't, I was sure that it would have been undone by this time. He'd only just discovered how my frock was fastened when in trotted the faithful Marie-Louise with a basket of logs. Once more, the tough policeman sprang to his feet. The old cook looked quite unconcerned. Of the three, Mr Derval was the most embarrassed. His face was as black as thunder.

'What a shame,' I thought as I watched him strutting furiously to the window. 'It's his job to punish criminals, yet I bet he would gladly choke old Marie-Louise to death.' As she left for the third time, he shut the door behind her and locked it, pocketing the key. 'Oh what a fool I am,' I said to myself. 'Fancy leaving the key in the lock.'

'Now', he said menacingly, 'we won't be disturbed.' He switched off the light, and we sat in the firelight. After a few minutes, he said, 'This fire is too hot. Let's sit on the settee.'

'I'm so cold,' I said.

'Don't worry. I'll warm you up,' he replied and, putting his arm round my waist, led me over to the divan.

The rest of his words were drowned in the noise of Marie-Louise thumping on the door. 'Come quickly, mademoiselle. Something dreadful has happened in the kitchen.' I sprang up from the livid policeman's grasp and switched on the lights.

'Open that door, please. Perhaps there's been an accident.' He obeyed. He picked up his hat and made for the door. 'I'm sorry I settled your affair with the Army,' he snapped. 'Perhaps another night you can repay me for my trouble.' He seemed desperately anxious not to be mixed up in any accident and beat a very hasty retreat. I tore downstairs to the kitchen, not knowing what to expect, and roared with laughter when I saw what had happened. Our cat Nuisance, whom we had all taken for granted to be a tom, had given birth to five kittens.

'Good old Nuisance,' I said fondly. 'That was perfect timing.'

The next day, all the boys turned up.

'Where on earth were you all yesterday? I tried to find you and couldn't,' I asked. Nobody spoke. 'What's the secret anyway?' I continued.

'If you must know', blurted out Johnny, 'we went womanising. Not Neil, he went to a cinema, but Tony and I. We haven't been with a woman since we've been here. That is, until last night and we had to find someone.'

'And what did you find, Johnny?'

'Two damned nice bits of fluff,' he replied proudly.

'Well, I don't want to lecture you, but you know what they say. "One night with Venus, three years with Mercury." Think it over and you'll see that it isn't worth it.'

'But what are we supposed to do, Anne? We've been stuck here three months doing nothing with this bloody war hanging over our heads. We've got to the stage where we don't damned well care what happens to us tomorrow.'

'Do you know they've opened a very exclusive boite not far from here to solve all your problems?' I said.

'Who wants to go to those places and pay as you go in as if it were a cinema. It's not the same. It's commercialising the whole thing,' said Johnny rebelliously.

'At least it's safe. Never mind. Forget it. What do you want to do tonight?'

'Can we stay here if we go to the nightclub?'

'Of course. It's a pity you didn't stay here last night.'

'Why?'

'Oh, forget it boys,' I answered.

The next day, I received orders to report at the ambulance depot the following morning at eight.

I knew this was what I had been waiting for. My first assignment.

Punctual for once, I marched into the commandant's office. Colonel Lammans was rather an effeminate man, with narrow shoulders and a well-filled-out body, a womanly body. He reminded me of a priest. He would certainly have looked better in a priest's cassock than in uniform. He looked nervy and sulky.

'Your orders, Miss Angelo, are to go to Bar-le-Duc, no farther,' he stressed. 'You will stop at a point marked on your map and wait for a driver coming from the other direction. You will exchange ambulances and return to the depot. You must be at that point at one o'clock this afternoon precisely. Not one minute before or after one. It is imperative that you do not hang around in that area, so do not get there before time. Is that understood?'

'Perfectly,' I said, wondering what it all meant and desperately anxious not to seem ignorant or naive. 'Shall I be bringing any wounded back with me?'

'It is your job to carry out orders and not to ask questions,' he replied trying to adopt a very military manner. I thought of Enid's words. 'Nobody ever hears about the wounded. Maybe there aren't any.' Still, I could always look, orders or no orders.

I set off. I had to keep up a constant speed if I were to arrive there on schedule. I was lucky. Apart from an occasional army truck and a few of my pet aversions, the dispatch riders, I had the roads to myself. I wondered who would be in the wrong this time should one of these riders take it into his head to smash up my ambulance. Probably me again. For the simple reason that I was not part of the illustrious French Army. But nothing happened, and I arrived at Bar-le-Duc at a quarter to one. I drove slowly through the village, heading for the clump of trees marked on my map. It was about a kilometre beyond Bar-le-Duc, and I was there in a matter of six minutes. I saw the clump of trees about twenty metres from the road. There were half a dozen of them growing in a field. I drew up as close to them as I could, against the grass verge, and stopped the engine. There was no sign of the other ambulance coming along the road from the opposite direction; and after a few minutes, I decided to get out and walk over to the trees. My legs were stiff, and my eyes were tired. Before leaving the ambulance, I decided that right or wrong, I would have to satisfy my curiosity and look into the back to see what I was carrying. I was quite certain of one thing. I wasn't carrying wounded men. Apart from the fact that I had no orderly with me, it would not have made sense to bring wounded to the Maginot. From it, yes, but not to it.

I walked round the vehicle to the back and was more than a little worried to find that it was padlocked. 'Good God, maybe I'm carrying bombs, and I don't know. I'd better get over to that clump of trees and wait just in case. I certainly don't feel like standing by, just to prove to myself how brave I am.'

The ditch was rather wide; I couldn't jump it, so I jumped into it, intending to scramble up the other side, but I got no farther. Out of nowhere, a plane was diving. I wanted to get out of the ditch and run to the trees, but I couldn't move. My legs were like jelly, and I was paralysed with fear. I stared at the plane which zoomed down, getting nearer and nearer. With the first burst of its machine gun, my legs gave way, and I fell flat on my face. Bullets tore up the grass verge and sprayed me with earth and stones. Then there was a deafening explosion, and the sound of the plane's engine died away. I tried to get up, but my legs were still like jelly, my stomach kept turning over and over. I was still too petrified to move. Besides, I had an idea that perhaps I was wounded, maybe I had lost a leg or something. I didn't know, I couldn't feel anything, and I was too terrified to find out.

I didn't know quite how long I'd lain there. The first thing I knew was that a soldier was leaning over me, giving me a drink from his flask. I didn't know what I drank. It tasted like firewater.

'Are you sure you're all right?'

'I don't know. What happened?' I asked stupidly.

'Oh, the usual. I'm quite prepared to bet that this place is alive with Jerry's spies. No matter which route we take, they know, and this is the result. Still, you're lucky. Your predecessors hadn't enough sense to jump out in time. I don't think you're hurt. Here, take my hand.' He heaved me out of the ditch.

'Good heavens, what a mess,' I screamed, staring at the mass of twisted steel and smouldering tyres, which was all that was left of the ambulance. 'What do I do now?'

'You'll have to get back the best way you can,' he told me. 'I'll have to take my ambulance back with me. There's no other way for me. You'll be all right. You will probably get a lift, or even a train.'

'But what about your wounded?' I asked. 'You can't take them back to the Maginot.'

'Oh, they can wait. I'll have to leave you and get back. Cheerio. Good luck.' With these parting words, he was gone, and I felt more lost than ever. If I'd not been so frightened of a repetition of the last few minutes, I would have sat down at the roadside and cried with rage and self-pity, but I started to walk away from it back to Bar-le-Duc.

I began to realise why we'd had such extensive physical training. Those instructors must have foreseen that we would probably have to walk back from each trip. Still, I hoped I would find some means of transport at Bar-le-Duc, but I was unlucky. There was nothing at all. My only hope was to walk to the nearest town some five kilometres away, where I could get a train. I trudged on, hoping for a lift from anyone at all. I would even have welcomed a dispatch rider, but all I could see coming down the road behind me was an old man on a bicycle. I stopped him. He seemed very surprised to see me on foot. My uniform was no longer immaculate, I was mud stained and weary; a rent in my tunic disclosed the miracles of padding, which gave me such perfect shoulders in uniform.

'Have you had an accident?' he asked kindly. He had such a placid expression on his face and spoke so softly that I had an impulse to bury my head on his shoulder and cry. Instead, I said, 'Can you give me a lift on your bicycle? I've been walking for ages, and I'm still at least five kilometres from the station.'

He smiled benevolently. 'I only wish I could oblige you, but I can scarcely keep myself on this ancient bicycle. I had intended to get a tricycle this year, but then the war came.'

I looked at him, and a brilliant idea flashed through my mind.

'If I make a pillow for you with my tunic and use it as a cushion on the bar, I could ride the bicycle if you could balance on the crossbar. Do you think you could?' I asked.

'I'll try,' said the old man, eager to be of some assistance. 'We shouldn't meet anybody along here, which is just as well. They'd think we had escaped from a circus.'

We started off. The old man was a bit nervous, but he did his best not to overbalance. I found it very hard work pedalling up the hill and wondered when he'd last oiled this rusty old bicycle. The old man was as excited as a schoolboy. It was the first time he'd ever been taken for a ride, and I could imagine the fun he was going to get out of discussing it with his cronies. I was very grateful to him and shook his hand warmly as I bade him goodbye and made for the station.

I went straight home. I knew that I ought to report to the depot before going home, but I felt I must get cleaned up first and steady my nerves before presenting myself minus ambulance to Colonel Lammans. I expected a terrible slating. I knew I shouldn't have disobeyed his orders and shouldn't have arrived too soon at the destination. Yet my common sense told me that if I had arrived there dead on time, the chances were that I would not have heard the plane with my own engine running and would have been blown up with it. Anyway, I wasn't in the mood to be told that I must obey orders blindly or resign, war or no war. It was all right for him to sit pretty in his comfortable office.

Marie-Louise was relieved to see me. 'Monsieur Derval from the Surete has been ringing up ever since you left,' she told me.

'I'm just in the mood for that swine,' I answered furiously. 'If he rings again, tell him I'm back. He'll know anyway. But tell him from me that unless he wants to go out of here on a stretcher, he'd better not come along till I feel like seeing him.'

'I don't like this quietness, this waiting.' She drew a letter out of her apron pocket. 'I had a letter from my son, Jacques, yesterday. He says he is so bored and wants to come home for a little while. He's done nothing at the Maginot for the last six months. He says the Germans fire for a quarter of an hour every evening and they fire back. That's all that happens. They listen to the Germans singing German songs all day, and the Germans have also put up notices. "Go home to your families. We don't want to fight you." It's all very demoralising for our men. I wish he could come home.' Marie-Louise started weeping uncontrollably.

'Don't cry, Marie-Louise,' I said gently. 'It's all for the safety of France, to make all our homes safe once more.'

'But how did they come to be unsafe?' she asked, dabbing at her eyes with her apron.

'It's no use asking me that, Marie-Louise. I don't understand war at all. I saw a little of what it's like for the first time, and I can't understand how peace can be born of such destruction. Anyway, I'm going straight to bed, so if anyone turns up, I'm not here.'

'I'll get you something to eat while you're getting ready for bed.'

When I arrived at the depot next day, Colonel Lammans welcomed me with a smile. 'I'm so glad you are safe. It was most unfortunate, the whole thing. We're working on a plan to make these expeditions safer.'

'You know what happened?' I asked, feeling more and more bewildered.

'Naturally, I shall not need you before next week. I'll write you in good time.'

'Thank you,' I replied, feeling very dazed, and walked out. 'Somebody's crazy', I thought, 'and it can't always be me. Anyway, I can live for another week according to him. He'd better make these trips safer. I'm not sticking my neck out for any old scrap iron. For wounded soldiers, yes, but not for whatever it is we are carrying. I still don't know what it is either.'

* * *

Gerald, 1940

CHAPTER 7

Gerald

I WAS NEARLY HOME—IN rue Nationale approaching rue Alphonse Mercier—when I saw another car coming fast off my right. I tried to stop, but there was a bright flash and a bang. I woke up flat on my back in bed.

'She's conscious, Doctor.' There was a nurse looking down at me. I had a frightful headache and blood in my mouth. My face was all swollen up, and I could hardly see out of my eyes. Some of my front teeth were gone.

He was in Army uniform. He put a hand over one of my eyes, quickly took it away, and watched. Then the same with the other. He pressed my face and moved my jaw. He tapped my knees and elbows with a little rubber hammer. And scratched the soles of my feet. He listened to my chest. Then he covered me up again.

'She'll be all right,' he said. 'A touch of concussion, but nothing serious. Keep her flat, sister. And keep those curtains drawn. She should be able to sit up in a couple of days. We'll get the dentist to see what can be done about those teeth. But other than that, there's not much we can do. I'll look in, in about a week or so. If you need me, don't hesitate.' And he put his things in his bag and went.

It was late morning. She gave me soup through a cup with a spout. She wouldn't let me lift a finger, and she wouldn't give me a pillow. Marie-Louise came to see me. She said it was an Army car that'd hit me. They'd brought me home. The officer had carried me up in his arms. They'd put the Buick in the garage.

The next day, it was nearly dark when I heard voices out in the bureau. Sister was talking with someone. It was an English voice, real

English, well educated, with no accent. She came and asked if I felt up to seeing a visitor. She said a British major wanted to see me. I didn't know any British majors, and I couldn't imagine what one wanted with me, but I was intrigued by the voice. So I said yes.

'Yes, Major. Come in,' she said. 'But don't stay long, please. She has to have rest and quiet. Here. If you'll give me those, I'll put them in water for you.' Out of the corner of my eye, I saw him give her a gorgeous great sheaf of flowers. He came in and looked down at me.

He was about fifty, lean and suntanned. An outdoor sort of face. The eyes were blue, with crinkles at the corners. His hair was fair surrounding a dignified bald crown. He had a good jaw and mouth. His major's cap was under his arm, and he was clean-shaven.

'Hallo,' he said quietly. 'And how are you?' And he was really concerned. His tone nearly made me cry. I was feeling awful, and I knew I looked it. My lips were all split and scabby, my face was all puffed up, and my eyes were going black. I wondered who he was and why he was so interested.

His eyes narrowed, and he stooped a bit to look at me more closely. He was really worried.

'Are you all right?' he said. 'Can you hear me?'

'Oh yes. Yes, of course. I'm sorry.' It was mostly a lisp. It was my four top front teeth that were gone. 'I was wondering who you are and why you're so interested. I don't think I know you although you remind me of someone.'

'Oh, is that what it was? Oh, that's fine. I thought . . . for a minute . . . well, never mind. And so I remind you of someone, do I? I hope it's someone nice. I'm the one that brought you home. We ran into you. At least my driver did. The police wanted to get an ambulance, but I looked in your purse and found you lived here. I said it'd be quicker if we brought you. Your housekeeper said to bring you up here. I just wanted you to know everything's all right. It was my driver's fault, not yours. Everything'll be fixed up. Your car's in your garage. We'll attend to that. All you've got to do is rest and get well. I'll shove off now. But I'd like to call in again, if I might. Would that be all right with you?'

I said it would and asked if he could say when. But he said he couldn't. He didn't know. And then he went.

And that's how I found what I was looking for. It was something like that whisky bottle in the sea. I could have wished we hadn't come together so violently. I'd been rather proud of my teeth. But if that's the way it had to be, that's the way it had to be. It certainly made sure we'd meet again. He had to come back. And when he did, the circumstances tied us further together. It had to develop.

It was five days later. In those five days, I gave myself an awful time wondering about him. Sister wouldn't tell me anything. Except not to ask questions. All she would tell me was that he was with the British Expeditionary Force. They all were. He'd got the doctor, and the doctor had put her on to me. She was going to stay until I was all right again. But she did what she could, though.

It was mid-afternoon, sunny and bright. I was sitting up in bed, reading. As soon as I heard the voice, I knew. She told him to wait; she'd see if I was awake. She knew jolly well I was because she'd only just left me. She shut the door behind her and got my bed jacket, mirror, and hairbrush.

'Here,' she whispered. 'Quickly. Slip this on and do your hair. Your major's here to see you. But be prepared for a shock. He's not quite the same.' She gave me time and then let him in.

It was an awful let-down. It nearly killed the whole thing. He came in like some scruffy barge hand or canal worker. He had an old cloth cap in his hand. His hair was all tousled. He hadn't shaved for at least a couple of days. His hands and face were dirty. His shirt was dirty. He had no tie or collar. The red-flannel singlet was as grubby as the shirt. The coat and pants were shabby and worn. His eyes were tired and bloodshot.

'Hallo,' he said. 'Yes, that looks much better. Good. I've been worried about you.' He came forward with his hand out to shake hands but saw how dirty it was and lowered it. He glanced down at himself. 'I'm afraid I'm not very presentable, am I? Sorry about that, but I thought I'd better come while I was in the area. I can never be quite sure.'

He looked round and saw the chair at my dressing table. 'I say, would you mind very much if I sat down? I'm a bit knocked up.' Without waiting for an answer, he went and got it, set it down by me, sat on it, and, without another word, went fast to sleep.

I didn't know what to make of it. I couldn't imagine what he was doing in that condition, but he was obviously exhausted. I felt sorry for him and let him sleep until he nearly fell. Then I woke him. For a split second, he was like a cat in a lion's den—scared stiff. He covered it up by bending and picking up his cap.

'So I dropped off, did I? Sorry about that. Certainly didn't mean to. Now let's see. What were we talking about?'

'We weren't talking about anything, Major. We didn't get a chance. You came in, said you'd been worried about me, got the chair, and went to sleep. Tell me. When did you sleep last?'

'Oh, a couple of nights ago. Why?'

'Yes, that's what I thought. And how much time do you have now?'

'Time? Oh, time's nothing. I shouldn't have anything now until one thirty. But why do you ask?'

'One thirty?' My clock said quarter to four.

'Yes. One thirty in the morning. Why?' His voice was sharp and suspicious.

'Oh, nothing. I thought maybe you'd made a mistake. What I was going to say was, would you like to go and have a sleep now? You could if you wanted to. We've got plenty of rooms, and some are empty. You could have a bath too, if you like. They've all got en suite bathrooms. I could get you a pair of men's pyjamas and a razor. You could have a sleep and then have some dinner with us. We don't have much, but there'd be enough to go round. Would you like that? And while you're asleep, my housekeeper could freshen your clothes up for you. What do you say?'

He thought it over and said he'd like it very much. But he didn't want to shave. And he didn't want his clothes touched. Marie-Louise got him a pair of old Jacques' pyjamas and put him in the Blue Room over the entrance. She made dinner and brought it up to us. He stayed until about eleven thirty.

He wouldn't tell me what he'd been doing. He said it was just part of the job. And he wouldn't say what that was. He wouldn't even tell me his name. I asked him, but he only said I could call him Gerald.

'But Gerald what?'

'That'll do, won't it? In the meantime?' He had the quizzical look Peter used to get when he was teasing. 'And then I can call you Anne?' He'd seen it on my license. He was very interested in why I'd left Scotland. And what I was going to do in France. But he wouldn't tell me anything about himself. He said the present was too risky to talk about, the past was finished and done with, and the future was too uncertain. 'Let's just take it as it comes.'

He left through the back way. He couldn't say when I'd see him again. He had a bike he'd left on the patio. But before he got it, he dirtied his hands and face at one of the flowerbeds. I watched him from my windows. Then he got his bike and carried it down, hopped on, and rode away. He looked like a real hobo in his old cloth cap.

Being forced to realise that Army officers, some of them anyway, were pretty awful, made me think about Gerald. He was one of them. Did he have the same attitude towards women? Was he the man I thought he was, or was I wasting my time thinking so much about him? It appeared to me that the sooner I found out all I could about him, the better it would be for me. I began asking questions—who he was, where he was stationed, and how I could get in touch with him. But I got blocked even in that.

They had a big conference. The top brass from both armies came, and there were statesmen and politicians. The entire hotel was surrounded by swarms of soldiers from both armies. I was out on the drive, below the patio steps, washing the car, and HRH the Duke of Gloucester came out. He'd heard I was English and asking a lot of questions, and he came to check on me. It wasn't until I told him about nearly getting caught by Lord Louis Mountbatten over the ten gallons of whisky/benzene that he really believed me. That amused him. He said Lord Louis would have enjoyed it too if he'd known. He used some pet name for him. But he gave me a bit of a lecture about asking questions.

'You just stop it,' he said. 'If your Gerald didn't give you his name and where you could contact him, you can be jolly sure he had good reason not to. There are jobs to be done where a man's very life can depend on his being unknown and unsuspected. Yes, and much more than that could depend on it. The enemy has his eyes and ears the same way we have. And remember this too: what you don't know, you can't be made to tell.' And that was something I'd never even thought about. It meant that he thought I might find myself in enemy hands. Anyway, it certainly stopped me asking any more questions. Before he went back inside, he let me take his photograph.

His bit about 'can't be made to tell' worried me. If he thought I could find myself in German hands, it was likely it could happen. He'd know more than I would. It was another reason I wished I could find Gerald. He was really the only one I knew who could advise me. As far as I could see, I was better off in my hotel in Lille than I would be back in my father's clutches in Invergordon. But I didn't need to worry about Gerald. When I really needed him, he found me.

Mr Derval, that horrible policeman, called. He said he'd come about the accident, the one with Gerald's driver. He said it looked as if I'd have to be charged. But he may be able to settle this matter as he had the last time. He pressed to discuss it over a meal at my place that evening. And this time he was not going to take no for an answer.

He brought a bottle of cognac. He drank most of it and then locked the door and tried to get amorous again. I was fighting him off when the phone rang. Without letting go of me, he answered it and said we didn't want to be disturbed. He was strong, and things weren't going too well for me. I was holding on to both sides of the door into the bedroom. He was behind me with one hand round my waist and the other round my chin trying to drag me through. Suddenly there was a banging on the outside bureau door. It was Gerald.

'Anne! Are you all right in there?'

I managed to get out a feeble 'Help! Gerald! Please help me!'

'Open this door immediately or I'll smash it down! Immediately!'

My policeman thought about it for a moment and then let me go. I got that door open and came out into Gerald's arms. He had his revolver in his hand. He was in his uniform and had his driver with him. There were some French soldiers in the background.

When he'd heard what had happened and what the policeman had said about the accident, he took some sort of identification from his top pocket and held it for the chief to see. Then he told him to get out and that he would hear much more about the matter. The policeman slunk out like a whipped cur.

I didn't see what it was he showed the policeman, but the effect it had told me he was certainly Army and that he had some special authority over the French police. It made me feel marvellous. I'd been wondering about him ever since he'd turned up in his barge-hand clothes and riding a bicycle. Now I was satisfied on that score at least.

I got another dinner sent up, and he stayed until late. He knew a lot more about me than I'd told him. He'd found out a lot about Father and his work at the Navy Yards. He answered all my questions about the chances of the Germans ever coming to Lille. He said he thought it was very likely they would. There was nobody to stop them. By the time he left, I had a lovely feeling that I had someone who really cared about me.

*   *   *

CHAPTER 8

Another Brush With Death

B UT THE AMBULANCE corps had other plans for me, and one morning towards the middle of the week, I found myself once more in the driving seat, on the open road heading for the Maginot line, but this time on quite a different route.

My mind was full of Gerald. I wanted so very much to see him again that I had actually been praying and asking God to send him to me. I had never felt like this about any man I had ever met in my whole life. I felt quite sure that I would be capable of taking the vows and entering a convent for the rest of my life if I could not be with him. Yet, I told myself, he may be married, and he was not the type to live with another woman. With him, it would be marriage or nothing. I wondered if I would ever know. I knew it would not be easy to drag any information out of him, private or otherwise, but I could always get him tight. Drink usually loosened tongues; all I wanted was the opportunity to find out if there was any chance for me.

Had I not been so engrossed in thinking of Gerald, I would have noticed that the road on which I was driving was absolutely devoid of any cover whatsoever. There wasn't a tree or hedge for kilometres. When I did realise it, I was quite panic-stricken. The road stretched ahead like a long white ribbon, and I felt terrified at the thought of driving on in that open country. From the air, I stood out too clearly to be safe. I pulled up. Terror always played havoc with me, and I knew I must find a hedge or somewhere to ease my feelings. I had lived long enough in France to have become accustomed to the sight of women squatting at the side of the road whenever they felt inclined, but I had retained a sense of refinement. This refinement was peculiar and affected me when confronted with the minor indelicacies of life. Although there wasn't a soul in sight, I simply couldn't just squat down at the roadside. There were no trees, so the next best thing was to wander halfway across the field at the side of the road. It seemed the middle of the field was better; it wasn't so public, so that was the right thing to do.

It was fortunate for me that I wasn't like the French peasant women, because I had no sooner put a substantial distance between me and the ambulance than I saw a sneak raider dive down towards it. This time there was no machine gunning, just one single bomb which must have hit it dead on. There was one terrific explosion, and then the ambulance blew up before my startled eyes. I watched the pieces fall from the air. One wheel was rolling down the road, pieces of the body were soaring through the air and landing in the field. All that was left of it was a distorted mass of twisted metal.

I was livid with rage. Rage against the Hun who had done this foul deed, rage against Colonel Lammans who had convinced me that he would make these trips safer, and rage against this phoney war which had disrupted transport to such an extent that I did not know how I would ever get home.

As I walked on trying to find a town, I began to wonder if Colonel Lammans were not a Nazi agent. Walking slowly through the lanes, I could take stock of the surrounding country and was quite sure that no sane man would send an ambulance out on such a bleak route, unless, of course, he deliberately meant it to be easily spotted from the air. I loathed him, I would denounce him, I would have nothing more to do with him or his doomed ambulances. This was the end as far as I was concerned, and wouldn't I enjoy telling him what I thought of him if I ever got back. Besides, I didn't want to die, not now when Gerald had entered my life. I wanted to cry with rage. The thought that maybe Gerald would call while I was trudging the roads like a vagabond made me want to scream. But what was the use? I prayed he wouldn't call before I got home.

It took me till the next day to get home. I refused to report at the depot, sent back my uniform, and rang up Colonel Lammans. For ten minutes, the wires were burning, but I refused to stop until I had told him exactly what I thought of him and of his outfit; and then when I had finished, I rammed down the receiver without even waiting for an explanation. I then broke down, and, dropping my weary head on my arms, cried myself to sleep in the chair.

The next day, I was still all nerves. I rang up Enid Hunter and asked her round to tea. I felt I must talk to someone solid and sensible, and Enid was always so calm. Enid's first words when she saw me were typical.

'Good heavens, what's the matter with you? You look like death warmed up.'

'I've had a dreadful time,' I replied. 'You can't imagine so much happening to one miserable person in two miserable weeks.' I told my friend about the ambulances, about the Surete chief, about the French major, and, finally, about Gerald. Enid was a perfect listener. Never once did she interrupt, and only once did she raise her eyebrows in astonishment. It was when I referred to Derval as a buffer between myself and the French Army. When I had finished, I looked Enid straight in the eye and said, 'Be a pal, Enid, and tell me what is wrong with me. I don't go about looking for trouble, and yet trouble is drawn to me as though I were a damned magnet. What is your candid opinion? Don't worry about offending me. Just tell me frankly.'

Enid looked very glum as she replied earnestly.

'Theoretically, you ought to be a corpse by now, but as you're not, you must lead a charmed life. Nobody could go through so much and live to talk about it unless she had at least nine lives like a cat.'

'But that isn't the point, Enid,' I interrupted. 'What I want you to do is to explain to me why these things happen to me. They don't happen to you, do they?'

'I should hope not. I don't think I have sufficient luck to see me through even a fraction of your adventures. But I believe I can put my finger on your trouble. Call it your handicap if you like.'

'Oh, call it what the devil you like, Enid. Only, what is my trouble?'

'You're too trusting,' replied Enid, shrugging her shoulders. 'Take Derval, for a start. Did he show you any official report about your accident with the dispatch rider?'

'No,' I said, feeling more than a little foolish.

'Well, there you are, then. There probably wasn't any, and he puts the fear of death into you to get what he wants, and you fall for it—hook, line, and sinker.'

'Now explain the ambulances.'

'I can't explain them. It looks very much like sabotage to me, but you would never be able to prove anything. I think you've done the right thing in giving it up. But you're incredibly lucky, you know. I can understand why the others never came back. You must admit that things happen to you that don't happen to everybody, and I quite agree with you that you don't look for trouble. I know you don't.'

'How do you account for my meeting Gerald and knowing him, although I've never seen him in my life before?'

'At the risk of making you really mad, there's one suggestion I can make.'

'Yes?' I said eagerly.

'He's probably a German spy.'

'Oh no, Enid,' I wailed. 'Don't say such a thing even in fun, not that it would make any difference to me anyway. I'm beyond all reasoning as far as he is concerned. I love that man blindly and unreasonably. I don't even know his name, yet I worship him. Even if he is a spy, it won't make any difference to me. I just can't help it. I hope with all my heart that he isn't. The very idea is revolting, but I would still adore him. It's the man I love, not what he does. Besides, he's Irish.'

'In that case, he's much more likely to be a British agent than a German one,' replied Enid convincingly. According to Enid's one-track mind, anybody who was Irish couldn't possibly be anything but a hero.

'I wish you could meet him.'

Just then, the sound of the boys arriving downstairs broke the silence. Instead of the usual three, there were five of them.

'Go down to the kitchen, Johnny, and ask Marie-Louise to make stacks of sandwiches. You're the only one she understands,' I ordered.

Neil introduced the newcomers. 'This is Dr Paddy and Jerry, both Irish. They've only just come over and feel terribly lost. You don't mind, Anne, do you?'

'Not a bit. Make yourselves at home. You know Enid.'

Enid was quite enjoying Paddy's conversation, but her face dropped when he showed her a photo of his wife. That was quite enough to make her lose all interest in him, and she lapsed into her usual silence. The telephone rang, and it was Gerald. 'Good God,' I thought. 'On the very evening I would've liked to be alone. And look at the place! It looks more like a ruddy zoo than a quiet bureau.' It certainly did, and the chatter of these youths was deafening.

'Gerald is coming up, Enid,' I whispered. I felt excitement. My heart was thumping so loudly that I was sure everybody in the room could hear it in spite of the noise. He knocked at the door, and I sprang up to open it.

'Hello Gerald,' I said, drawing him into the room. He'd seemed to hang back as I opened the door and he saw the overcrowded bureau. The noise stopped abruptly as he entered. The boys scrambled to their feet, making a feeble attempt at coming to attention at the sight of a superior officer. They looked a sorry sight with their tunics all undone, their belts thrown all round the room, and their mouths full.

'Gerald', I said, breaking the silence, 'this is Enid Hunter, and these are some of my boys. Don't mind the state they're in. They come here to relax. I'm foster mother to half the BEF.' He sat down, and Enid offered him some sandwiches. The boys were very ill at ease.

'If you boys are going out for dinner, you'd better get cleaned up and started. You know where the bathroom is. Think of Marie-Louise, and don't make too much mess,' I said, making it very obvious that I wanted to get rid of them. They hurried out, apparently relieved at the excuse I'd given them for leaving.

'I suppose you aren't coming with us?' said Johnny, glaring at Gerald.

'Not tonight. Another night.'

'I suppose we can't—,' Johnny went on, but I cut in on him.

'No, you can't. Not tonight.' I knew perfectly well what they wanted. They wanted permission to come back and sleep there for the night, but I wanted the house to myself with no interruptions from anyone. They streamed out. Enid laughed.

'What's so funny, Enid? It's your turn now to be hoofed out.'

'You are staying to dinner, aren't you, Gerald?'

'If I may.'

I was overjoyed. 'What about you, Enid, you don't want to stay for dinner, do you?'

'How could anyone refuse such a warm invitation?' my friend joked. 'You make it extremely difficult for me to say no, but I must get home.' Gerald laughed at my clumsy attempt to get rid of Enid, but Enid was no spoilsport.

'Your mania for saying what you think will get you hanged one day. You mark my words. Oh well, I'd better leave you in peace. Come and see me out.' She collected her bag and gloves and told Gerald she hoped to see him again.

'What do you think of him?' I asked excitedly as we went downstairs together.

'At last', my friend told me frankly, 'you've picked somebody out of the top drawer. Gerald has generations of breeding. He's an aristocrat to his fingertips. You're damned lucky. Find out if he has a brother.'

On my way back to the bureau, I called out to Marie-Louise, 'How long will it take you to prepare a nice little dinner for two?'

'About an hour, but there isn't anything very exciting in the house,' replied the old woman.

'But you must get something, something nice, anywhere. Beg, borrow, or steal it if you have to, but find something. Get it from the Army, but get it.'

The old servant chuckled. 'Very well, leave it to me.' She vanished in the direction of the kitchen.

I flew back to the bureau, wondering if Gerald was getting impatient at being left alone. But no, there he was, as I had left him, perfectly comfortable in a big armchair, quietly sipping a cocktail, his long legs stretched out in front of him. I couldn't help feeling how well he fitted in that room. He seemed to belong to it, and he certainly looked at home. The moment I entered, I felt a physical delight within my body, and I was conscious of being particularly and exquisitely happy. I sat down on the floor in front of the fire and looked up at him.

'I still can't understand a young girl living alone in such a big place. It just doesn't make sense.'

'But I've told you this is my home.'

'I understand your point perfectly, but, don't tell me to mind my own business if I say I don't think you've got this war properly into focus. Do forgive me if I say what I think, but I'm nearly old enough to be your father, and I was here in the last war.'

'Please go on,' I broke in. 'I should like your advice.'

'Well, to start with', Gerald went on, 'your being here isn't going to prevent this place being blown to atoms if there are raids. Secondly, if it doesn't get razed to the ground and this town is occupied by the Germans, you'll either be in a concentration camp and this house would be swarming with Huns who would undoubtedly loot the place, or, even worse, you might be picked up one night as a hostage and shot. So you see, you'll lose this house anyway. But if you stay, you may lose your life as well.'

'You make it sound ghastly.' I was on the point of tears. 'I love this place more than anything else in the world. In fact, it's the only thing I've got to love.'

'But surely a girl like you doesn't have to remain single all her life? It almost seems like sacrilege to me to hear you talk of loving this house as if it were a human being. There must be dozens of men crazy about you. If you tell me there are none, I most certainly will not believe you.'

'It isn't easy to find the right man. I've tasted what it can be like with the wrong one. I don't want to make the same mistake again,' I replied quietly. 'But supposing I ask you a few questions, will you answer them?'

'I'll try,' he said, looking straight at me.

'Well, forgive me for being personal, but you have what I would call a suffering face. Are you unhappy?'

'I didn't know that it showed on my face. The only answer I can give is that I'm not one of those fortunate mortals ideally married and blissfully happy. I'm not happy, but I think it's probably largely my own fault.'

'Do you feel like talking about it to a stranger?'

'Somehow I don't feel that you're a stranger, Anne. I seem to have known you for years, but I don't think talking about myself is going to make my life less complicated.'

'No, but it could make it less unbearable,' I replied softly.

Just then, the conversation was interrupted by Marie-Louise bringing in the hors d'oeuvres. She'd arranged everything beautifully, and Gerald seemed ravenous.

'When did you have a meal last?' I asked him.

'Very early this morning. I've had a beast of a day, but I've made up my mind to see you this evening, so I worked like a demon to get it finished,' he replied between mouthfuls. When Marie-Louise brought in the 'piece de resistance', I looked guiltily from the tiny chicken to the old woman. I raised my eyebrows, and Marie-Louise shrugged her shoulders. Deciding that the sooner we ate, it the better, as we had definitely not bought the chicken during the last month, I proceeded to carve it. Marie-Louise seemed to have taken her orders far too literally. Although I enjoyed good food, I was glad when the meal was over and we settled down to our coffee and liqueurs. I sat, as usual, on the floor—only this time, I sat at Gerald's feet, my head resting on his knee.

'Do you feel like continuing our conversation regarding your private worries, Gerald?' I asked, feeling extremely curious.

'I don't think so, Anne. Not tonight. Another night perhaps. It seems such a pity to spoil such a perfect evening with my sordid life story.' He couldn't see my face, but I frowned. But to me, Gerald's word was law, so we spent a pleasant evening contrasting the two countries, France and England. I tried to convince him there was no country like France. Gerald almost convinced me that England was a country worth dying for. It was past midnight before he left, promising faithfully to come back the following week. I knew this time that he would.

Life moved on in a pleasant round of eating and sleeping. Early bedtimes and long quiet nights. What I felt for Gerald was something I had never felt for anybody in my whole life.

One evening the following week, the doorbell rang. I knew it was Gerald. Even the bell seemed to have a joyful ring when he was outside. I tried to tell myself that it was silly to feel so excited, but I couldn't help it. For a moment, I stood motionless, feeling something akin to panic starting my heart thumping madly. Then I raced down the stairs and stopped short, breathless, as Gerald was admitted by Marie-Louise. I looked at him, and my heart seemed to somersault. I couldn't speak, only stare at him as he came towards me, his hand outstretched. He smiled, and the hall seemed full of sunshine. By the time we reached the bureau, I was more composed. I wanted to throw myself into his arms, but I didn't dare. I was terrified of doing anything which might offend or embarrass him.

'I can't stay long,' he told me apologetically. 'I'm dreadfully sorry. I've been looking forward so much to spending another long evening here. You make me feel like a human being again when I'm with you.'

'Can't you get yourself billeted near here, Gerald?' I said, trying to sound flippant, but hot tears were stinging the back of my eyes. I'd waited night after night for him, not daring to go out in case he should call, and now he had come, he could not stay.

*   *   *

CHAPTER 9

Husband And Wife

A MONTH LATER, MY relationship with Gerald had progressed very little. I sometimes wondered how I'd had the courage to wait night after night, week after week, just for the occasional glimpse of him. I'd never considered myself the faithful waiting type, yet nothing could drag me away from the house in case he should call. It never struck me as strange that I should lead such a monotonous life. In any case, in my own mind, I knew there was nothing I could do about it. I knew too that if I were to go out in the evenings, I would be as miserable as sin, and anxious to go home in case he was there, so I did the only thing I could do. I waited and waited. Still, the joy on his face each time he called me felt it was worth waiting for. I adored him more than I thought it possible to adore any human being, but I still didn't know what his feelings for me were. I'd tried to draw him out, to get him to talk about his family, his home, but it was no use. It was always 'another time'.

On this particular evening, he seemed rather nervous.

'What's worrying you, Gerald? Can't you tell me?' I asked when I could bear the tension no longer.

'I'm going on leave tomorrow. I've ten days. I'm not looking forward to it, but I must go. I've things to straighten out, once and for all. It isn't fair to you that I should go on like this without at least making an effort to find out what my position is going to be for the rest of my life.'

'I don't understand,' I said softly. 'What has it to do with me?'

'Everything,' he replied. 'Can't you see how desperately I love you? I'm not free to love you. I want you more than I have ever wanted anything in my life before, but it's not fair to you. As long as I'm married, I haven't the right to love you or to expect you to love me.'

'But I do love you, Gerald. I love you so much I don't want to live without you. A hundred wives couldn't keep me away from you. What does one matter? We could be just as happy together with or without a wife in the background. She couldn't spoil our lives. Only we ourselves could do that, and we wouldn't, so why worry?'

'Darling, I adore your philosophy on life, but it just isn't as simple as that. You don't know what the conventions are like. It's wrong in the eyes of most people. It would smirch us forever.'

'But I don't care what people say,' I said abruptly.

'But I do,' said Gerald. 'It would mean social isolation.'

'Not in France, Gerald. It doesn't mean a thing here. I want you, darling. I want you always.'

'If I didn't love you so much, I would listen to you, Anne, but I can't let you ruin your life for me. I don't live in France. We would have to live in England. You don't know what such a relationship would mean over there. You can't know, you're so young.' He took me in his arms for the first time and tenderly kissed my lips.

When we had both regained our composure, Gerald said quietly, 'You see, that's why I must go home tomorrow. It's doubtful if we can ever marry, but I'll tell her she must give me a divorce. I'll do my utmost.' My eyes filled with tears. I knew women. I knew Gerald's wife would not give him up, I had a feeling that she belonged to that soul-destroying species of female who, not wanting their husbands themselves, made sure that no other woman could ever have them and kept them chained to their vows for the rest of their miserable lives. I also knew that unless Gerald was free, he would never consent to live with me. His principles would not permit anything which was not entirely above board. The thought of the future without him was unbearable. But it was in the hands of the gods. I would pray for his freedom as I had never prayed before.

For the next few days, Gerald was seldom out of my thoughts. I wondered how he was getting on with his wife. I wondered what he would be like in a temper. I'd never seen him in a temper, but I was quite sure that he had one. What Irishman had not. I wished he was back for more reasons than one. Apart from missing him dreadfully, I wanted to know the worst. This suspense was awful.

Five days had gone by. I could neither eat nor sleep. It was very late at night, but I tossed restlessly in my bed. I had a strange feeling that Gerald was not far off. I decided that I must be going crazy. Too much worrying. But sure enough, a few minutes later, I heard a car draw up at the door. It was past midnight. I sprang out of bed and looked down from my balcony. I could not see much in the blackout, but I called out Gerald's name. He called up to me to come down for a minute, and I absolutely flew downstairs to let him in. I hadn't even waited to snatch up a dressing gown; I just ran as I was in a nightgown, more revealing than concealing, and threw myself into his arms on the doorstep. He took off his greatcoat and wrapped it round me. I wasn't quite sure why he did it. I was sure I looked much better without it. We went up to the bureau, and then I saw his face properly in the light. It was worn and haggard, and his eyes were so red that I wondered if he'd been crying. I dismissed such a ridiculous idea from my mind. He was no woman; he was a real man. He sank down into an armchair, covering his eyes with his hands. I put my arms round his neck and kissed him tenderly.

'What happened, Gerald? Why are you in such a state?' I asked, feeling very worried at his wild appearance.

'It's no good, darling. I've had a hell of a time, and all for nothing. I haven't closed an eye since I left here.'

'This is dreadful, darling. I'll get you a hot drink, and you can stay here tonight. There's an empty room next door to mine. Until you've had some rest, we won't talk about it. Tomorrow perhaps.'

I didn't expect him to agree, but he was obviously too tired to refuse, and within half an hour, he was tucked up.

Next morning, when I peeped in to see if he was awake, I found him still fast asleep. So I let him sleep on. At about midday, I ran a bath for him and asked Marie-Louise to bring him up some breakfast. The old woman seemed to have taken a fancy to him, and the tray she brought was quite a work of art. She wouldn't give it to me to take in but insisted, much to Gerald's embarrassment, on bringing it right up to his bed.

'I hope you haven't anything to do this morning, Gerald', I said, laughing, 'because it's already afternoon.'

He sat bolt upright, as if realising that he had no right to be there, but he soon recovered himself and remembered that he was on leave. 'How on earth did I get here?' he asked.

'You were no trouble. You obeyed like a lamb, and you've slept the clock round,' I replied. 'Listen to me, darling. Why not spend the rest of your leave here? You surely don't want to go back to work before you need to.'

'Oh no, Anne, I don't want to plant myself on you like this. I'm very grateful to you for putting me up last night. I was all in, but I can't impose on you.'

'But, dearest, I want you to stay. You must stay. You can do just as you please, go out, or stay in, or just eat and sleep, but please stay,' I pleaded.

'There's nothing I'd like better, my dear, if you're quite sure I won't be in the way.'

'Positive darling,' I replied, bubbling over with happiness. 'Your bathroom's next door. You'll find everything you want there, and don't be alarmed at all the gadgets. You'll learn by your mistakes.'

We spent the entire day doing nothing, and after lazing about, Gerald was beginning to look human again. After dinner, I asked him to tell me what happened during his short leave.

'She was drunk when I arrived, and stayed that way for days. When eventually she did sober up, I asked for a divorce. I told her about you. That was a big mistake. I should have kept my mouth shut. She flew at me like a virago, accused me of living with you, and then'—he paused—'she said something about you, which made me see red. I caught her by the throat, and, God help me, I nearly killed her. I stopped just in time, as her face was turning blue. I don't know quite why I stopped, because I wanted desperately to kill her, only somewhere deep down in us all, what we are taught to believe in our earliest years, remains with us all our lives, no matter how much we may change in the meantime. We're taught not to kill, among other commandments. Maybe that's what prevented me from killing her, I don't know. All I do know is that she's not even worth killing. She refuses absolutely to divorce me. What are we going to do, Anne? Up till now, it didn't matter to me one bit being tied to her. I had nothing to live for anyway. My career was ruined, and I had nobody to think of but myself. This may sound very selfish to you, dear, but in a way, I was glad when this war came along. It gave me something to think about. Not having anything to live for, I signed on for this particular work I'm on, hoping not to get back alive. I'm bitterly sorry now that I did, but how was I to know that you would come along and I would want to live again. Because, darling, I don't want to die now. Now that I've seen my wife, I know that she'll drink herself to death in maybe only a year or two, and we could have waited, but in the meantime, she's safe in Ireland, and we're both here with the Germans practically on our doorstep.'

'But, darling, must you carry on with your dangerous work? I don't know what this work is. I don't want to know. You would have told me anyway if you were free to do so, but surely you're not compelled to carry on with it?' I asked, feeling that everything was too involved for my mind to unravel.

'I must, dearest', he said quietly, 'right to the bitter end.'

'But, darling,' I persisted, 'you surely don't have to be brave deliberately. Can't you play for safety somehow?'

'I'll be very careful, my love. I have someone to come back to now,' he replied tensely.

'Gerald', I said, suddenly getting up, 'let's get married tonight.' Gerald stared at me. 'Not legally,' he explained.

'Just let's pretend. The rest of your leave will be our honeymoon.'

'Darling, Anne, you're too sweet, but I can't let you do it. It's not fair to you.'

'Gerald, you must. After all, the next few days may have to last us all our lives. Let's take our happiness when we can, Gerald. We might never see each other again after the War. One of us might not be there, so let's make the most of it, darling. It can't hurt anybody, just to please me, Gerald. Say yes, darling.'

'Good God, stop tempting me, woman. Surely you can't expect me to say, "No, damn you, I won't live with you for five days". You know damned well there's nothing I want more, but it's wrong, and you know it.'

'No, I don't know it's wrong,' I said. 'Who said so? For all we know, maybe it's wrong to get married. It's all a man-made law anyway. And who says that particular man was right? Maybe he was a lunatic, and the world followed his example. But what does it matter anyway? Surely, in God's eyes, it can't be wrong to be happy. Surely, he doesn't want a world of miserable people. Don't be so conventional, darling, and honourable. Conventions and misery go hand in hand, as far as I can see.'

'All right, my love, if you want it that way,' said Gerald.

'Good,' I said, bubbling over with joy. 'I'll get dressed for my wedding, and Marie-Louise can bring up some champagne.'

'You're a little fool, but I love you all the more for it,' he replied, kissing me again and again.

I came down a few minutes later, dressed in a lovely white gown. Gerald held his breath as I entered.

'You're the loveliest thing I've ever seen,' he whispered, holding me close.

'I am not, darling. It's the frock,' I replied.

'Not only the frock. It would look like a rag on anyone else.'

I opened my hand. In my palm, he saw a small plain gold ring. It had belonged to my mother, but I had never worn it. It didn't match any of my more expensive jewellery, so I had kept it at the bottom of my jewellery case. I held it out to him. He took it reverently.

'Now can we start?' I asked.

He did not reply, so I went on. 'Do I take this man as my lawful wedded husband? I do. Now it's your turn. dear.'

'Do I take this woman to be my lawful wedded wife? I do,' he said solemnly. He placed the ring on my finger. We kissed tenderly, then, turning to the champagne, he poured out two glasses. 'To the bride and bridegroom. May they live happily ever after,' he said quietly.

I had a lump in my throat. It was all very well making a pretence of the marriage ceremony, but somehow to me this ceremony meant more than any real ceremony could ever mean.

'Let's get merry, Gerald, and let's dance,' I said, turning on the phonogram.

The hours passed. We were blissfully happy. The world outside didn't seem to matter. For a few hours, we forgot the war, forgot the problem in our lives. We even forgot the future with all its dangers. We only thought of the present and enjoyed every second of it.

By midnight, we were both tired and had one thought in our minds. To sleep. I would have liked to have gone to bed much earlier, but Gerald didn't seem to be in any hurry. Maybe he was, he didn't show it, but at last we were in my bedroom. I went into the adjoining room for his pyjamas.

'Am I sleeping here?' he asked.

'Of course, darling, unless you're one of that species of males who must have a room to themselves, but we're on our honeymoon, remember? Anyway', I went on, 'there are two beds in here, so you can sleep alone if you like.'

This was the first time I had ever found a use for the two beds in my room. They had always been there; I had never bothered to find out why, and until this evening, the only use I had ever found for them was on the summer nights. As one bed got too hot, I would get up and get into the cool one.

I left him and went into my own dressing room to prepare for bed. When I came back, he was in bed staring at the ceiling. He looked really uncomfortable. I wondered if he'd ever had any girlfriends. I hoped he had, for I didn't want to suffer the least disappointment tonight when we had so little time left. I walked over to him between the two beds and, switching off the light, got into bed beside him. Then I wished I hadn't turned off the light. I would have loved to see his face.

It was late when we got up next morning. I woke up first and looked at Gerald's sleeping head on the pillow beside me. The old strained expression had gone. He looked so peaceful and so calm lying there I hadn't the heart to wake him. Not until Marie-Louise brought in our breakfast, raised her eyebrows, and shrugged her shoulders in a way which plainly meant 'I can get used to anything, and it's none of my business anyway', did I wake him up. He looked round the room in amazement, and then, remembering, drew me down to him and kissed me over and over again. His eyes were smiling and kind, with a look of happiness about them that I'd never seen before on his face. I felt deliriously happy.

How we wished time would stand still, but no amount of wishing would put back the clock, and in what seemed a matter of hours, we were spending our last night together. Neither of us could sleep. We didn't want to waste a single minute of our last few hours together. I got up and made some coffee and went down to the bureau for the cognac. We were both trying hard to take our minds off our separation in a few hours' time.

*   *   *

241 rue Nationale, Lille, in northern France. This was taken
the day before the German Army marched in and occupied
the city in May 1940. The Buick out front was Anne's.

CHAPTER 10

The Refugees

I T WAS SOON afternoon, and Gerald was gone. I knew he would be back in a few days' time, but those few days were interminable. I wondered how I was going to live through the rest of my life if anything should happen to him. Eventually, he did arrive, but only to spend a few hours.

'Things are going from bad to worse,' he said. 'We can expect the Germans to break through any day now.'

'Through the Maginot,' I asked.

'I doubt it. There are plenty of places for them to walk through without sticking their necks out at the Maginot. When it does come, it'll hit us like a tidal wave, and we won't be able to stop it,' he said despondently.

In no time, he was gone, leaving the same old blank space he left each time he went away. I was worrying myself sick over his safety. Even the boys had come to say goodbye as they were moving on.

The next few days were a nightmare. I stood on my balcony with Marie-Louise, looking down on the streams of refugees who passed in an unbroken line for hours and hours. I felt stupefied as I watched. The cars were so riddled by bullet holes that they looked like sieves, and I wondered how the drivers could still be alive in them. There were carts, vans, drays, and bicycles, all piled up with the most fantastic collection of household equipment I had ever seen. I couldn't, for instance, see the sense in dragging along a huge grandfather clock on a handcart with children perched precariously on top. The number of mattresses that went through could have furnished the houses of a complete town. There were chairs, even a piano on a van, birdcages and cats, and very old infirm people, all desperately trying to get away from the Hun. But what chance had they on foot against the onrush of steel behind them?

'Where are the Germans?' I shouted to one old man, who looked up.

'Not twenty kilometres from here', he replied, 'and it's murder and slaughter for all civilians.'

I was terrified. It wasn't so much the sight of this bedraggled procession which frightened me so much as the cries, the awful, delirious cries which came from the carts and vans. The piercing screams of children. I saw heaps of children lying huddled together on lorries, and all crying shrilly as if panic-stricken. They all looked so desperate, and the wailing and moaning went on and on, hour after hour, unending, seemingly everlasting.

'What are we going to do, Marie-Louise? How can we stay here?'

'I don't know, mademoiselle, but if you want to go, you must go. I'll stay on here. I've no other home, and this is the only place my son can find me if he is spared.'

'But they will murder you, Marie-Louise, if you stay,' I protested.

'Oh no, why should they? I'm too old to do them any harm, and if you don't mind, I would rather stay.'

I decided to stay too, but that evening, a very wild-eyed Gerald arrived.

'I'd hoped that you would have gone, Anne. You must not stay here, you must go home tomorrow morning at the latest. After that, it'll be too late,' he cried.

'But I don't want to go, Gerald. I'm afraid, but I must stay.'

'Don't be a little idiot. There's nothing you can do here. They are butchering everybody in their path. For God's sake, do as I say,' he stormed.

'But what about you? If I go, I'll never see you again. I won't know where to find you. As long as I'm here, I'll see you sometimes, but not if I go. I can't go,' I wept.

'Darling, I'm leaving France in two hours' time. I have my orders. If you go in the morning, you'll still get a boat for England. You stand a chance of reaching the coast before the Germans. But for heaven's sake, don't waste any time. You can make it in your car, but take plenty of petrol with you. There's no petrol on the way. The refugees have run the pumps dry. Don't worry about me. Things are easier for me than for you. I only wish I could take you with me, but blast this war, I can't. But I'll find you, darling. I will find you in England. Take care of yourself, you're so precious.' Tears streamed down his face as he spoke, and that was all that was needed to start the tears in my eyes too.

'Take this revolver,' he continued. 'You may need it. Shoot the first Hun who tries to take your car away from you. Without it, you're sunk. You'll never make it on foot.'

I looked horrified as he offered me the weapon. 'But I'm terrified of those things, Gerald. I've never touched one. I don't think I want it.'

'Darling you must take it. I'll show you how to work it. All you want is a steady hand for a steady aim.'

'I know, Gerald, just a steady hand,' I replied, trembling all over.

'Well, I'll leave it here for you. Now I must go. Be careful, dearest, and God bless you till we meet again.' Gerald was trying to unfasten my arms from around his neck, but I clung to him.

'Don't go yet, stay a little longer. Surely, a few minutes can't make so much difference,' I pleaded.

'Darling, you must be sensible. It isn't good bye, my love, just au revoir. Turn round and I'll go. Talk, darling, and keep on talking, and it won't hurt so much,' he said as he freed himself at last.

'All right, darling,' I replied. 'Supposing we make a date to meet on the twenty-fourth of the month following the end of the War. I can't think where . . .' I stopped, unable to pretend any longer.

I turned around. He was gone. I ran frantically from the room, calling his name. I caught up with him just as he was stepping into his car.

'Gerald', I cried, tears running down my face, 'don't leave me, take me with you.' Marie-Louise came running from the house and tried vainly to drag me into the house.

'Anne, please be sensible, don't stay out here, there are planes all over the place, and just look at that red glow in the sky. It's shell fire. Go in darling, before it's too late,' he pleaded.

'I don't care what happens as long as we're together,' I moaned. Then he pushed me towards Marie-Louise and jumped into the car and drove away. I looked after him, petrified with fear. 'Marie-Louise,' I screamed, 'he's driving towards the Germans. What'll happen to him?'

'Don't worry, mademoiselle. He knows what's best to do. God will look after him for you.' I didn't feel so sure about that, especially when I looked at the streaming masses of refugees who kept passing in an unbroken line before me.

I rang up Enid Hunter. I had to talk to somebody, but the caretaker told me that they had all left that morning for Brittany. Enid had tried to ring me but had been unable to get through. I knew I should start deciding what to take with me, but my brain refused to work. All I could do was sit and think of Gerald, and the hours were passing. After some time, however, I looked around. There wasn't much money in the house, and I wouldn't have time to go to the bank in the morning. I intended to leave at daybreak. I took my bracelet out of the safe. It was the only piece of jewellery that I kept in the house. The rest was in the bank. 'Well, maybe it's safer there,' I thought. 'I can always come back and get it after the War.' I threw all sorts of clothing into suitcases and decided to take some silver and pictures. They would always raise some money if necessary. Although it was the middle of the night, I went round the garage, and, placing a twenty-gallon milk churn on the floor of the car, proceeded to fill it up with petrol from the forty-gallon drum.

On my way back, I passed by old Uncle's home and woke him up. 'Listen, Uncle, I'm leaving in a few hours,' I said. 'Would you like to come with me?'

'It's very good of you, my dear, but I would be far too much trouble to you. I would much rather stay here. I'm so old, that should I die tomorrow or next year makes very little difference. But you have all your life before you. You go on, my dear. I'll pray for you every day.'

'Will you stay with Marie-Louise, then?' I asked.

'Maybe. Thank you. I'll think about it.'

I returned home. I looked round the dear old house, stroking a chair here, a settee there. I rubbed my cheek fondly against the curtains. For a moment, I was tempted to go back on my word to Gerald. I wanted to go on living here, come what may, but I didn't weaken. I went round the rooms, packing up valuable ornaments and locking them in cupboards. I gave an ironic laugh. 'Just as if locks and keys could keep out the Hun.'

The thought of going back to England would not have appealed to me one bit but for the fact that Gerald would be there. He would make any country a paradise. I had to admit that leaving France was going to be a terrific wrench. People in other parts of the world just did not realise that life here was more pleasant than almost anywhere else. I wondered what would happen to France should the Germans win. They'd start off definitely by re-educating the children and fouling their minds. I knew how the Germans hated liberty, how they hated justice and equality. They were so wrong, believing that force ruled the world, and France would be the last country in the world to knuckle down to the Nazi way of life.

It was soon morning, the tenth of May. In spite of the early hour, the 'lodgers' were gone. I was amazed at not having heard them go. Marie-Louise appeared with breakfast. 'I suppose this'll be your last breakfast here, mademoiselle,' she said sadly. 'And to think that at last, we have the house to ourselves and you won't be here to enjoy it.'

I stared stupidly at the old woman. Somehow I could not realise that I was leaving the house, perhaps forever.

'I suppose I ought to get started,' I said dully. 'What are the roads like?'

'Crammed tight with refugees. I don't see how you'll get through,' the old woman replied, shaking her head.

'Are you sure you won't come with me, Marie-Louise?'

'Certain, mademoiselle. I must stay.'

'Oh well, I had better start. I'll get the car round if you could start taking some of these cases down. I'm sure I must have put in all the things I don't like and don't want, but I can't think straight,' I said, pulling on a coat.

As I brought the car round, an elderly man and woman with two little girls were standing outside the house. 'Mademoiselle', he said, 'have you room in your car to give us a lift to Paris?' He handed me a card and went on, 'We are desperate to get away.'

I read the name: Mr Paul Chardon, champagne manufacturer. I

looked at him, perplexity written on my face. Madame Chardon noticed my expression.

'Mademoiselle', she said softly, 'we were due to leave this morning, but our chauffeur left with our car in the night. It was our only hope. For the sake of the children, please take us to Paris. I beg you. You don't know how cruel the Germans can be to children. We were here in the last war, and we saw it with our own eyes. Amusement to them was cutting off children's hands before their wretched parents' eyes. Please, mademoiselle, for their sakes.' Tears were streaming down her face as she clutched the little girls' hands.

'All right,' I said. 'When will you be ready to go?'

'We're ready now,' interposed Mr. Chardon, intending to take no chances. 'We live on your way out of town, so perhaps we could collect our cases on the way.'

'There won't be much room,' I said, rubbing my forehead. I could scarcely hear them speak for the noise and wailing which came from the endless refugees column, and to crown it all, loudspeakers vans were standing at all the street corners blaring out to anyone who would listen, 'Stay in your homes. Keep calm. Don't block the road. You will prevent our army from advancing to stop the Hun. Get off the roads.'

But nobody stopped to listen. People rushed around more madly than ever. The mere word 'Boches' seemed to fill each and every one of them with terror, so that they all rushed about getting nowhere except in each other's way. I dashed into the house to get away from the noise, if only for a moment, but couldn't shut it out. Hastily I bundled everything into the car, leaving just enough room for my passengers.

'Get in quickly,' I said. 'The sooner we get started, the better.' They got in with sighs of relief and profuse thanks all round. I kissed Marie-Louise, who was holding out a French helmet and Gerald's revolver.

'Take them,' she told me. 'You may need them.' I took them, wrinkling up my nose in disgust.

*   *   *

CHAPTER 11

Fleeing From The German Advance

I F I HAD imagined for one minute that I would get to Paris that evening, I was never so mistaken in my life. We had been on the roads for five hours, and according to my map, we had not covered 100 kilometres. We were jammed between a horse and cart in front and a battered old car behind. No matter how hard I tried to get away from them, it was no use. They were spread out across the road, and they moved en masse. I had no idea where the beginning of the column was. All I knew was that when it came to a halt, I had to stop with it.

'We won't get to Paris in a week at this rate,' I muttered aloud. 'And just look at my radiator. Steaming like a kettle, and not a drop of water anywhere in sight.'

'Mademoiselle', said Madame Chardon timidly, 'I have six bottles of champagne here. If you like, the next time we stop, we could put a couple of bottles into the radiator. What do you think?'

'I think it's sacrilege', I replied, 'but thanks very much. We've no choice.'

'Mademoiselle, have a biscuit. I'm so sorry I've nothing more substantial to offer, but in our panic, we forgot to bring food.'

My stomach did a somersault. 'Good God. I did too. I brought pictures. I brought knives and forks, and no food at all. And we might be on this road for days. Still, surely, we'll get to some shops eventually.'

'We will', said Mr. Chardon, 'but the head of this stream of people will be just as hungry as we are.'

The column stopped. After what seemed to be ages, I got out to investigate. 'If it starts off again, will you take the wheel?' I said to Mr Chardon. 'Pick me up again along the line. I'll see you,' I said, and as I walked along the ditch, I realised that this column was endless. There was a lane leading off from the main road. I wandered up it and found the British Army. I was surprised. They were the first soldiers I'd seen so far.

'Can you tell me where I can get some water for my car?' I asked the corporal on guard at the wooden gate.

'Ask the captain over there,' he replied, letting me into what seemed to be a farmyard. I repeated my request to the captain. He was very much the same type as young Johnny.

'Certainly not,' he rapped out. 'All you filthy fifth columnists pretending to be refugees. Get out of here before I have you locked up.'

I lost my temper. 'You crazy idiot. If you are a specimen of what has been sent out here to win this war, you can forget it, chum. You are too stupid for words. Go back to the classroom where you belong,' I stormed and walked back to the car. It had still not moved. The look of relief on my companions' faces when I flopped onto the seat was touching.

'Why are we stopped so long?' asked Madame Chardon anxiously.

'I don't know,' I replied. 'There's no beginning and no end to this column. Maybe the beginning is in Paris, and they won't let them in. Some of these refugees are in a dreadful state. There's an old woman lying on some straw in a handcart a few metres ahead, with no covering in this blazing sun, and she's howling. It sounds just like a dog at night. I can't see her living through this. There are hundreds of them with blood soaking through their bandages. Apparently, they were machine-gunned on their way through Belgium, and everybody is screaming for water. All the children are crying, and the horses are ready to drop. Some are lying in the ditches. They can't go on. They've been walking for days. They're screaming hysterically to their friends to go on without them. Everybody seems to have lost someone in all this mess. Why don't we move? What the devil is holding us up?'

My nerves were getting frayed, and it didn't help matters knowing how terribly afraid my passengers were. The little girls had fallen asleep, each clutching their mother's arm. There were stains on their faces where the tears had dried. I wondered why they had been crying. Was it hunger, tiredness, or fear? All this nerve-wracking chaos was no place for children, yet they were the most important.

At last we were on the move. We'd never managed more than first gear since we had set off. I was trying hard to remember whether a car used more or less petrol than normal when driven so slowly. I hoped it was less, but I had a feeling that it was more, just because it was so vitally important that it should be less.

By the evening, we had arrived at St Pol. I was furious. I'd had no intention of going to St Pol, but each holdup had apparently meant a detour, and here we were. We got out and lifted the bonnet. The engine was red hot. We could have fried eggs on it, if only we had some eggs.

'Senegals,' shouted Mr. Chardon, pointing to the coloured troops on the market square. 'They will make those Germans run for their lives, if anybody can.'

'How?' I asked.

'Well, in the last war, they were terrified of meeting coloured troops who apparently enjoyed cutting off their ears,' he replied, smiling for the first time.

'Would you like to look for some food, which I doubt exists, and I'll look for water and petrol,' I said.

He agreed. The troops were helpful with water, but there was no petrol, no food, and no rooms to be had anywhere. We spent the night in the car in the square.

At six o'clock the next morning, I looked at the map. 'If we can get onto the road to Amiens, we'll be all right.'

'What wouldn't I give for a cup of coffee,' said Mme Chardon, with parched lips.

'Where are all the evacuees?' asked Mr. Chardon, looking pleased at the thought of having lost them. How wrong he was. We hadn't gone more than a few kilometres when we were again diverted and in no time had caught up with that soul-destroying sight—the refugees. Only this time, we were at the tail end of them. The procession moved more slowly than ever and, by midday, had come to a halt.

'This is the limit,' I fumed. 'What sort of a road is this, anyway? It's too narrow to be even a lane. There's no hope of overtaking all that mess ahead of us.' I sounded the horn furiously, but it was no use. All I got in return was a storm of abuse. And the language—well, I'd thought I had heard everything. Apparently, my fellow wanderers had a finer range of oaths than I had ever possessed. I buried my face in my hands. The heat was terrific. My head throbbed, and my eyes were burning and dry. I looked at the sky, hoping for some signs of rain. Instead, my heart missed a beat. I stared at the sky, speechless with terror. There were at least five parachutes floating down towards us. I tried to tell the others, but I couldn't. My mouth was bone dry, and I wanted to be sick. I poked Mr. Chardon in the ribs and pointed to the sky. He fumbled for his glasses.

'Germans,' he muttered, 'God help us all now.'

Madame Chardon and the children started to cry.

'For God's sake, stop it,' I yelled, finding my tongue at last. Their faces, white with terror, turned towards me, as if asking what they should do. I didn't want to frighten them any more than they already were.

'What a clever idea,' I remarked, keeping my voice as steady as I could. 'No one but a Jerry would think of having sky-blue parachutes and sky-blue coverings over their uniforms so that they wouldn't be seen till the last minute. I'll bet you anything you like half this mob hasn't seen them yet. Won't it be funny if they land in some of the carts?' Inwardly, I prayed that they wouldn't be carrying machine guns. It wasn't in my nature to sit still and wait for something to happen. After the first few terrifying minutes, I got out of the car and walked along the ditch to see what I could find out. I saw the Huns searching the cars and carts ahead of us. I went up to one of the drivers who had been searched. 'What are they looking for? Are they all armed?'

'Soldiers and arms,' he replied, raising his eyebrows as if to imply that the whole idea was ridiculous. I stood rooted to the spot. 'Good God. Gerald's revolver is in the pocket of the car. I must get to it. But what the hell can I do with it? I can't very well swallow the ruddy thing, and I dare not stick it in my corsets, it might go off.' My legs would not hurry; they seemed to have turned to jelly, but in spite of them, I got back before it was our turn to be searched. I threw the helmet into the ditch, just in case they should think we were hiding a soldier. But the revolver was another matter. I did not want to throw that away. I took it out of the pocket of the car. What a wonderful opportunity. There were six bullets in it and only five Germans. I looked at it in my trembling hand. The more I tried to stop trembling, the more my hand shook. What was it Gerald had said? 'A steady hand for a steady aim.' I burst into a fit of hysterical laughter, 'Steady hand,' I screamed, endangering the lives of all around me as I waved the revolver all over the place.

'Stop it, mademoiselle,' shouted Mr. Chardon, giving my face a vigorous slap. 'I'm sorry', he said when I had calmed down, 'but the Germans are coming towards us.'

I was incapable of thinking. In any case, there was no time to think. 'What'll I do with it?' I asked, too terrified to make any attempt to hide it.

'Sit on it,' he suggested. I closed my eyes and waited, and wondered what would happen should the heat explode the bullets. I wondered what would happen if they asked me to open up the boot of the car. I wished I were not so ignorant in the matters of firearms. And I also wished I could stop fidgeting. If I couldn't stay still, what on earth was to prevent the trigger from rubbing on the seat and going off?

I felt almost glad to see the two German faces in the window. They looked all over the car and were very polite. They complimented us on our foresight in bringing along enough milk to last some time, and after saluting us, they moved off. We all breathed a sigh of relief. I put the revolver back in the side pocket and, turning to my companions, said, 'I say, if they are all going to be as nice as that, we'll be all right. But do you think Germans are born without any sense of smell? Imagine mistaking that can of petrol for milk when we're almost suffocated by the stink!'

We moved on again, but not for long. I got out as usual. Anything was better than waiting. The column of refugees looked like a long black ribbon threading its way as far as I could see, and then on the horizon appeared two planes flying low. They were so low I wondered how they could miss this seething mass of humanity. It did not take a second to realise what they were doing. They were machine gunning the entire mass of unfortunates who had no chance of getting out of the way. I heard the sharp *rat-a-tat* of the guns as they spat out death in all directions. I dived back to my passengers, yelling at them to get down on the floor. They stared in bewilderment. They didn't seem to grasp what was happening.

'Get down,' I yelled. 'Aeroplanes machine gunning.' I leaned through the window and pushed one of the little girls onto the floor. The others followed like dazed sheep. I hadn't time to get into the car, so I rolled under it. In a matter of seconds, it was all over. I got up. For a moment, I was afraid to look in the car. I did not know what I would find.

'Mademoiselle. Are you all right?' shouted Mr. Chardon.

'Yes, what about you?'

'None of us touched, by the mercy of God. But look at what you missed.'

I stared. There were four bullet holes in the roof of the car. They must have come through at quite an acute angle and gone out through the windscreen. They'd all passed over the driver's seat, and I shivered at the mental picture of what my head would have looked like.

'Good Lord, what a mess!' I cried. 'And we thought the Germans were so nice. It's quite true what they say about the only good German being a dead one. The swine. But what's happened to the refugees, they are so quiet? Surely, they can't be all . . .' I stopped. My whole being was filled with rage and loathing against those murderous Huns who had done this dastardly crime. First, they had sent down parachutists to make sure they were all unarmed, then in they came and attacked.

'The low-down fiends,' I muttered between clenched teeth, making my way along the line of refugees. Very few had escaped. There was an occasional woman here, a child there, screaming over the bodies of its parents; but hundreds and hundreds had been massacred in cold blood. Horses and dogs lay dead on the road with human bodies stretched out across them, all riddled with bullets. Blood was flowing in a stream along the side of the road. The sight was too horrible for words.

The few survivors were wailing and screaming over the bodies of their dead. I could bear it no longer. I picked up two children who were apparently now all alone and brought them back to the car. Their crying started the two other little girls off.

'Please stop crying,' I pleaded. 'I can't think straight. We can't get along that road. I couldn't drive over those unfortunate people, and we can't turn back. Do either of you know in which direction Paris lies? Or the coast? I don't know myself.'

After a few minutes, Mr. Chardon pointed across the field. 'That way, mademoiselle, but how are we to get there?'

'We have no choice. We'll have to go across country, over those fields. I hope we don't break an axle. But it's our only chance.'

We took some boards out of a nearby cart to span the ditch and were soon rattling and bumping over the fields. We had to crash a gate on the other side to get out, but were thankful to find ourselves once more on a road, or more correctly, a lane. It was good to get some speed up for a change even though we didn't know where this lane would lead. On and on we went, and after several hours, we found ourselves in Abbeville.

'At last,' I breathed. 'Now we can go to the coast, or Paris.' My passengers made no reply. I remembered with a start that these people wanted to get to Paris, not England. Still, as far as I could see, none of us had any option. We would just have to go wherever we could.

Abbeville seemed strangely calm. Windows were shuttered, and there were no people on the streets. All the shops were locked up.

'There's something strange about this place,' I remarked. 'We'd better just go straight through and get onto the road either to the coast or to Amiens, whichever is open.' But it was no use making plans. Wherever we went, the roads were barricaded. I was tempted to drive straight through them but decided that it might not be wise. Perhaps they were closed for our own safety. How could I tell without a soul anywhere to question?

'It's no good,' I said. 'We'll just have to go back on the road we came and see where the other end of it goes.' Back we went and, to our horror, found ourselves in St Pol. But what a difference. All the Senegalese troops, plus hundreds of French soldiers, were lying on the pavements without helmets, without guns—in fact, none of them had any equipment at all. I parked the car and went over to speak to them.

They told me they were prisoners and the Germans had taken the town. I couldn't believe it at first, but I soon did.

Something sharp was sticking in my back as I stooped to talk to the prisoners. I straightened up and turned around. It was a German with a bayonet. He didn't say anything; he just kept prodding me in the back till I was once more in the car. Then he mounted guard over us, as if to make sure that none of us would move again. I wished he would take off his helmet. I was sure I wouldn't be so afraid of him if only he wasn't wearing that terrifying-looking helmet. The mere shape of it was frightening.

In no time, German tanks and lorries came streaming through the town. I started marking the numbers on my map. There were thousands. A German officer had taken charge of the square and was directing them with his baton, which he produced from the leg of one of his jackboots. As I watched them, spellbound, pouring through, hour after hour, I wondered what chance the French and British combined had of stopping them. Much as I hated these Germans, I could only stare at them with admiration. Their timing was perfect. They were disciplined and drilled to the last degree, and their speed and precision were a source of amazement. It looked like the perfect army. What a pity that it should be the enemy.

Eventually, they had all gone through. The officer in charge came over. He didn't speak French, but his English was perfect.

'Where can we find some food and somewhere to sleep?' I asked him, making a great effort to appear friendly.

'You can't stay here', he replied good-humouredly, 'but if you follow me, we're going to spend the night at a farm a few kilometres off.' My reluctance to follow him anywhere must have shown on my face because he went on, 'We're going to blow this place up in half an hour.' That decided me.

'All right, we'll come along. But don't go too fast.'

We watched him get into a car. It was a new Citroen. We wondered where he had stolen it. I heaved a sigh of relief as I realised that they were apparently taking only small cars, which meant a lack of petrol. We couldn't get into the farmhouse, so we had to stay once more in the car. There was no food anywhere, and as we sat there, a roar of bombs told us St Pol was no more. Even though we were kilometres away, we could hear fragments of bombs and debris falling around us.

In spite of our tiredness, we couldn't sleep, and at four o'clock, I decided to get the car ready for the next day. But the Germans had also decided to get up early, and so I had to wait till they had finished with the water tap in the farmyard.

There they were, lined up at the tap, stripped to the waist. Each man produced a toilet case on a leather strap and proceeded to shave himself. They greased and brushed their hair before dressing, and all the accessories came from the same toilet case. It was incredible to think of men grooming so perfectly at a time like this. By five o'clock, they were all ready to leave and streamed out of the farmyard, without having taken the slightest notice of me. I might have been a cow belonging to the farm.

It was pure luck which brought us onto the road to Amiens. There wasn't soul in sight for hours on end, but the solitude was too good to last. Along came roaring convoys of cars and lorries swarming with guns and soldiers. They shouted to me to move over.

I stopped at a fork in the road. The signpost said four kilometres to Amiens. One of the officers came over.

'Take your car off the road, mademoiselle. We shall be busy for the next hour.'

I stared stupidly at him. What did he expect me to do with it? Put it in my pocket? 'But where?' I asked, looking all round.

'Put it in the front garden of that house over there. Go through the fence. It won't be difficult with a tank like yours.'

I wondered how many companies had gone through in the last hour. It was endless. They poured down one of the roads at the fork with the same precision and speed that I had seen at St Pol. I wondered how many motorized divisions there were. I also wondered where they were going. Certainly not to Amiens. Certainly not to Paris. When it was all over, the officer in charge came over again.

'What do you think of the German Army?' he asked.

'It's the most impressive army I have ever seen,' I replied. 'But where on earth is it going that way? This is the way to Paris.' The officer was so buoyed up with success that he became very talkative.

'We're not going to Paris. That can wait. We are going to England.'

'What on earth for?' I asked, dumbfounded.

'To wring Churchill's neck and give Chamberlain a new umbrella,' he replied, full of self-importance.

'But you have to cross the channel.'

'We have hundreds of boats waiting for us at the coast.'

I did not say anything. What could I say anyway?

'You have a nice car there,' he remarked, looking it over thoughtfully.

'It isn't a car, it's a tank,' I said guardedly.

'Really. Heavy on petrol?'

'Drinks like a fish', I said, 'wallows in oil, and as for water, well, you have to drive alongside a river to satisfy it.'

'Oh,' he replied. 'Not much good to us, then.' I nearly jumped out of my seat at the thought of his contemplating taking our sole means of transport and survival.

'No good at all. It would only get in your way. You need small fast cars. This one is only fit for the scrap heap. By the way,' I went on, 'we're starving. We haven't had anything to eat for three days.'

'Really,' he said, pretending to be amazed. He called over a German corporal and ordered him to bring us something to eat. He reappeared with a huge box of biscuits and half a kilogramme of butter. The officer went over to his car and brought back four huge bars of chocolate for the children.

'We Germans love children,' he said as he handed them each a bar. I couldn't believe my eyes.

'Haven't you seen all those children killed on the roads? All those refugees?' I asked, more perplexed than ever.

'I did,' he said with a catch in his throat. 'I think it's inhuman. The English swine who committed those atrocities deserves no mercy. But we will avenge your countrymen, mademoiselle.'

'Well, I'm damned,' I thought. 'The nerve of these monsters, putting the blame on the RAF. I hope you roast in hell.' As for his remarks about avenging my countrymen—of course a German wouldn't detect my English accent when I spoke French. Only a Frenchman could do that.

'Where can we find something to drink?' I asked him. He promptly held out his water bottle. It was filled with delicious coffee. I wondered if it was poisoned, but even that couldn't stop me taking a good drink. Even the thought of putting my lips where his had been couldn't stop me. He handed it round to the others, and between them, they finished it.

'Thank you,' I said. 'That was the most delicious coffee I've ever tasted. Now, if you can tell us if we can get to Paris by the Amiens road, we'll be more than grateful.'

'You can't get to Paris by any road. All the bridges over the Somme are down. You'd better go back home, mademoiselle, wherever you came from. This is as far as you will get.'

My heart sank. After three days of agony, we couldn't turn back. 'There must be a road somewhere,' I thought. 'They are very thorough in their methods, but surely they've missed a bridge somewhere. I must see for myself. I won't believe this fellow. In any case he's too sweet to be a German, and I don't trust him. Maybe he'll throw a bomb once they leave us.'

Just then, the officer received a signal from some others, and turning to us, he clicked his heels, saluted, and left.

'Did you hear what he said about the bridges?' I asked Mr and Madame Chardon.

'Sounds dreadful,' the man replied. 'But if the worse comes to the worst, we can always swim over.'

'And leave the car and the children?' I retorted.

'Oh no.' He sounded horrified. 'I thought there might be a boat or something on the other side. Oh, I don't know. I feel too weary to think.'

'Well, don't think,' I said, getting very jittery. 'We'd better have a look before we decide what to do.'

In a matter of minutes, we had arrived at Amiens.

'My God,' I cried, 'just look at the mess.'

We all stared in horror. The town had been bombed into a mass of rubble. Nothing but the shells of buildings remained. Steel girders stood up like shadows painted on the sky. The acrid smell of burning wood made my throat hurt. The streets were littered with rubble and overturned carts, power lines, cars, and corpses. Animals and humans lay dead. I went to see if I could clear the road a little to get through.

'You'll have to help me, Mr. Chardon. We can't very well drive over the dead.' He obeyed, and together we lifted as many of the dead as we could manage and placed them at the side of the street. It was impossible to move the horses which lay there, their stomachs slit open and their big eyes staring. I felt sick with the horror of it, and panic clutched at me. I had never seen so many eyes, eyes stunned by fear. I must get out of here quickly. My reason would snap if I didn't. Monsieur Chardon walked ahead while I drove through, gritting my teeth as I bumped over the carcass of a dead horse here, a donkey there. Then a car blocked the way. I could see a pair of legs sticking out from under it. I got out and, taking the legs, gave them a tug. I promptly reeled backwards on the road. From the waist up, there was nothing. The sight of half a corpse was far more nauseating than a hundred complete ones. I covered my eyes with my hands and screamed hysterically. Monsieur Chardon pulled me away, and we continued our task of driving through the ruins. It was hard work, but at last we were through the worst. The rest of the town had not suffered quite so much. Breathing a sigh of relief, I found my courage returning, a little.

'I think we might forage for food. God knows how much longer we may be on the roads, and there isn't a living soul in this town. I'll go down this side of the street if you'll go that way,' I suggested.

'All right,' replied Mr. Chardon wearily.

I noticed a small grocery shop quite near, with its door blown off. I entered, stumbled on something in the darkness, and fell, hitting my face on something cold and clammy. For a second, I was afraid to get up. I lay where I was and took some matches out of my pocket and struck one. I screamed with terror. I was lying on the dead body of a man whose head had been blown open, and lying beside it were his brains. It wasn't till the match burnt my fingers that I realised what I was doing and, stumbling to my feet, I rushed blindly to the car. It didn't matter how much food there was in that shop. I'd noticed piles of butter and cheese out of the corner of my eye during that brief second when I'd struck the match. Food was no longer important. I felt I would rather starve to death than try to find food again in this town. I screamed to Mr. Chardon to get into the car, and my fingers trembled as I fumbled with the gears.

'We must get out of this town. It's ghastly,' I gasped through clenched teeth. I drove like fury in and out of potholes, over planks and rafters strewn across the street. Even the wires were down and made a criss-cross pattern across the road, but I had to get away from it all, no matter what damage I did to the car.

We were almost out of the town when we heard the drone of aircraft. Precisely at the same moment, I saw a huge crater looming up ahead.

'Good heavens, surely, they're not going to attack that place again. We are the only living things in it, and we can't get out. Look at that hole in front of us.' My companions were too terrified to reply. 'Hold tight,' I yelled. 'We're going into that bombed house. They say bombs never fall in exactly the same place twice.' I turned the car sharply and, racing the engine, tore straight at it. With an almighty bump, we broke about a metre of the wall, which had remained standing; and we were in, surrounded by masses of smashed china, broken furniture, and one spotlessly clean and undamaged bath.

We were not a moment too soon. The roar of exploding bombs nearly burst our eardrums. The children were all screaming. Accompanying their screams, the sound of falling masonry on the roof of the car made us feel that the end had come. And then, miraculously, it was all over, and no one was hurt. I looked out. The rest of the town was blazing furiously. Clouds of smoke rose up over the houses. Under the ceiling of smoke, the houses sprouted spirals of red flames. Softer flames hung from the windows; others flew up from the eaves. The heat was fast becoming unbearable.

'We'll have to get out of here,' I shouted, my voice barely audible above the crackling of the burning timber. I went out into the street to see what the road was like. 'We'll have to chance the crater,' I yelled, driving towards it.

'You can't, we'll only get stuck at the bottom,' shouted Mr Chardon.

ANNE ANGELO

I stopped for a moment. Just then, there was a terrific crash. We all choked as dust filled the air. The far side of the house in which we had sheltered had caved in.

'Good God', I yelled, 'just look what we missed.'

Monsieur Chardon went over to look. 'I believe', he called, rubbing the dust out of his eyes, 'you could get out through that house and into the courtyard on the other side. I'll explore a bit and see if there is another street there.'

I waited. It seemed an eternity, but at last he came back. 'We're saved,' he cried, rubbing his hands together like an excited schoolboy. 'We can make it a bit flatter with planks, and then it won't be so hard on your poor car.' We got to work. My hands were torn and bleeding, but I didn't notice it. All I wanted was to get away from this place if it meant eating every obstacle in my way.

We bumped through, and with great sighs of relief, we were once more on the open road. Here a different sight met our eyes. For kilometres, the road was littered with abandoned cars. I wondered how their owners must have felt to have got so far and no farther. New cars, old cars, surrounded by open suitcases, clothes, cutlery, even hairbrushes sticking out. What had the people been searching for when they had thrown out what must have seemed less important items? There were rugs, blankets, and even furs, lying on the verge. 'What a chance for a looter,' I thought. 'Not even a lock to pick.'

There was no sign of life for several kilometres, and when it did appear, it was in the form of a German sentry. He stopped us and told us to turn back.

'But we're going to Paris,' I insisted. 'We can't turn back.'

'You can't go to Paris. No bridges.' My heart sank. What could I do if they would not let me pass? They were armed, and I couldn't very well knock them down. 'But why not?' I reflected. 'We've knocked down walls, why not the master race?' I prayed for courage to kill these two in cold blood, but my prayers were wasted. The sentry asked his companion to look at the other side of the car, so I didn't dare to move.

'Not good,' he said. 'No bridges.'

I pointed to Amiens. 'No road.' He shrugged his shoulders. An idea struck me.

'Are there any farms around here?' I asked him. 'We could perhaps get work on a farm until the roads are clear again.'

Apparently, he agreed for he pointed to a farm which stood out against the sky some kilometres away.

'Can we go there?' I asked him eagerly, offering him a cigarette to keep him in a good mood.

'Ja ja, you go.' I didn't wait for him to change his mind. I raced off, half expecting him to shoot after us, but nothing happened. Soon we were turning into what seemed to be a cart track. The track turned out to be a switchback, and on we went up and down till we arrived at the farm, which appeared deserted.

I wiped the perspiration off my forehead. 'How would you all like to turn farmer for the duration?'

'We could do worse,' replied Mr Chardon. 'We're fairly safe from bombs here, we can't go forward, and we can't go back, so we might as well stay here. It looks abandoned. I wonder why?'

'Those cows are making an awful row. I wonder what's wrong with them?' I remarked.

'No wonder,' replied Mme Chardon sadly. 'The poor beasts haven't been milked for days. Just look at them.'

I looked. They could scarcely walk and looked as if they were in acute agony. I had never realised that a cow had such an expressive face before. We were so busy examining the cows that none of us heard a footstep behind. A voice saying 'Pardon' made us jump.

'French,' I exclaimed, 'with Germans just down the road.' He looked at me as if I were an escaped lunatic.

'It's true,' said Mr Chardon. 'They are just down on the main road.'

'Impossible,' the man snorted. 'Wait one minute.' He reappeared with three French generals and members of their staff. I stared at them, unable to believe my eyes.

'May I see your identity cards?' said one of them. We all produced cards, passports, and other papers.

'We're not fifth columnists,' I said furiously. 'We're refugees from

Lille, probably the only refugees still alive. Considering the number of Germans we've met, we must lead charmed lives to be still here. We've given up trying to get to Paris. The bridges are down so we intend to stay here. Now you know everything.'

'But, mademoiselle, the Germans are a hundred kilometres from here.'

I pointed to the little road. 'If that switchback is a hundred kilometres long, then you are right, but they are just down there on the main road. Can't you send someone to find out if you won't believe me?' I said, getting more and more angry.

'I will,' he said. 'In the meantime, tell me about these Germans you have met.'

I gave him my map with the numbers jotted down on it.

'And you say they were going to England?' he asked. 'Which way?'

I showed him the fork marked on the map.

'By Abbeville,' he said, looking very worried. 'That explains why the roads out of Abbeville were all blocked. It was to keep them clear for the Huns.'

'But who was doing all this?' I asked.

'Their fifth column, of course. They got in among the refugees and blocked whichever road they wanted to keep clear for the Germans and cluttered up the roads our troops and the British were on. It's so simple. Those damned Boches are too thorough.'

'Can you give us any idea why they didn't shoot us down like the others?' I asked after a while.

'Probably. They have orders to treat the French courteously. For instance, you will be able to say that they behaved like perfect gentlemen, won't you?'

'Yes, but what about all the people who were massacred? Will people believe the story about the RAF being responsible?'

'Probably.'

'Yes,' I said slowly. 'I see it all now. They certainly do think of everything.'

They were still discussing German tactics when one of the men came back to report that he had seen the Germans.

'You'd better leave here, mademoiselle,' said the general quickly.

'But we're starving, we have no petrol, and we can't get to Paris, and we certainly won't go back to Amiens. I would rather die, so where can we go?'

'My men will escort you to St Just. From there, you can easily get to Paris, and I'll order some food and petrol for you.'

Food came in the shape of a couple of dozen duck's eggs, a huge loaf of dark-brown bread, and two bottles of wine.

'Just our luck,' I fumed. 'A few days ago, we could have fried eggs on the engine, now we have the eggs, and the damned engine is as cold as a tomb. And all that milk to be used and not a soul knows how to milk a cow. Can I try to milk it? These poor children are starving.'

'Go ahead,' said one of the soldiers, 'but we've tried before you.'

I tried, but I was afraid to squeeze or pull too hard, so I didn't get a single drop. All I got was the cow's tail full in the face several times. I gave up in disgust.

'Couldn't we stick one of these kids under a cow and see if they remember what they did as babies?'

'No good,' said the soldier. 'We've tried it.'

'Hell. Is there anything you haven't tried?'

He shrugged his shoulders.

Our escort was ready. Three cars appeared out of nowhere. Pieces of straw clinging to them gave me a very good idea of where they had been hidden. They gave us 100 litres of petrol. The generals came to shake hands with me. 'You've rendered us a great service, mademoiselle. We have already notified London. My men will see you safely to St Just. Then it should be easy for you. Good luck, and thank you again.'

We were soon in St Just, and our escort turned back. I wasn't quite sure why I had been given an escort. I didn't know whether it had been for my safety or the safety of the generals.

We spent that night some kilometres out of the town, sleeping in the car. We'd learnt by this time that it was much safer this way. A few kilometres away, the Germans started to bomb yet another town.

It was late the next evening when we reached Paris. 'Look,' I almost shouted. 'Restaurants, people, living people for a change. Look at all the troops. Thousands of them. All in the wrong part of the country.'

In spite of the lateness of the hour, we all streamed into the first decent-sized restaurant we came to.

'Watch me make a pig of myself,' I said. 'I'll eat myself sick.' And sick I was.

I dropped the Chardons off at an address they had given. 'Do you think you could keep these children and put them in a home or something?' I asked. 'I can't take them. I don't know yet where I'm going to stay.'

'Of course, mademoiselle. We'll be delighted. It's the least we can do. Would you not stay with us?'

'No, I don't think so. I should try to get back to England.' They kissed me affectionately and thanked me profusely as I left them.

I didn't know quite where to stay in Paris. Suddenly I remembered my old friend Paul. I made my way to his flat at 8 rue Quentin Bouchard. In spite of the nearness of the Germans, Paris was always Paris. People thronged the streets, all out for amusement. Feverish, nervous amusement perhaps, but nevertheless there was a I of gaiety everywhere. It took me some time to get to the flat. I didn't know Paris well and lost my way several times. I hoped Paul was in. Furthermore, I hoped he was alone.

I rang the bell. Paul appeared. 'Good Lord, Naive of all people. What on earth are you doing here? What a disgusting mess you look.'

I eyed him ferociously.

'I wonder what you would have looked like if you had been four days and nights on the road? Bombed, machine-gunned, and starved.'

'Don't be silly, Naive. There are no Germans between Lille and Paris.'

I could have hit him, but tired as I was, I dragged him out to look at the car. The sight completely wiped the smile off his face. He suddenly became all nerves, and fired question after question. I felt dazed. He was white with terror.

'Oh, relax, Paul,' I said wearily. 'They're on their way to England. I'm tired. Can I stay the night here?'

'If you want to,' he said without enthusiasm, 'but you know there's only one bed, and I hate anybody sleeping in my flat with me.'

'Good Lord', I screamed, 'don't be afraid of me. The way I feel tonight, I couldn't hurt a rabbit. I can sleep in the bath.'

'Don't be vulgar, Naive. Maybe you can do with the divan.'

'Thanks, I will. But I'd better get deloused first.' I felt so angry that I wanted to make him feel really uncomfortable.

'You surely haven't brought any livestock along with you. Not in my lovely flat. You couldn't do such a thing,' he groaned.

I gave him a filthy look. 'Can you help me unload the car? I'm so tired, and I want to go to bed.' He helped, somewhat unwillingly. The strain nearly killed him.

'What made you bring those pictures along?' he asked, gazing at them.

'I thought I might sell them if I were stuck for money.'

'I'll give you a hundred francs for them,' said Paul, trying to appear generous.

'You know very well they're worth thousands,' I retorted. I turned my back on him and went into the bathroom. I reappeared half an hour later dressed in a pair of his silk pyjamas.

*   *   *

ANNE ANGELO

CHAPTER 12

Paris Falls

I THOUGHT ABOUT TRYING to find work driving ambulances, but after my past experience, I hesitated. Anyway, I felt I needed to rest a few days and regain my thoughts.

Life in Paris was so pleasant I hadn't the heart to tear myself away. I knew I ought to leave and make for Brittany, but as long as the Germans didn't come near Paris, I lingered on. Paul had become quite pleasant after our bad start. I had a feeling that he was pleasant because he was afraid. Knowing that I had come through from Lille when thousands had perished in the attempt, he probably felt that if the worse came to the worst, he would get away safely with me. So he turned on the charm. I enjoyed being made a fuss of, but the time came when Paris was being threatened. We both packed hastily and set off for Brittany. The following day, the fourteenth of June, the Germans took Paris. There was no bombing, there was no fighting.

Day after day, at St Malo, I searched for a boat to England, but the boats were too busy taking off the scattered remnants of the BEF to bother about civilians. There were boats taking refugees to the Channel Islands, but I had a hunch about them. Something told me not to go. I had a feeling that sooner or later, the Germans would occupy them, and they would become a glorified concentration camp. It was England or nowhere. In the meantime, the BEF were immobilising their cars and lorries and pushing them into the sea. Then came the news of the German advance. They were within seventy kilometres of St Malo. I hurried off for my car, but I was too late. There was no petrol to be had. There was, however, a huge reservoir of petrol on the outskirts of the town. I and others hurried towards it. Once more, we were too late. The

BEF had set it on fire, and the flames were high in the air. I sat down by the roadside and cried with rage. Pulling myself together, I went back to the docks. While I had been searching for petrol, an English destroyer had come in and taken off all the people who had waited for days for a chance of escape. This was the last hope. 'The best thing I can do is to throw myself into the sea,' I thought bitterly.

There was nothing for it but to go home. Home at that moment was one of Bonne-maman's villas. I didn't relish the thought of staying with such a large crowd. All Madame Crecy's sons were there, complete with wives and children, nursemaids and governesses, including Enid Hunter.

'No luck?' enquired Enid.

'Not a hope,' I replied. 'My last chance of driving to the south went up in smoke before my eyes, and the Germans will be here tonight. Short of swimming over to England, I can't see how I can get there.'

'Well, you asked for it, didn't you?' said Enid, who was just as bad-tempered as the others.

'What the blazes do you mean?' I snapped.

'Well, you didn't have to stay so long in Paris, did you now?'

I flew into a rage. 'Shut up, Enid. I'm going out to wait for the Germans. I'd rather talk to them than to you.' With those parting words, I went out, slamming the door viciously behind me, and made for the sea front. I was angry with myself for flying at Enid like that. I knew why I'd done so. It was because I knew in a way that Enid had been right. I knew now that I shouldn't have lingered in Paris, but it was so much easier to be driven to do things as the emergency arose than to do them when there was no hurry. Had the Germans been right behind me in Paris, I was quite sure I would have left at once. But they hadn't been, and so I'd waited until they were before I moved again.

A week later, tempers had not improved. It wasn't so much that Germans were everywhere that upset people. These Germans were friendly, courteous, and obliging. There was no friction between them and the civilian population. There was no need for any. The local children loved these Huns who spent their time and patience amusing them. Outwardly, they behaved as if they loved every single one of

ANNE ANGELO

them. I felt very suspicious. I couldn't believe they could be so human. There was a reason for their good conduct somewhere, but there was no point in trying to find it. It was something more than the presence of the Germans which was gnawing at the hearts of the people. There was a sense of impending doom. The future of France was at stake.

I wandered into the living room. The entire family were collected there, their ears tuned to the radio. Marshall Petain was speaking in a harsh spluttering voice. He had taken over the government. Some of the women burst into tears of joy. Petain's voice, cold, trembling, went on.

'I give myself to France. It is with a heavy heart that I say we must stop fighting. I have asked our opponent if he is ready to sign a pact with us as between soldiers, and so put an end to hostilities.'

'How ridiculous,' muttered Monsieur Marc Crecy. 'An army is not asked to stop fighting before the armistice is signed.' He stormed out of the room. Everybody started talking at once. One or two for the armistice, the others against it. I didn't care either way.

It didn't take the Germans long to get organised. Within two or three weeks, petrol was once more to be found, but there was a snag to it. I could get petrol to go home, provided home was in occupied France, but I couldn't go to the unoccupied zone. The demarcation line had come into being.

I asked Paul what his plans were.

'I would like to go back to Paris,' he said. 'After all, the Germans are here, and they are in Paris. I might as well go home and enjoy the occupation in my own flat. What are you going to do?'

'I think I'll go back to Lille. As you say, they are here, there, and everywhere, so I might as well go home too.'

'Good. I'll come along. If we both take our cars, we can help each other on the road. Let's get our tanks filled up,' he said eagerly.

Enid Hunter came out of the villa as I was putting the finishing touches to my preparations for the journey.

'I expect I'll see you in a week or two. We're all going back. I'm sorry about you, though. You're here now for the duration,' she said quietly.

I put down my oil can and looked at Enid wonderingly. 'Surely, Enid, you must believe a little in fate at your age. Can't you see I'm not meant to go home? For some reason, I must stay in France. I don't know what that reason is, but I will someday. I suppose I'm a fatalist. I've tried to get out and didn't succeed, so I resign myself to staying put. After all, maybe Gerald is still in France.'

'I hope not', said Enid nervously, 'for his sake.'

At seven o'clock the next morning, we were ready to leave. I was so laden with Paul's belongings as well as my own that I couldn't find a square inch of space anywhere in which to put the spare tin of petrol.

'I'll take it for you, Naive,' said Paul. 'I have lots of room.'

'I should think you have after piling all your stuff onto me,' I retorted.

'Don't be so bad-tempered, woman. You know all those heavy things will spoil my upholstery.'

'Oh, very well, Paul, you always win, but don't go too fast in case I break down. Oh, before I forget. Keep a safe distance in front of me. My brakes are done in.'

'All right. You've had weeks to get those brakes fixed, but you didn't. I'll keep out of your way.'

During the next few hours, Paul behaved perfectly, waiting each time I fell behind. We were halfway to Paris when we encountered our first spot of bother. At least I did. We were in the hilly country of Normandy. I was going downhill at a terrific speed, trying to keep an even distance between me and Paul. I was furious with him for going so fast. Around the bend, the gates of a level crossing were just closing. I couldn't see Paul, and I couldn't stop. My brakes were utterly useless. I couldn't change down; I was going much too fast. I had no alternative but to crash straight through the gates.

It wasn't until I was climbing the next hill some distance away that I managed to stop and look behind. The smashed-up gates had derailed a German troop train. I heard their shouting and swearing in the distance and was off like a shot. As long as the tumult at the crossing went on, I had a chance of getting away undiscovered. There was still no sign of Paul. In the back of my mind, I had a shrewd suspicion that he had seen me crash the gates and made off, not wishing to be involved in anything. I cursed him. It was all his fault, anyway, loading me down

ANNE ANGELO

with his luggage and then expecting me to do a hundred kilometres an hour, nonstop, in my poor old car.

About an hour later, I hit my second spot of trouble. The old familiar pinking sound of the engine greeted me. I'd run out of petrol. Paul, blast him, had my spare tin. I cursed him all over again, but that didn't help. He, of course, was nowhere to be seen. There was nothing I could do but wait. I must have been there for at least two hours before there was any sign of life at all. It came in the form of a German lorry.

'Benzene,' I yelled at them, but they had none. They said there was a place about three kilometres down the road where I could get some, and they offered me a lift. I declined. I couldn't leave the car. I didn't dare. Anybody might take it, and then I would be properly stranded. I waited on. After a while, a man came along on foot.

'What's the matter?' he asked in a broad Irish accent.

'Good Lord,' I exclaimed. 'What are you supposed to be, a deserter or something?'

'That's my business,' he told me. 'You wouldn't be going to Paris, I suppose?'

'I am', I said eagerly, 'but I've run out of petrol. If you would like to go down to the dump about three kilometres away and bring some back, I'll give you a lift.'

'Sure, anything to oblige a lady,' he said and was off. An hour went by before he returned, carrying a German can of petrol.

'Thank God,' I said. 'I'll get the tank filled up when we get to the dump. What were they like?'

'Welcomed me like a long-lost brother,' he said jovially. 'Couldn't be kinder.'

'Good,' I said, letting in the clutch.

It was getting late when we arrived on the outskirts of Paris. There we were, stopped. The curfew was on, and no one was allowed to go in or come out till the morning. The German sentries were very polite, but firm. I could spend the night in a nearby empty house if I liked, and they would keep an eye on the car until the morning. I declined their offer. I spent yet another night in the car while my passenger spent the night drinking in a nearby cafe. When I got to Paul's flat the next morning, my rage knew no bounds.

But one look at him, and my rage turned to pity. His eyes were red as if he'd been crying all night.

'What on earth is the matter, Paul?' I asked.

'Didn't you see that ugly little sardine of a car outside?'

'Yes, but what about it?' I asked stupidly.

'That beastly little thing is now my car. I was stopped yesterday by some young German officers. They decided that their colonel would like my car so they told me to get out and change cars. That's all.'

He was once more crying like a child. In spite of feeling sorry for him, I had a violent desire to laugh.

'That's what you get for running away from me. It's a judgement,' I muttered under my breath.

*   *   *

ANNE ANGELO

CHAPTER 13

The Forbidden Zone

THE NEXT DAY, I went on alone to Lille. There seemed to be more Germans than ever all around the north. Marie-Louise welcomed me back with open arms.

'I'm so glad you have come back. There's so much for you to do here.'

'Me,' I exclaimed. 'How?'

'My son is here. He got away and is trying to organise something to help the others who were trapped in France. Your countrymen, mademoiselle. There are hundreds in hiding.'

'But', I stammered, 'where's your son hiding?'

'In your room,' the old woman announced happily.

'What are you talking about, Marie-Louise?' I could feel the last remnants of my patience dribbling away.

'Mademoiselle', explained the old servant, 'you have drawers in your room.'

'Yes, but I don't see the connection,' I said with a look of exasperation.

'Be calm, mademoiselle,' Marie-Louise went on. 'You have big cupboards in your room. Under those cupboards, there are drawers, and under those drawers, there is enough room to hide fifty men. The space is about sixty centimetres high and stretches from your room right across the house to the garden. It's a wonderful hiding place.'

'Wonderful?' I repeated, then suddenly jumped to my feet. I shook Marie-Louise till the old woman's few remaining teeth rattled in her head. 'You haven't got men in there already? For heaven's sake, Marie-Louise, you couldn't be so stupid. Can't you see, it's the firing squad for all if you get caught? For goodness' sake, say something.' I stopped shaking the old woman, who was trying to find words to reply, and, turning my back, I went upstairs. I would find out for myself. 'That crazy old woman wants locking up,' I thought.

It took all the strength I had to pull out the bottom drawers. I made such a noise that I didn't hear footsteps come in behind me.

'Hello, my dear,' said Uncle, giving me a beaming smile. The sound of his voice had startled me. Nevertheless, I was glad to see him. I rushed into his arms.

'What's going on in this house?' I asked. 'Are you in on this?'

'Naturally, my dear. I wouldn't miss it for worlds.'

'But it's dangerous, Uncle. Don't you understand either?'

'I understand more than you do. If I can be of some assistance to my country, to this poor battered France, I'll die happy,' said the old man.

'It's foolish to measure life by one act, Uncle. So many people become heroes in an excited moment, or because at that moment, there was nothing else they could do. But surely it can't be worthwhile,' I replied, despondently.

'My dear girl. I think it's extremely worthwhile.'

'But why pick my house for your deeds of heroism? Surely you must know how it will all end?' I went on wearily. I had expected to relax on getting home. Instead, I'd walked right into the lion's den. 'Are there any men here yet?'

'No, not yet. Jacques is busy making air vents before they arrive.'

'Oh, no,' I moaned. 'Not through those marvellous ceilings.'

'Don't worry, he's a craftsman. If anything, he'll improve them.'

I turned my attention once more to the drawers. I had to admit with reluctance that they made a wonderful hideout. I did not, however, relish the idea of my room being turned into the theatre of operations. Still, I supposed I could use another room.

Jacques was busy. He explained his plan in detail whilst I lay on my stomach beside him. I was suddenly beginning to be interested in spite of my fear of the Germans. Jacques seemed to infuse some of his enthusiasm into me. I hadn't the heart anyway to tell them to get out. After all, just supposing I did forbid them to bring any soldiers here, and supposing one of the people who ought to have come was Gerald. The consequences of my refusal were unthinkable.

I went back into my room and found Uncle. He was still sitting where I had left him.

'All right, Uncle. I'll help, but I warn you, I'm scared to death.'

'Good girl.' He smiled. 'I knew you would.'

'But I won't sleep in here. I'll use another room.'

'I think it would be wiser if you slept in here. It wouldn't arouse suspicion should the house be searched.'

Those first few days after my return opened my eyes to the real horrors which were to follow.

Poor Lille! The battered town swarmed with invaders. Infantry men, pioneers, engineers, labour units, youth battalions, and the rest.

One and all were drunk with victory. The lords of creation! Just taking time to recover from the looting and the champagne celebrations before wiping out Britain—the last little obstacle in their path!

In dreadful contrast to these swaggering Nazis were the wretched survivors of the civil population.

They were stunned by defeat, deafened by the loudspeakers that kept telling them how the British had betrayed them; starving; wandering from house to house for news of loved ones.

It broke my heart to see the poor French being trampled in the mud by these brutes who gorged and goose-stepped and sang 'We're Marching Against England.'

Yes, for a few weeks, the Nazis believed they were masters of the world.

They treated me with amused contempt.

It tickled their sense of humour that a British girl should be at liberty and be made to entertain the future conquerors of her country.

'Would you like a free trip to London?' said one.

'Just tell me the name of a good British tailor,' said another.

Many were sentenced to death when I was living in Lille, and thousands of others were rounded up secretly and sent to concentration camps for their underground work against the invader.

Food was still of primary importance for our wretched existence. Every day I walked to the Grande Place to my favourite shops. They were usually empty, and here and there the Star of David was painted on windows and doors. I wondered how the Germans knew who were Jewish and who were not, I was afraid to ask, but it seemed to me that they hadn't finished rounding up the Jews. One day I watched from the opposite side of the street while they dragged men, women, and children screaming from their hiding places, not even allowing them time to gather up any warm clothing, and pushed them with the butts of their rifles into trucks which seemed to have a peculiar stench. A young Nazi shrieked orders and obscene names at the bewildered and frightened families. I watched him, hating the evil expression on his face. I'd never seen such a maniac. More families were dragged out of somewhere and lined up shivering with the others. Nobody was brave or foolish enough to argue with the guns. I saw my old friends Hans and Christina, who owned a delicatessen, being bundled into a truck. One soldier was dragging Christina by her beautiful long blonde hair. I'd known them for years but didn't know they were Jews. How did the Germans know? How could they! He gave Hans a final kick and swaggered over to the driver, whistling. The truck moved forward. My whole being was tearing apart with anger, frustration, and wretchedness. I was overtaken by a chilling numbness. The prisoners moaned as they prayed to be delivered from their inevitable fate. I trembled involuntarily and turned away. They were only a few. I found out later that there were hundreds of thousands of others from Lille and elsewhere whose destiny had been a death camp.

Nine people out of ten in that part of France were seething with hatred against the Hun.

The Nazis pretended all was well in the Forbidden Zone, but they gave themselves away.

Every day I used to see the closed vans driving up to the Bourse—men, women, youths, and girls dragged out to be tried for some so-called crime against Hitler.

The real horror of the Zone was that the Nazis were convinced they were behaving 'correctly'. They were often genuinely puzzled by the hate they caused.

This order came from Hitler himself, soon after the occupation, when the town had been plundered and looted, the civilians vilely treated, and trouble was brewing.

German soldiers: You are ordered to treat the vanquished French with the utmost correctness. At the same time, you will ruthlessly suppress all anti-German activities.

So we had the frightful contrast of Nazis trying to play gentlemen and then, whenever they got panicky, breaking out into inhuman cruelty.

They plumed themselves because they always said 'Please!' when asking directions, because they gave way to old people walking along the pavement, because they no longer looted the few goods left in the shops but paid for them in worthless francs, because they were never allowed to get drunk and run riot in the streets.

An instruction was issued that German soldiers were to win French sympathies by speaking freely about their own families at home.

The idea was that the French would be touched by this human side to the Nazis.

So for weeks on end, the Germans who always obeyed orders most thoroughly were stopping civilians in the streets, pulling out pictures of their wives and children, and trying to be sentimental in clumsy French.

Mind you, they did this willingly enough, for they had a queer sentimental streak in them, and several times, I saw them weeping as they displayed the photographs.

But the same soldiers would stand by callously while the Gestapo terrorised the innocent, while girls were rounded up for a terrible fate; while the sick and old were thrown into the streets in bitter cold to make way for officers who wanted better billets.

Three days after I returned to Lille, an order was issued ordering French people on bicycles to dismount and stay by the kerb whenever they heard the warning bell of a German armoured detachment.

I was in the rue Vauban.

A German storm trooper, slightly drunk, elbowed an old woman off the pavement into the road. He laughed and passed on.

Two military police crossed the road, arrested him, marched him off. And French people around me murmured, 'Good, they are trying to behave correctly.'

A few minutes later, the clanging of a bell was heard. An armoured column was passing through.

Remembering the order, the people on bicycles jumped down and wheeled in to the kerb. All except one stout man who must have been very deaf. He kept on his way, though Germans shouted angrily at him.

Suddenly he heard an armoured car coming on at breakneck speed. He turned in quickly to the pavement. But that Nazi at the wheel was a fiend. He steered in, mounted the pavement, and deliberately ran down the cyclist.

It was horrible, cold-blooded murder, at which women fainted. But the German soldiers were all laughing.

'That will teach the fools to obey our orders,' shouted a German officer.

The French people told me, 'Hitler made mock of us once with his tanks, his paratroops and his bombers. We're not going to have him laugh at us again by acting too soon. When we strike, it will be to settle accounts.'

It's the things that happened since the defeat that made collaboration impossible.

The people in the Forbidden Zone remembered the callous mass burials, with no attempt at identification; the looting; the burning.

They recalled how the old and the sick were thrown into the streets to make room for German soldiers.

'The Nazis were fools!' the French said contemptuously. 'They might have gone on and beaten the British, but they lost their chance through behaving like drunken savages.'

Everything was put aside in the frenzy of plundering. It wasn't impulsive. It must all have been thought out long before.

Each week, every soldier was issued with a sack already labelled: 'A Present From France.'

They plundered shops and houses, filling their sacks to the brim and then lugging them to the station, where special trains were awaiting to take the loot back to the Reich.

In between, they gorged themselves on food and drank champagne by the bucketful.

*   *   *

CHAPTER 14

The French Resistance

I SEIZED MY CHANCE and filled my rooms with the best people I could find. I didn't want any more officers or soldiers billeted on me, especially with a language problem. I couldn't supply meals, but I could supply lodgings and services.

This served a double purpose; it did the unfortunate a good turn, and it kept the Germans out.

Again and again, the Huns were on the point of 'requisitioning' the place.

Once, when German troops were definitely scared of British bombers, they went through the city taking over houses with good wine cellars, into which they could dive for shelter.

My cellar was exceptionally good. There was no wine left, so there was plenty of room!

'Excellent, excellent!' said the Nazi who came round, until I pointed out a skylight of thick glass that gave on to the pavement.

'A bomb through that would kill everyone in the shelter,' I said. 'That's why we never use it.'

Immediately, he struck my house off the list. He was taking no chances.

If he had looked around, he would have seen there was a back compartment to the cellar which was absolutely ideal for the purpose.

A few days later, two RAF pilots arrived. They were very young, but so very confident.

'If we can get some French papers, we can make for the South of France and get back. Britain needs pilots. She needs us desperately. Can you imagine what it must feel like to make plane after plane and have nobody to fly them? There are so few of us and it takes time to train pilots. The Huns certainly will not sit back and wait.'

I felt lost. Among my varied acquaintances, I knew not a single forger, yet I had to get papers for these boys. I went in search of Uncle. I found him drinking soup in the kitchen.

'Look, Uncle, you suddenly rope me into something I know absolutely nothing about. These men need cards. I'm expected to get them. How? What sort of organisation is this anyway? Can't you tell me who's in it? Do I know any of them? I'm so much in the dark I'm a menace instead of a help.'

'All I can tell you, Anne, is that there are about a dozen members at present, but our numbers are increasing. I can't tell you who they are, it isn't safe. If I were you, I should try the postman for identity cards. He has proved himself very pro-British, but feel your way first. Don't plunge into it. Don't tell him these men are here. Always play for safety.'

I spoke to the postman the next day. I'd known him for years and had a feeling that he had, at some time in his life, held a more elevated position. Over a glass of beer in the kitchen, I made him talk about himself. He hated the Germans bitterly. He'd lost his entire family during the evacuation and had come back with one thought in his mind. To avenge them.

'I need identity cards desperately,' I said, having convinced myself that he was on my side. 'Have you any friends in the Town Hall?'

'I have one,' he replied. 'He worships money, but he would do the thing properly. What I mean is that the cards would be genuine. They would be cards with names on record. Of course, the original owners of those names wouldn't be living anywhere in this district. There are lots like that. I know. I used to work at the Town Hall many years ago.'

'Good,' I said. 'How do you go about it?'

'Well, first of all, you'd better take photographs of these men. I'll develop them for you. I'm keen on photography, and in the meantime, I'll contact my friend. Of course, if he's pro German, we'll have to kill him, but I don't think it'll be necessary.'

I opened my eyes wide in astonishment. He spoke of killing as simply as if he were discussing changing a shirt. And he looked such an inoffensive little man too.

It took time to get papers for the two pilots, but eventually, the day came when they were ready to start their journey. I smiled as I looked at them. They were wearing Paul's suits. Suits he had left there before the war.

'Now remember, you two, once you get to Paris, the lorry driver will drop you right inside the Halles, the market. Go into the Cafe Rosa, have a coffee, and ask for Felix. Tell him Anne sent you. That's all I can do for you. The lorry driver can be trusted. Felix can be trusted, so do as he says. You'll probably go over the demarcation line by lorry, but he'll tell you all about it. For heaven's sake, don't forget that you are both Italian. Use your hands a lot when you talk. Okay?'

'Thanks a lot,' replied the one I had nicknamed Tom. 'If we get through, we will never forget what you've done. Now we go out by the garden and round the back street to the garage. Are you quite sure it's safe? I mean for you.'

'Don't worry about me. I'll keep any snoopers busy at the front of the house. You should see me drunk and disorderly, I'm really good. Thank God Hitler's proclamation the other day said that all citizens of France had to be treated with respect and courtesy, except, of course, those helping the enemy. Never mind, you worry about yourselves. As the clock strikes six, get moving. Good luck. Let them have it when you get back up there.'

It was nice to have the house empty of British servicemen again. Not that I expected it to stay like that for long. Still, it gave me breathing space. My nerves were on edge with listening to the everlasting *thud* of German jackboots as they patrolled the street night and day. I'd got into the way of listening and holding my breath as they passed the door. The thought that those steps might stop outside the house and the bell ring was telling on me. I had to keep calm, but I was so afraid of them. A letter from Paul saying he was arriving the following day made me feel better. I needed moral support very badly, not that I expected much from Paul. I'd seen how cowardly he could be. Still, he would be

ANNE ANGELO

someone to talk to. Marie-Louise and Uncle were all right in their way, but I needed to laugh sometimes.

Uncle spent his days in the cafes listening to the conversations all around him and picking up scraps of information. The Germans took no notice of him. He looked so inoffensive and was so very old. At dinner that evening, I heard all his news.

'The Boches are very worried about the presence of enemy agents in the district. There's talk of taking hostages,' he said sadly. 'They know there are a lot of soldiers hidden by the civilians, so we'd better be careful for the time being. They intend to search all houses.'

'We're all right for the moment,' I said, feeling very frightened. 'I hope they come when there's nobody here.'

'I hope so too,' he replied.

'By the way, Uncle, Paul will be here tomorrow. He has some business to attend to or something.'

'Do you think I ought to move out, Anne? I don't think he'll be very pleased to see me.'

'Of course not, Uncle. Perhaps he won't stay long.'

'I hope not, Anne,' said Uncle. 'We may get a batch of men to hide, and somehow I wouldn't trust Paul. I don't mean that he's a traitor. It's only that he's afraid, and he would talk to save his skin.'

'I think you're right, Uncle.'

Paul arrived for lunch the next day. He looked so funny stepping out of the miserable little car he'd been landed with. A visitor arrived late that afternoon to see him. Paul went down. He reappeared in the bureau about ten minutes later white with rage.

'What's the matter, Paul? You look as if you've lost something.'

'Don't talk to me,' he raged. 'Do you know who that man was? I'll tell you. He was the owner of that little scrap heap of a car outside. The Germans had stolen it from him. He had all the papers to prove he was the rightful owner, so he's taken it away.'

'Couldn't you stop him?' I said, marvelling at the smallness of the world. 'Surely, if the Jerries gave it to you in place of yours, it then belongs to you, bad as it is.'

'It's his, and it has gone, and I'm the loser. I'm sick to death of this war and everybody in it. I'm going out,' yelled Paul.

He came back a few hours later, however, bursting with excitement. 'Naive,' he yelled. 'You'll never guess what I've just seen. The Packard. My Packard. It's standing outside the Town Hall. I'll try to see the Kommandant tomorrow morning and get it back. They're behaving very decently.'

'Decently,' I said sarcastically. 'You haven't seen anything yet. This isn't Paris. For your information, this is the forbidden zone, the Red Zone, the secret zone, or whatever you like to call it. The real name for it is just plain hell. They can pretend to behave correctly now when they have finished plundering and looting the place. Now that they've got tired of treating the people vilely. Oh yes. They are trying to behave like gentlemen, but when they get panicky, they break out into inhuman cruelties. You haven't seen anything yet, Paul. All you see is the German who says "Please" when asking for directions. The Germans who give way to people walking along the streets. The Germans who pay for the few remaining goods in the shops, but pay for them in worthless francs. The Germans who are never drunk because they are not allowed to run riot. You probably don't know that while hating us all like poison, they have instructions to win over the civilian population, to mix with them, to talk about their families. Even I have seen snapshots of their loved ones back in Germany. Only, I am no fool. I had great difficulty in refraining from laughing at their clumsy sentimentality. As you're new to this zone, Paul, I'd better tell you that if you hear a bell clanging, it's a warning that German armoured detachments are going through, so get off the road. Ignorance of their laws and regulations won't help you.'

'It's incredible,' breathed Paul. 'I've found them so charming, so friendly, except, of course, for losing my car, but I'm sure that I'll get it back.'

'Like to make a bet on that, Paul?'

'No, thanks,' he said wearily. Just then, the doorbell rang.

'Are you expecting anyone, Paul?' I asked, my heart thumping. I didn't know why, but I was suddenly very frightened.

'No, are you?'

'I'm always expecting visitors. Unwelcome ones,' I replied quietly.

I listened. Heavy footsteps were marching up the stairs. They didn't knock. They simply walked in, clicked their heels, and asked, 'Are you Mlle Angelo?'

'Yes.'

'You are a British subject. You are going to prison.'

'What for?' I screamed, backing away from them. Paul was speechless in his chair. 'I haven't done anything.'

'No questions,' rapped out the more sinister-looking of the two. 'Come.' He came towards me and grabbed my arm. I kicked him viciously in the shin. How I wished I were wearing Marie-Louise's clogs. I would have broken his leg. He caught hold of my hair in one hand and with the other he twisted my arm round my back till I felt sure it would break.

'Paul', I screamed, 'do something.'

But Paul didn't move, and I was marched down the stairs into a waiting lorry. In no time I realised I was being taken to the prison of Loos. I'd often passed by the horrible place and pitied the poor people who were locked up in such a hole. Apparently, I was now going to have the doubtful pleasure of getting an inside view of the place.

*   *   *

The prison at Loos.

CHAPTER 15

The Prison At Loos – The Cachot

I WAS BROUGHT BEFORE a hulking bull-necked officer. They emptied my pockets. They searched me thoroughly, and none too gently. He got up and twisted my arm till I almost fainted with the pain. 'Throw her into the cachot.'

I felt sick with pain and fear. What on earth could a cachot be? Not something filled with wild animals, surely! I screamed and kicked like a madwoman as they thrust me into a coffin-like cell a little over one metre high, about half that square. It was pitch-black. I'd heard of these cells. They'd been used about three hundred years before in the days of torture.

It seemed as if I'd been condemned to all the horrors of hell. I couldn't bear being shut up in a cold, dark place. I felt I was choking. If only I could have stood up straight. If only I could have stretched my legs or arms, but it was impossible. I had to spend the entire night sitting back on my heels, my body too numb to allow even a few minutes' sleep. I wondered how long I could stand it.

The next morning, I was transferred to a larger cell shared with three other women, all French.

'What are you in for?' asked one of them.

'I don't know. What about you?' I replied.

'All we said was "Tete de lard". It means fat head, or perhaps a little stronger. So we're in for insolence. In their own words, for making an insulting remark reflecting on the courage of the German Army. Can you beat that? Still, they can't keep us in forever. I happen to know that they are overcrowded already, and there are hundreds more pouring in every day. So they'll have to let us out to make room for others. They're afraid of riots.'

'I suppose this cell is made for one person?' I said, looking around. One camp bed with two grey blankets in one corner, a tiny ledge intended for a table along one side of the cell with a stool chained to the floor. One small washbasin and one toilet. Not another thing in the entire room. 'How on earth can four people sleep on one bed?' I asked. As for privacy, well the only thing to do was not to eat or drink. In any case, the food was dreadful.

The wardress was bringing in lunch. 'We could rush her,' I whispered.

'No good,' replied one of my cellmates. 'We'd never get past the guards.'

'Here you are, mesdames,' said the wardress, putting down her enormous tray. 'With my apologies.'

We stared at the tray. Four bowls of greasy soup—or, rather, water with pieces of fat floating on top, and five or six grains of rice. Four round balls of dark-looking bread and four spoons.

'Congratulate your cordon bleu on this master piece of a meal,' I said sarcastically. 'And tell me something, what are you, a Frenchwoman, doing working for the Boches?'

'I have no choice, mademoiselle. The entire prison has been taken over by the Hun, including the staff. We either obey as employees or join our prisoners. What would you do?'

'I would poison their soup,' I said vehemently. 'You have a chance to do something for your country.' The plump woman looked at me, raised her eyebrows, and left us.

I looked ruefully at the ball of bread I held. 'How on earth are we supposed to eat it. There isn't a soft place anywhere in it to start on. I'll bet you they've mixed cement with it to make the flour go further. And I am starving.' I tipped the greasy soup down the toilet. The others, after disdainfully turning up their noses, followed my lead. We were each left with the ball of bread. I tried throwing mine on the floor in an attempt to break it, but it only bounced. Finally, we decided to play bowls with them. We had no books or papers to read, and the balls of bread helped to spend many tedious hours.

Supper at four o'clock was exactly the same as lunch, and like lunch, it went down the toilet. Our 'bowls' had increased to eight, which made it more fun. But we couldn't play for long. At five o'clock, we were ordered to bed. I looked at the small narrow bed and looked at my well-built companions.

'We'd better try to get in,' said one of the others. 'Two at the top and two at the bottom.'

If only that bed had been wider, it would have worked. As it was, there was no room for anybody's feet. I spent most of the night taking somebody's toe out of my mouth. That was bad enough, but when someone had firmly planted her foot under my chin and forced my head back until I thought my skull would smash against the wall, I decided it was time I got up. I spent the rest of the night on the floor. I had never known that a stone floor could be so bitterly cold.

The following days were all exactly like the first. The only thing that changed was the number of bowls we had to play with.

'If they don't let us out soon, I'll go mad,' I stormed. 'The worst thing about prison life is loss of freedom. To know that one can't go out and come in when one likes is, to my mind, the most soul-destroying part of the whole business. I don't mind the food being inedible. I don't mind sleeping on the floor. But that door is locked, and I can't get out—that is what is so killing.' Picking up a bowl, I hurled it viciously through the bars of the window. The glass smashed. 'Look,' I screamed hysterically. 'A new game. Let's smash them all out.' It was all over in a matter of seconds. Not one bowl remained, and not one pane of glass either.

We all sat down and waited for the inevitable reckoning, but nobody came near us.

'Surely, the Boches must have heard our sweet music,' said one of the women.

'I wonder why they haven't bothered?' I said. 'I can't figure out these people at all. They slay you for less. I would much rather they shouted their heads off and put up some cardboard. If they don't, we'll freeze to death tonight. It was a silly thing to do, but I do find the sound of breaking glass so satisfying.'

'Do you? I've never thought about it,' said one of the others.

'What I've been thinking about', I said thoughtfully, 'is the possibility of getting out of that window.'

'Do you think the bars are wide enough apart?' asked my companions.

'I've got so thin lately', I said, 'that I'm sure I could get through them sideways, if I can get my head out. Shall I try?'

'Yes, do,' they all chorused. 'We'll make a human stepladder for you.' They all put their arms round each other's waist, and I climbed up. My head was rather a tight fit. It would have been much easier without ears. Soon my shoulders were through, but my bust was in the way. I struggled and tugged, but all I managed to do was to get well and truly wedged. My cellmates were shouting to me to hurry as they couldn't hold me much longer. But I was hopelessly jammed.

Just then, we heard the rattling of the wardress's keys. Apparently, she was used to attempted escapes for she didn't seem surprised when she saw us all.

'Come along, all of you. You're released,' she said.

'Help,' I shouted as my companions made a dive for the door, leaving me dangling in mid-air. The wardress came over and tugged at my legs. I had never realised that the weaker sex could be so strong. The woman practically ripped my nose off in the process of extricating me from my perilous position.

I was taken before that hulking officer again. How I loathed that man.

'You can go and live in your house', he told me in very good English, 'but you must sign this paper that you will not leave the city boundaries. You are a hostage. Will you give that promise?'

'Yes,' I said, without the faintest intention of keeping my word to this brute.

'Do you know what is meant by a hostage?' asked the officer after I had signed the paper.

'No.'

'It means that if any British agents get up to any tricks, if any other

British try any games, you will be punished. Perhaps you will be shot. Do I make myself clear?'

'I just don't understand.'

'You are a hostage for the good behaviour of all the other British in the zone. If they can't behave, then you will suffer.'

'Do you really mean that I would be punished for something I didn't do?'

'You will see,' he roared. 'Now go, and remember what I have said.'

*   *   *

The Bourse from the Grande Place, Lille.
Headquarters of the feared Gestapo.

CHAPTER 16

The Stolen Car

I WAS GLAD TO get home. I decided that never again would I be rude to or upset a German as long as I lived, but it was so easy for me to make resolutions when I was safely in my own home, where I couldn't even see a German. As soon as I saw one outside, I felt my hatred for them mounting and mounting inside me till I was afraid for myself. It was as much as I could do to keep my temper under control whenever I met one in the street. It was difficult to choke down the desire to kick them, to kick them hard, to spit in their eyes, to abuse them.

Paul had kept out of my way for a day or two after my return, but eventually, we met face-to-face.

'Thanks for helping me out of gaol, Paul,' I said sarcastically.

'Don't be so bitter, Naive. What could I have done? Had I said one word, they would have bundled me along with you, and where would that have got us?'

'I think you're the worst coward I have ever met, Paul. But I don't suppose you can help it. Did you get your car back?'

'No. They wouldn't let me see anybody with any authority at all. It makes me so mad. It's always standing there, all alone in the square unguarded, yet I haven't the courage to step into it and drive it away.'

'Is the ignition key in it?' I asked.

'Yes. I look at it every day and get more and more furious.'

'Would you like me to steal it for you, Paul?' I asked him quite seriously.

'Would you really do that for me, Naive?' Paul sounded incredulous.

'No, not for you, but for two thousand francs.'

'You make me sick,' grumbled Paul. 'All you ever want is money.'

'That's not easy for you to understand, Paul. You are rolling in it. I'm nearly broke, and I'll do it for two thousand, but not a centime less. Think about it. Only, you'll have to hide it for the duration. Maybe your friends could cover it over with bales of linen in their mills. You'd have to arrange that. I'd get it there. Tell me tomorrow if I'm not back in jail again. I've got to the stage where I don't know where I'm going to spend the next night.' I left him to work it out on paper and went down to the kitchen. Uncle had been waiting for me.

'We're expecting six men,' he said.

'But Paul's here, Uncle. It isn't safe,' I protested.

'Get rid of him, my dear.'

'Just like that,' I said, snapping my thumb and forefinger. 'Try to stop them coming for a day or two, and I'll see what I can do.'

'All right, Anne, but we haven't much time,' he replied.

The next day, Paul had decided on having his car.

'You understand, Naive, if you're caught, I don't pay over the money.'

'Naturally,' I replied. 'I want it in cash, mind. No cheques.'

'Don't you trust me?' he asked. I gave him one of those looks that means so much more than words.

'What happens if they find it when it is hidden, Naive. I shall, of course, expect you to refund the money,' he said calmly.

I nearly exploded. He wasn't one bit concerned about the risk I was taking; all that mattered to him was his wretched money. 'That would be your loss, Paul,' I answered. 'Once I deliver it to the mills, it's up to you and your friends. My part of the job is to steal it. You're not paying me to hide it. Do we agree?'

'All right,' he replied. 'I'll probably lose my car and my money in the end, but there's no point in arguing about it.'

'That depends on how good your friends are,' I replied. 'By the way, you'll let me know this afternoon where I have to drive it to, and if I were you, I should go back to Paris. By train, naturally. When you get your travelling pass, make rather a fuss about having to go by train, etc. Once you are in Paris, they may come around asking questions, so don't let them frighten you into telling them where it's hidden. If I get involved, believe me, Paul, I shall swear I had nothing to do with it, and I will produce witnesses to prove that you did the job yourself. So leave me out of it for your own sake.'

'I shouldn't like to do business with you again,' he replied bitterly. 'You're no longer the sweet innocent girl I used to know. You are as hard as nails.'

'Never mind the compliments, Paul.'

That same evening, I set off. The car was there, all alone, in the Grande Place. I went across to it. As I got closer, I saw there were two Wehrmacht soldiers patrolling in opposite directions along the footpath. I went round the back of the car and up the steps into the building. As I went, I saw the keys were in the dash. I knew the building well and went straight to one of the women's toilets. I didn't dally long. I was afraid somebody might drive the car away any minute. When I came out, I walked very briskly and businesslike down the steps, straight to the car, opened the door, and sat in. I started it up and drove it away. I didn't even look at the sentries on the footpath. I drove it out to Marcq, where Paul's friends had linen mills. They hid it for me in one of the warehouses under some tarpaulins. I caught the first tram back to my place.

I waited for Paul. He'd gone to the Cintre bar to spend the time drinking with some German officers he knew. Nobody would suspect him. He came home sometime later and paid over the agreed sum. It was the easiest money I'd ever earned. There were bound to be repercussions, but 'Sufficient to the day' had become my motto.

Paul left for Paris the next morning. He was out of the way just in time. Four Germans came to the house to look for him. They explained that it was in his own interests to help them find the car, as doubtless, he would have it returned to him in the very near future. I hoped he wouldn't be fooled by their trickery. I told them that he was in Paris.

Within five minutes of the Germans leaving the house by the front door, two British soldiers came in by the back. I rushed them upstairs.

'What on earth made them send you here in broad daylight?' I asked hurriedly.

'It was too risky to stay where we were another minute. We should have come here last night,' one of them told me. Just then, Jacques appeared and showed them how to get in behind the drawers should they hear the doorbell ring. They tried it out and found it quite simple to operate. Four more arrived during the day. Two of them actually by the front door.

They were supposed to be furniture removal men. They carried tables and chairs in under the noses of the German sentries. By some means or other, the real removal men were waiting in the kitchen to change places with the British men as soon as they entered. They then carried on with the removing. If I hadn't been so frightened, I would have seen the funny side of it. Having once taken in all the furniture from the lorry, they calmly proceeded to take it all out again. One of them even went up to a German sentry patrolling in front of the house and began talking to him, telling him that the people in the house were undoubtedly quite mad. They ordered furniture, and when it was brought in, they changed their minds. I could see him from behind the curtains in my room, tapping his head and looking up to the sky as if in sheer desperation.

Our organisation had improved in efficiency with time, and in less than a week, the soldiers had gone. I hoped they would get through, but there was no way of knowing. Once they were in Paris, they were out of our hands completely.

Uncle was rather worried. He'd heard that the Germans intended to take a census of all the inhabitants in the zone, with a view to billeting their troops and families who were arriving from Germany.

'Of course, if we could arrange for the police to certify that this house is full up, I believe they would accept it,' he said.

'The police,' I said incredulously. 'Why?'

'I believe', he replied, 'that they've given the French police sweeping powers to win them over and get them to collaborate.'

I sat bolt upright. 'I know the very man, unless, of course . . .' I broke off, remembering Mr Derval of the Surete. Somehow, I felt that he would rather see me drawn and quartered than help me again. I cursed myself for having been a fool and not having 'managed' him better. Still, there was a chance that he might hate the Germans. One never knew.

I went over to his office. He received me in quite a friendly manner, but it didn't take me long to discover who's side he was on, and it wasn't mine.

'What do you think about the Germans and this occupation, Mr Derval?' I asked.

'They are behaving extremely well,' was his reply as he sat back in his chair, his hands clasped on his paunch. 'Frankly, France can do with new blood and the people here with a little discipline. Together, France and Germany—we would be invincible.'

I watched him anxiously, seized by rising anger. What had happened to give treachery these new powers in France?

'Would you like to drink to the end of a long feud and the beginning of a new peace?' he asked, bending over his desk and reaching out for a bottle of Pernod.

'No, thank you,' I said angrily.

'No other Frenchman rejoices as I do,' he went on. 'I mean that I am a loyal Frenchman, and I rejoice boldly. Mind you, I don't say that the Germans are civilised. By some miracle, they managed to escape that. Liberty, which we have been chasing after for centuries, flourishes only on the other side of the Rhine, liberty to obey and prosper.' He paused to take a drink.

'I don't know what half of that means', I said dryly, 'but I gather you agree with them, and with all they do. In fact, you're on their side.'

'Quite correct,' was his self-satisfied reply.

'Then I'm wasting my time, Mr Derval,' I replied. Infuriated by my contempt for him, above all by my pleasure in showing it, he missed the hatred in my eyes. 'You're not afraid of the day of reckoning when it comes in the shape of the British Army?' I asked.

He laughed. 'My dear girl, even you must know that the British Army is obsolete. It will never set foot on French soil again. You may be sure of that.'

'I wouldn't be so sure of that, Mr Derval. And don't forget you'll be tried as a collaborator, and possibly as a traitor.'

'Mademoiselle, your eloquence is deadly, but surely, you can tell me what you wanted in coming here?'

'Actually', I said fearlessly but foolishly, 'I wanted a letter signed by you stating that I have no room in my house to billet Germans and their families. Mind you, it'll be in their own interests because there are patriotic people still left here who might succeed in either blowing up the entire house or even poisoning them. Surely, as their friend, you would like to prevent such accidents happening.'

'I think they are quite capable of taking care of themselves', he retorted, 'and I have no intention of helping you. You were not particularly sociable at our last meeting, mademoiselle, were you? I have not forgotten.'

'Neither have I', I said furiously, 'so unless you give me that letter, I'll tell your wife that you were having an affair with my friend, Enid.'

'I'm sorry to spoil your little effort at blackmailing me, but my wife was evacuated to the South months ago. So unfortunate, isn't it?' He looked at me with murder in his eyes. I turned on my heel and left, wishing I could kill that little worm. I felt I'd made a mess of the whole thing.

'It's no good, Uncle. He won't give me that paper. What can we do?' I asked the old man anxiously.

'I don't know, my dear, but we'll think of something,' he reassured me.

'Couldn't we have some dreadful disease in the house,' I asked eagerly.

'Perhaps we could, but who would we use as a victim?'

'Marie-Louise,' I said quickly. 'We could keep her in bed for a few days and hang sheets up over the door. You could be the doctor, and I'll answer the door for the time being. How would that work?'

'If I know anything about the Germans, it'll work perfectly. Our trouble will be Marie-Louise,' he replied knowingly.

It took us the rest of the day to convince Marie-Louise that she had 'scarlet fever'. We all helped to make the sick room ready. We made the old woman look as feverish as possible with the help of rouge and liquid powder, and settled her down in bed. We weren't a minute too soon. The doorbell rang. I went down to answer it.

'What rooms have you vacant in this house?' demanded one of the soldiers.

ANNE ANGELO

'I don't know,' I replied. 'At least I don't know if it's safe for you to come in. We have scarlet fever in the house.' They pushed me roughly aside and started up the staircase. Marie-Louise was in the room facing the top of the stairs. They opened all the doors on their way, asking who used them.

'This is my aunt's room, but she's very ill,' I said, keeping a straight face with great difficulty. In spite of the risk, I found the whole thing very funny.

They pushed into the room, and the wet sheet hanging over the door hit them right in the face. It reeked of carbolic.

'Doctor, Doctor,' wailed Marie-Louise, sitting up in bed. She looked dreadful. Uncle came out of the dressing room looking very efficient in a white overall, a white band round his head and glasses hiding his watery old eyes. As he entered, with a hypodermic in his hand, he looked at the Germans, who were staring, rooted to the spot.

'Gentlemen', he said sternly, 'this lady is very ill and extremely contagious.'

The Germans turned and fled down the stairs two at a time and slammed the door behind them. We exchanged glances and then burst out laughing. For the moment, we were saved.

*   *   *

From Anne Angelo's story published in *The Weekly News*, Dundee, September 1941.

CHAPTER 17

Goering's Beauty Chorus

G ERMAN WIVES WERE searching the shops for items to send home.

German blondes, all lipstick and face cream, were patrolling the rue Nationale, keeping an eye on the civil population. These blondes were Gestapo agents. There were hundreds of them.

Men, women, and children—gaunt and starved—shuffled along in sabots and rags, searching hungrily for any scraps of food left by the greedy Boche. Hatred on almost every face.

I saw the first batch of Gestapo girls arrive. Four hundred of them. Marching like soldiers through the Grande Place to their billets in the town.

They were big, powerful specimens, these Nazi maidens of the Women's Security Group. There was precious little glamour about them, I assure you.

Some of them were wearing spectacles, more than half of them with very pimply faces.

I wonder why so many Germans today come out in masses of pimples. Something to do with their diet at home, I suppose.

In spite of the misery of the people of Lille, how we laughed at that first batch of Snoopers.

'Hitler's secret weapon!'

'Goering's beauty chorus!'

That was the kind of jeering remark that was passed.

The Nazi girls were given three months' schooling in Lille, during which they had to pass out as proficient in the French language.

The successful ones were then put into 'civvies' and assigned to their jobs.

Some were planted in factories to watch out for sabotage; others went into workshops as extra forewomen to spy on the hands.

They boarded trams and listened to conversations; they infested the boulevards with their ears flapping back.

They kept an eye on hotels and private houses; they mixed with French people in shops, cafes, and restaurants, reporting on 'malicious rumour-mongers'.

No doubt, some were successful. On the whole, however, they were a failure.

You could nearly always pick them out at one glance—for a Nazi maiden is a Nazi maiden, no matter how she may try to dress differently.

French people would spot them, shrug shoulders, then either move well away, or deliberately lead them up the garden with some fantastic rumour.

And the French had their own back for this snooping by giving pitying glances at the German girls' clothing or get-up.

The sequel to all this gave us a laugh, and heaven knows we had little enough to laugh at in the Forbidden Zone.

As time went on, the Snoopers yearned to be glamour girls!

A French girl, even with the shabbiest clothes, can somehow manage, with a silk scarf and a few cosmetics, to look 'different'. And I guess it must have made the old Eve stir in the Nazi breast.

The change began. The German girls bought smart dresses, silk stockings, and chic hats. Flaxen hair was turned to platinum. They haunted the beauty parlours. And one day they were bold enough to take to lipstick and rouge!

'Our womenfolk are not painted hussies!'

How often had I heard German soldiers say that, boasting of the fact that Hitler would never let Nazi maidens degrade themselves by powder and lipstick.

Now these Gestapo girls had fallen for the temptation.

The girls were reprimanded, ordered to be natural. But they

ANNE ANGELO

persisted, pointing out that they betrayed themselves as German at once if they went about without makeup.

The girls were backed up by German staff officers, who wanted attractive companions for the dance clubs and cabarets.

Nazis sneered at the French as an immoral race, but nothing was more disgusting than the way in which German girls were apparently expected to associate with Nazi officers.

Finally, the Snoopers scored a decisive victory which led to more trouble.

A deputation of Frenchwomen went to the Maire, complaining bitterly that German girls were monopolising the beauty parlours and buying up all the face creams, powders, and lipsticks.

'They starve us—and that is bad enough. But if we cannot keep up appearances, we might as well be dead!'

French people could laugh at the Gestapo girls, but I had to take them more seriously.

Again and again, they were put on the job of following me around, eavesdropping when I met friends in the city.

By this time, the Nazis had got it firmly fixed in their thick skulls that any trouble in the Zone must be due to wicked British agents.

So they kept me under observation in the hope that I would lead them to some 'underground organisation'.

My first encounter with a Snooper was at my home in rue Nationale.

She seemed a bit more intelligent than the average, and she posed as a destitute Alsatian refugee, wanting a job as a maid. But I saw through her at once.

'Very well,' I said. 'But can you carry out the duties? Meals, mending, and twenty bedrooms to clean. Fortunately, the Germans have robbed me of all the silver, so that doesn't need to be cleaned every day.'

Her face fell.

'Twenty bedrooms? But it takes an hour to do one.'

'In Germany, yes. In France, no,' I said meaningly. 'A trained French maid takes only twenty minutes.' That was true. The French maid was like quicksilver as she worked.

This Snooper just gave me an angry 'I'll pay you back for this' look and stalked off.

From then on, I was frequently watched by these girl spies. They used to sit at adjoining tables in the cafe where I met my friends.

Once, I got annoyed and deliberately talked at them, passing some remarks to make them sit up.

That evening, a Gestapo officer called at my home, quoted my exact remarks, and warned me that I was on my last chance.

'You must be more guarded,' he remarked, to my surprise. 'It is no pleasure to me to send women to concentration camps. But you cannot reasonably expect to air your views within a few metres of the headquarters of our High Command.'

For the first time in my experience, a Gestapo officer was not raging and fuming, but talking common sense. I suspected a trap. I was wrong.

He was a disgruntled, discontented German, utterly fed up with the whole war. And afterwards, I met quite a number like him. 'Win or lose, I shan't get home for years,' was how he looked at it.

*   *   *

ANNE ANGELO

CHAPTER 18

British Women Give Nazi Salute

I T WAS A fortnight before I got any more British. I'd shifted old Jacques from up on the top floor down into the Blue Room, in case the Germans came and wanted to know why it was empty. I always kept it locked. Then I got a message. There'd be a signal by my back gate around a certain time. If everything was clear, I was to give a certain answer. There'd be two of them, and I'd have them until the next night.

It was so simple. I got the flickers from the torch and gave my response. I was up at my bedroom window overlooking the garden. When I got down into the garden, I saw a shadowy figure go out through the back gate, and two others came out from among the shrubbery. They were two crews from a fighter bomber who'd been shot down. They had civilian clothes over their uniforms. I couldn't give them much to eat; I hadn't got very much. But they had good hot baths and a good night's sleep before they went on their way the next night. After that, it became quite a commonplace thing. I got all sorts of people, mostly Air Force, but also some Army and some people who I didn't know what they were—people who weren't either French or English, civilians with briefcases which they hugged to themselves as if they were gold. Sometimes I'd have them for a couple of days, but it was mostly just for the one night. At one time, I had nine up there under the wardrobe floor waiting to be passed along.

One night there were two soldiers, a sergeant and a corporal from the BEF, who'd been cut off at Dunkirk. As soon as I got them into the house, in the light, the corporal recognised me. It was Angus Kilmarnock from Invergordon. It'd been Angus who'd helped Peter and me look after Geordie Ross while Geordie's mother had been down in prison in Inverness. Angus was in his full battledress with nothing to hide it. The guide who'd brought him had lent him his overcoat but had taken it back when he left him in the shrubbery. I gave Angus the full-length leather coat and sou'wester I'd got from the brothers on the *Saucy Shrimp*. He said if he got back to Invergordon, he'd tell them I was okay.

British soldiers came and went all the time. Fortunately, the refugees kept to themselves, but somehow the Germans began to associate the big double-fronted house in the rue Nationale at Lille with the ever-increasing numbers of British soldiers escaping from the forbidden zone. Time after time, they came to the house to cross-examine me. I was getting more and more angry. I'd gone to such lengths to keep the Germans out of my house, and yet, though not actually living there, they were in and out more than ever. In desperation one day, I lost my temper and kicked one of them viciously with my heavy brogue shoe. I was promptly marched off to the local concentration camp. I screamed and fought throughout the entire journey, but they took no notice. Instead of going to prison, I arrived at a huge boys' school.

There I met a lot of people I knew, people I'd met at the British club; but there were no men there. Only their wives and children.

'I say', I cried, 'what are all you people in for?'

'Nothing,' they replied. 'Unless it's because we have British passports. The funny thing is that we are all French married to Englishmen. Some of us have never been to England. None of us can even speak English.'

'What about me?' said a good-looking girl standing at the back. The voice sounded familiar. I looked round.

'Good heavens, Madame Pericles, you of all people. What are you doing among us?'

'I had the misfortune to be born on your island of Cyprus off the coast of Greece. My parents are both Greek, my husband was Greek, and here I am, considered a British subject.'

'That's a bit thick,' I said. 'But where are we all going?'

'As far as I know, we're all here for questioning,' replied Madame Pericles. 'Just as if they couldn't question us in our own homes. I don't

ANNE ANGELO

know what my clients will think when they call to see me and find I've disappeared. It's bad for business.'

We were standing around gossiping in the dormitory when two soldiers ordered us outside for exercise. Those of us who dared, laughed at the idea of exercising like criminals, but we all had to troop out. We walked round and round the enclosed playground until we'd had enough of it. Madame Pericles and I sat down on the ground.

'They must have had very well-behaved boys at this school,' I said, 'judging by the state of the wire netting. It's perfect. Not a ruddy hole anywhere. Such a pity. The Boches are all playing football. They wouldn't miss us.'

'You've given me an idea,' exclaimed Madame Pericles. 'Supposing we start climbing up the netting. We won't get out, but we will spoil their game.' She proceeded to take the lead, and the rest of us followed her. Again and again, the Germans had to stop their game to pull us down. At first, they were quite gentle, but after a time, they lost their tempers and flung us brutally to the ground. We gave up climbing.

Two days later, we were on the point of murder. Alone, we might have put up with the camp, but the wailing of hungry babies was more than any of us could stand. What those mothers must have felt; hearing their children crying all day and all night with hunger must have been agony. Needless to say, nobody had had even a crust of bread to eat since their arrival, and the eternal waiting to be questioned went on and on.

That afternoon we were all rounded up in the hall waiting for the Kommandant. He arrived and, in perfect French, announced, 'All those who would like a hot meal, please raise their right hands.'

Up went the hands almost before he had finished speaking. There were blinding flashes. German photographers had 'snapped the scene'. The women had their miserable hot meal of sausage and black bread. 'The only thing about this meal that's hot is the pepper,' I said with disgust. Actually, there was so much pepper in the sausages that, hungry as we were, most of us could not eat.

'They don't believe in wasting anything, do they?' said Madame Pericles. 'I'll bet you anything you like these sausages were meant for themselves, but as they were inedible, they gave them to us. What I wouldn't do to get even with these filthy swine. I *will* get even when I get out of here, or die in the attempt. That is, if they decide to let us out. They are just as likely to ship us to Siberia or somewhere equally unpleasant.'

'Yes,' I agreed. 'I have ways and means of liquidating some of them if I ever get out of here.'

'Promise me that you will let me help,' cried Madame Pericles. 'If I'm considered to be an enemy alien, then I might as well behave like one. Believe me, I have a fierce temper.'

'Then maybe we can arrange something,' I said thoughtfully.

The next day, there were posters up all around the camp. Near each poster were little groups of Germans roaring with laughter. I went over to see the cause of their merriment. I felt stupefied as I stared at it. There, in front of my eyes, was a photograph of all the women in the camp, their right hands raised, and underneath was the caption: 'BRITISH WOMEN GIVE THE NAZI SALUTE TO SHOW THEIR ADMIRATION FOR OUR BRAVE SOLDIERS.'

'What will they think of next?' I muttered furiously. These fiends were cunning as well as cruel. If only I could get out.

At last, the great moment came. We were to be questioned by the Kommandant. We had to enter in pairs. Madame Pericles and I walked in together. He sat at a desk piled high with records. I wondered how he'd obtained all his information.

'Madame Pericles and Mademoiselle Angelo,' he said without looking at us.

'What does all this mean?' Madame Pericles burst out. 'I am not British, and I have never been to Britain, yet here I have been locked up. Why?'

He looked up, first at her and then at me. He leaned back in his chair until he was balancing it on the two back legs. He started tapping his teeth with his pen and smiling. How I would have loved to push him over.

'Not bad,' he murmured. 'Not bad at all.'

I stared at him in surprise while his eyes travelled up and down my figure and that of my companion. Madame Pericles was as blonde as I was dark. We made a terrific contrast, and we both had lovely figures. This, however, was no beauty competition, and we resented being on show for his benefit. A germ of an idea was growing in my mind, however.

'What are two nice girls like you doing here?' he asked suavely. 'Surely, there has been a mistake somewhere.'

I saw my chance and took it with both hands. 'Of course, there has been a mistake,' I said sweetly. 'I'm sure a gentleman like you would never have allowed it had you known. Would you now?'

'Certainly not,' he replied.

'Look', I said, turning on my charm, 'if you will let us both go home, we'll invite you to dinner tomorrow night. I'm sure you could do with some relaxation. Your army works so hard. Would you like that? Madame Pericles would be there too, so you could bring a friend.'

'Delighted,' he said, beaming.

Another thought occurred to me. 'Won't your fellow officers be annoyed if you fraternise with us, though?' I asked, pretending to look worried.

'I shall not tell them,' he replied smoothly.

'Good,' I said joyously. 'What's your favourite drink? I have French, Italian, and German wines. I even have vodka. I prefer German wines myself, and I expect you do too.'

'Naturally.' He smiled, looking pleased with his conquest. 'I will draw up your release papers, and you may go home at once.'

'Thank you so much,' I breathed. 'Tomorrow at seven thirty, then.' We marched out, and within ten minutes, an orderly brought us our release papers, and we were free once more.

*   *   *

CHAPTER 19

Gestapo Officers Come To Dinner

'WHAT'S THE IDEA of inviting that snake to dinner and roping me into it too?' asked Madame Pericles as we rode home on a tram.

'I thought you wanted to "liquidate some of the Boches",' I replied calmly. 'Here's your chance.'

'Oh, but I couldn't really kill anyone,' the girl replied, trembling.

'You won't have to,' I told her. 'You only have to entertain them.'

'Oh, so we become decoys, do we?' she said, brightening up. 'That suits me fine.'

'Good,' I replied. 'Then come to dinner tomorrow, be nice to them, flatter them, you know how to do it. You'll probably have to fight for your honour if I'm any judge of eyes, but don't lose your temper, play for time.'

Once again, I was very glad to be home. Jacques and Marie-Louise were equally glad to see me. Uncle was upstairs in the hideout room. I telephoned him to come down. He looked extremely worried.

'I'm so glad you're back. I was beginning to be afraid for you,' he said.

'Nothing new here?' I asked.'

'We're very worried, mademoiselle,' replied Marie-Louise. 'There's a leak somewhere.'

'What do you mean?' I exclaimed. 'They haven't found out, have they?'

'There's no one here at the moment,' said Jacques.

'Just a minute, Anne,' said Uncle. 'We all believe the Germans have a suspicion that something is going on. They've raided this house night and day ever since you were taken away. And we had two visitors. We had a terrible job getting them away. I have a feeling there's a snooper in this house. We don't know who it is, and we must find out. With so many refugees, it's difficult. I've gone over your list time after time, but they all appear to be genuine cases.'

I took the list. After a pause, I said, 'Most of these people are married couples, except for these two girls here. They say they are students. I used to tell the police here that when I first came to France, otherwise, they wouldn't have let me stay. Maybe I'm wrong, but I'll shadow those two from now on. At least I'll take one, and Jacques can take the other.'

'Good idea,' Jacques put in. 'Nobody bothers to pick me up with only one arm. Maybe it's the best thing that ever happened to me. These girls upstairs are really very good-looking. They haven't even the usual pimply faces and spectacles. Anyway, if they do happen to be members of the Women's security group, we'll know how to deal with them.'

'In the meantime, we have another problem,' I said. 'There are two Gestapo officers coming to dinner here tomorrow at seven thirty. Any plans?'

My companions nearly shot through the roof.

'But it isn't safe,' cried Marie-Louise.

'What a chance in a million, and what a perfect answer to our problem of clothes for the two men we're expecting. With this constant watch, the men will be here for the duration, unless, of course, they can appear as German officers. We haven't much time, but if we hurry, it can all be arranged. I wasn't a medical orderly for nothing,' said Jacques.

We all stared at one another. We knew Jacques would not stop at murder; he was a perfect match for the Hun. I hoped it would all go off all right. I was quite in the dark about Jacques's plan. Still, tomorrow I'd know as much as it was good for me to know.

It was quite impossible to get much sleep that night. I was afraid of the plan going wrong. The prospect of facing a firing squad was not pleasant. Quite apart from that, the German soldiers did a routine search of the house three times during the dark hours. I wasn't afraid of them that night. Let them come as often as they wished, but not tomorrow. I wondered if these men were under orders from my prospective guest.

If that were so, it would be all right. He would most likely call them off while he was there. But supposing they were a separate branch of the Gestapo? It was not a nice thought.

I was glad when the morning came. I waited till one of the 'students' left the house and then followed her. My heart missed a beat as the girl stopped to talk to some Germans at the Grande Place, but I nearly passed out when my quarry walked up the steps of the Gestapo headquarters and was saluted on her way in.

'What a fool I've been,' I told myself furiously. 'And under my own roof. God knows I should have foreseen this, considering they did the same thing during the evacuation. The dirty little double-crossing Nazi bitch.'

I went on to my hairdresser. I had to look my best for my important guests that evening.

'Good morning, madame,' said Madame Jose as I entered.

'Do something with me,' I asked. 'I look the worse for wear. This war has aged me fifty years in the last week. Get me back to normal.'

'Leave it to me,' said the hairdresser. 'You will be ravishing when I have finished.'

'Tell me, Madame Jose, do you get many of the Gestapo girls in here?' I asked.

'Lots and lots,' she replied. 'We had one in here only yesterday. She was here over five hours. She spent over a thousand francs. But we don't want her money. First, she wanted her hair dyed platinum. We started. Got half done. She didn't like it. So she said she would have it golden brown. No good. Then we changed it to chestnut. She liked that and bought bottles and bottles of everything she set eyes on. Bah. She'll regret it.'

'Why,' I asked curiously.

Madame Jose laughed. 'The dye cannot be guaranteed. I've a feeling that her hair will go all colours of the rainbow by next week, unless it falls out altogether.'

I laughed loudly. 'Don't get absentminded and have an accident on me. I'm Mademoiselle Angelo, remember? Tell me how you can tell these German girls when you meet them.'

'Well, it used to be easy. At first, you know, they weren't allowed to wear any makeup. Now you can't tell them from French girls. Of course, they were backed up by the German officers who liked attractive companions for the dance halls and cabarets.'

I went home and told my confederates all I had learnt.

'Leave her to me,' said Jacques. 'I'll be waiting for her on the way home in the blackout tomorrow. Tonight we must concentrate on our guests.'

It wasn't until late afternoon that Jacques's plan had taken shape. There would be white German wine for my 'guests'. I was not to drink any of it. Within an hour of drinking it, the Germans should be fast asleep. I was to ring the kitchen. That was all I knew.

At a quarter to seven, Madame Pericles arrived looking very lovely in a black dinner gown. I chose white. Of the two of us, I felt that Madame Pericles was the more appropriately dressed.

As the clock struck seven thirty, the two Germans arrived. Marie-Louise served dinner.

'Do you know', I said, 'we don't even know your names.'

'Just call me Erich, and my friend here is called Reinhard.'

'I can't imagine such nice men as you being in the Gestapo. You don't look the sort. They are cruel, ruthless bullies. You are perfect gentlemen. Besides, I can tell by the scar across your face that you were a Prussian officer.' In such a friendly atmosphere, they relaxed, drank copiously, and their tongues loosened.

'Quite right, my dear,' answered Erich. 'No one is more fed up with this war than I am. I'm a soldier. I never thought I should sink so low as to become a Gestapo officer. It was because I was a lawyer that they gave me this work.'

'Why didn't you refuse?' I asked, beginning to feel quite sorry for him.

'In Germany, one never refuses to do as one is ordered. Either I became a Gestapo officer, or I faced a firing squad. How I hate Nazism and all it stands for. First it was Poland, then Norway, and now the Zone. I am so sick of it all. I only live for the day when I can go back to my wife and my home.'

'And your children?' I asked.

'Unfortunately, I have none, so Hitler takes half my income as punishment, as though I were responsible for Nature. Even if we do manage to cross the Channel, which I doubt, we'll have our hands full for years keeping the British under control. I don't mind telling you that a great army of Gestapo has already been trained for this job. They will show no leniency. But win or lose, I won't get home for years. Unfortunately, it's the fanatic Nazi tail that wags the German dog. There are thousands who feel as I do, and all of them, like myself, will go on obeying orders to the very end.'

'What's your candid opinion about the nature of this war?' I asked. I was beginning to like my guest, in spite of his nationality.

'Frankly, mademoiselle, I think you British are the most stupid in the world. You shouldn't be fighting against us. You should be fighting with us against Communism. Russia, if you like. You mark my words. No matter which of us wins the War, the winner will have to turn round and fight Russia before lasting peace can be guaranteed, and this war will have been fought for less than nothing.'

Marie-Louise had entered with the coffee. There was still no sign of my guests falling asleep. I found myself inwardly hoping that they wouldn't.

'Are you very hard up for food?' asked Reinhard.

'Hard up,' Madame Pericles almost shrieked. 'We are positively starving. We have probably eaten a month's rations tonight, haven't we, Anne?'

'Maybe three months' rations if they don't speed up deliveries a bit,' I replied.

'I'll arrange for you to have some of our supplies,' said Reinhard, taking out his notebook. Madame Pericles got up and put a record on the phonogram. I hoped the soft lilting melodies would help my guests to relax. But no, they wanted to dance. I was enjoying my evening immensely, until Erich got amorous. Reinhard followed his example, but Madame Pericles managed to control him more successfully than I did Erich. He pulled me down onto the couch, and his face was very close to mine as he asked me if I would like him to make love to me.

ANNE ANGELO

'Not tonight,' I said, praying for the drug to work. 'Not while our friends are here.'

I broke away from him. 'Let's dance again. Teach me the most popular dance in Germany. After all, I might come and see you after the War.'

'All right,' he said, gallantly, trying to rise to his feet. But his knees gave way, and he sank back onto the settee. 'Oh, I feel so drowsy. Maybe I drank too much.'

On the other side of the room, Reinhard was all out in the large armchair with a rather frightened Madame Pericles stroking his forehead. Within a few seconds, both the Germans were snoring. I waited a few minutes then rang the kitchen. Jacques came in, followed by four men, none of whom I'd ever seen before.

'Jacques', I pleaded, 'don't hurt these men. They are not Nazis, they are good Germans. Couldn't you turn them loose somewhere. Anything, only don't kill them.'

The four men had already removed the sleeping Germans.

'It's too risky,' said Jacques. 'And more important still, we need their uniforms and their papers. It's not like you to be so squeamish. Nazis or Germans, what is the difference?'

'It isn't that. They are harmless enough, and this is murder,' I went on.

'It is very small payment for all the atrocities they have committed,' replied Jacques fiercely. I let him go and burst into tears.

'Don't cry, Anne,' said Madame Pericles. 'You can't be too soft-hearted with Germans. They didn't show us any pity in that camp, did they? Think of all those poor children crying with hunger. Our departed friends didn't do much for them, did they? Oh, buck up. Let's have a drink.'

Of the two of us, Madame Pericles was by far the more composed, the more practical. I had to admit the truth of what she'd said. Erich had certainly obeyed the Gestapo orders pretty willingly. Perhaps he'd just been trying to get on the right side of me with his tale of hating the Nazis. After a couple of drinks, I felt very much better.

That night, two British soldiers left the house dressed as Gestapo officers. I took one look at them and fled.

'Look, Uncle, let's have a break, please,' I pleaded. 'Don't have any more soldiers here for a while. We'll be watched night and day. As it is, everywhere I go, I'm followed, and once they miss those two officers, this house will be turned inside out. Let's relax. You can be too foolhardy.'

'I think it'll be wiser too,' replied the old man. 'But perhaps we will not have any choice. In the meantime, Jacques still has to deal with that blonde spy upstairs.'

I felt sick at the thought of another murder.

*　　*　　*

CHAPTER 20

German Dirty Tricks

T HERE WAS HARDLY a French man or woman who would not take part in underground activities to get even with the invader.

Telephone wires were cut. Staff cars met with accidents. German soldiers disappeared. Arms were stolen. From the factories came word of sabotage, though not yet on a very large scale. The Nazis refused to believe that such a state of affairs could be due to their own savage blundering. An explanation had to be found for all this trouble. They soon hit on one.

'These things are all due to British agents,' they maintained. 'They are everywhere, plotting, carrying out sabotage, helping escaped British prisoners. They must all be found and shot. The same fate awaits anyone found helping them.'

Naturally, they wasted no time calling on me. I was cross-examined for hours at a time. I was bullied and threatened. Over and over again, they asked me if I were a member of any organisation, but never once did they get any satisfaction out of me.

'If you like, you can have me followed night and day,' I said. 'That should satisfy you that I have nothing to do with all this. After all, the French here are not collaborating with you in the slightest degree, so why blame non-existent British agents?'

'Two of our officers are dead. They were taken out of the canal,' shouted the Gestapo chief who was questioning me. 'Their uniforms and papers are missing. Who but a British agent would need a German uniform? Who murdered those men? Tell us the truth, or it will be the concentration camp in Germany for you.' I succeeded in looking completely innocent, although my heart was pounding with fear that I might give myself away.

'I wish I could help you, but I can't. Anything could happen in this blackout,' I replied, looking as if I meant it.

'What about all these British soldiers who have escaped?' he stormed. 'Somebody must have given them shelter. Confess. They came to your house, didn't they? How many have you assisted?'

'Really', I said wearily, 'your men search my house day and night. Surely, such clever men would find them if they were there. Surely, you don't think my simple little brain is a match for theirs. It's preposterous.'

'All right, mademoiselle, you may go,' he barked.

I returned wearily home.

'It beats me', I said to Uncle, 'why they don't lock me up once and for all.' I felt that a prison bed, provided I had it all to myself, would be a welcome change from this nerve-wracking freedom I enjoyed.

'They won't,' replied Uncle. 'And do you know why?'

'No.'

'Because you have friends among the French officials. They have persuaded the stupid Boches that as long as you are free, you are bound to lead them sooner or later to this organisation which makes them shiver. I know it's unpleasant to be under suspicion, but it's much better than a camp in Germany.'

'I suppose so, Uncle. Has our blonde friend upstairs vanished yet?' I asked, although I was afraid of the answer.

'Unfortunately for them, she has. She was found stabbed with a German knife. Jealousy perhaps.' He raised his eyebrows, nodded his head, and left me.

The Gestapo in the forbidden zone were changed as often as the troops. Apparently, the Nazis were afraid that they would grow sympathetic if allowed to remain too long in one place.

I knew I was being shadowed whenever I went out. They did it so clumsily. All letters which reached me had been opened. My telephone was tapped. I grew very, very careful. Twice in one night, there was a furtive tapping on my door. I didn't open it. The next evening, the telephone rang. 'Hallo,' I said.

I was amazed to hear an English voice reply.

'Mademoiselle Angelo, I'm afraid I cannot give my name on the phone, but good friends told me to get in touch with you. I called at your house late last night but couldn't get an answer from you. So I've risked phoning. Can I see you? It's urgent.'

My first thought was that it was a British soldier who wanted help in getting out of the Zone. But experience had taught me to be cautious.

'I'm afraid I don't quite understand,' I told him.

'No?' he replied. 'Then perhaps this will help.' He started to whistle. Not very well, but finally, I grasped the tune. 'There's a long, long trail a winding.' As I listened to the familiar tune, I felt almost sure that here was a Britisher striking the long, long trail home.

'Yes, I understand,' I whispered. 'But I can't discuss it on the telephone.'

'Sure, I'll come round,' he replied. 'I'll be very careful.'

While waiting for him, I felt very puzzled. I couldn't understand why he hadn't come to me through the usual channels. 'Maybe he's just arrived and hasn't managed to get in touch with the others in the organisation,' I thought. 'It's no use worrying. But to telephone—that's asking for trouble.'

He showed up. A fine, upstanding man, fairly well dressed in a lounge suit. He introduced himself. Apparently, he was a major in a well-known regiment.

'Where do you come from?' I asked, watching him suspiciously.

'I'm an escaped prisoner. I heard of you before the Battle of France. Actually, I was stationed in Lille. I went to friends when I escaped, and they told me you would look after me. Perhaps help me with identity cards, or maybe a German uniform to help me get through.' He referred to several officers with whom I had dined in those days. He described how he'd been taken prisoner and how he'd escaped.

'It's risky for you to stay here,' I warned. 'The Gestapo come often, and you know we would both be shot if we were caught.'

'In that case,' he replied, 'I think I know of another little hideout. It's the papers and the uniform that matter. Get those for me, and I will pay you a thousand francs.'

That did it. I felt my skin go goosy with suspicion and fear. 'An offer of money for my help,' I thought. Would a genuine officer do that? It had never happened before. On the contrary, it had been I who had always given them money! From that moment, I stalled. I arranged to meet him later at a restaurant. He went off very pleased with himself, but something about his thick neck and the way he carried himself made me extremely sceptical and uneasy. Yet his English was perfect. His story foolproof.

I told Jacques all I knew of the major.

'We will soon know if he is genuine. Go to the restaurant. I'll arrange to have him followed. In the meantime, stall,' he told me.

I met the major, but I still couldn't promise him anything. Nor did I involve myself. The following day, Jacques reported that the major had been seen dining and drinking with a number of Gestapo officers and speaking German fluently. He'd also been seen entering the Gestapo headquarters with a blonde girl.

Next morning, he rang me again.

'I'm sorry,' I told him. 'I can't help you. It's against the law.' For a day or two, he persisted in ringing me, but I always had the same answer for him. By this time, Jacques and the other members of the organisation were becoming alarmed. Enquiries showed that at least a dozen so-called escaped prisoners were at work trying to trap suspects. The news that they had caught a Frenchwoman and her son filled us all with terror. Both were shot within twenty-four hours, and posters went up warning the civilians to comply with the law, unless, of course, they wanted to share a similar fate. The Zone was seething with rage.

Members of the underground extracted a terrible vengeance. They lured an 'escaped prisoner' to a villa and threw him headfirst down the coal hole onto the concrete floor five metres below. He died. They sent an anonymous letter to the Gestapo saying that the body of a British officer would be found there. They also added that they had hopes of catching several others like him.

The entire town was put under a curfew for a week, starting at four thirty in the afternoon. I was questioned once more, but the Germans didn't dare tell me that it had been a Gestapo agent who had been murdered. That would have given away the whole wretched business. But the bogus major and his colleagues disappeared overnight. They were too terrified to continue.

I was a regular visitor to the Faculte Catholique. This was an emergency hospital where wounded British got treatment. Although I myself was starving, French people constantly brought me butter and eggs for the wounded. I was never allowed to see the men personally and had to leave the parcels at the gate.

As they recovered, they used to walk and play in the grounds, watched by great crowds of French people.

At first the Germans were sarcastic about the French still wanting to help the British, but as the flow of food continued, the Nazis became furious and finally drove us away. (The British were later shifted to Belgium.) I was accused of stealing and hoarding.

'You are only worried because you thought you had grabbed everything for yourselves,' I snapped.

Within a matter of seconds, I was marched off to the Gestapo headquarters and warned about spreading anti-German propaganda.

'We are arranging for you and all your British friends to be transported to a camp in Germany, or maybe Belgium. Perhaps we shall have a little more peace in this zone, then,' said this particularly revolting Nazi.

'When?' I asked.

'Within a month or two, you should be ready to leave.'

'I don't think I mind very much. I'm sure I'll see far fewer Germans in Germany than I do here,' I said.

'Silence!' he shouted. 'Unless you wish to be locked up for insolence.' I shut my mouth tight, but only for a few minutes.

'Do you know', I said, 'most of the women who were with me in a camp here a few months ago were Frenchwomen. There are no English women here except myself, yet they were there with me.'

'They had British passports!' he yelled, bringing his fist down on his desk. 'All holders of British passports will go. Now leave my office, and I don't want to see you brought here again, otherwise, we have our own methods of taming people.'

I started for home. I felt hopelessly lost. Although I had made light of the prospect of going to Germany, I didn't relish the idea at all. Suddenly, I had an idea. My footsteps quickened till I was home. I shouted for Uncle. As usual, he was drinking soup in the kitchen. I tore downstairs.

'Listen, Uncle, will you marry me?' I said.

The old man nearly fell off his chair. His bowl of soup fell out of his hands and spilt over the floor. Marie-Louise's eyes nearly popped out of her head.

'Have you been out in the sun too long?' she asked me.

'Oh, listen. I have to get a French passport. I've got to marry somebody in a hurry, and Uncle is the safest person I know,' I cried.

'But, my dear', he said, still trembling with the shock of my sudden proposal, 'I'm over seventy. I've managed to steer clear of marriage for half a century, and now, at my age, I get a proposal. Of course, I'll do anything to please you, but this all seems quite ridiculous to me. If you must marry a Frenchman, pick somebody young, handsome. You have lots of friends. Why pick me? I'm no use to you.'

'That's exactly the reason why I do pick you. You're not young, so you are terribly safe.'

'Dear me,' said the old man, shaking his head. 'To think I'm going to be a bridegroom at last, but not in a church. I draw the line at that.'

'Of course, Uncle,' I said happily. 'A civil marriage in the town hall. Thanks a lot, you're an angel.' I kissed him lightly on the top of his head. It was usually the driest spot. His nose had a perpetual drip.

For days I was in a rush, filling in forms, backwards and forwards to the town hall, until I decided that it must be easier to be married in a church. Finally, we got to the last stage. The Chamber of Justice. A hook-nosed individual sat there in judgement.

'Why are you marrying this man, mademoiselle?' he asked. 'A lovely girl like you, young and well-to-do, does not marry an old man unless it's for his money. This old man has none. What's your reason?'

I didn't like the look of the man at all, but I decided to be frank.

'I want to become a French citizen so that the Germans can't put me in a concentration camp,' I replied, looking very innocent but inwardly dreading this man. He rose, glared at me, and broke out into a storm of abuse.

'You British have the most colossal conceit. You are always making use of people. How dare you think that French people have been put on this earth for the benefit of you English? We have to decide whether or not you deserve to become a French citizen, and I can give you my answer now. Whether or not your marriage goes through, that does not interest me, but I shall do all I can to prevent your becoming a French citizen.'

I was filled with rage. I stood up and faced him.

'If you won't help me, then you are helping the Germans. I promise you, that when I get back to England, I shall give them your name as the biggest traitor in this town. They will know how to deal with you. You can bully a girl, but try to bully the British Army when it comes back again. Keep your rotten French papers and help the German Army. I hope they help you when your day of reckoning comes.'

His face was as white as the papers he held in his hands. With one last look of contempt, I turned and walked out with Uncle. Had I been alone, I would have run out of the place slamming all the doors behind me, but instead, I had to walk very slowly.

'I'm sorry, my dear, we did try,' he said, trying to console me, but I would not be comforted.

'Are we supposed to be married or not, Uncle?' I asked. 'We have signed so many books and forms I gave up bothering to read them. I was only interested in getting French papers, which apparently I'll never get.' There was a ring of bitterness in my voice.

'Don't worry, my dear,' replied the old man. 'If the worse comes to the worst, we can always smuggle you out of the Zone.'

'But I don't want to go now,' I said. 'Who'll take over the identity cards department and give these men the necessary money to live until they get clear? What exactly is your part in all this, Uncle? I've often meant to ask you. You don't help with the killings, do you?'

'Of course not, Anne. A man my age! I have neither the strength nor the courage. My job is to empty their pockets. It's surprising what I find in them sometimes. But of course, there has been so much looting both legal and illegal that it doesn't surprise me now, whatever I come across.'

*   *   *

Olga Morrison, whom I'd met in Oran while waiting to get across to Marseille several years before, was quite active among the Resistance at the Cafe de la Paix. She often came to my place. I was pleased to see her. Her two boys had been born in Berlin, and she and they spoke good German. This helped a lot if any patrols came while she was there. She was a white Russian. We were both doing what we could, although she was involved in some very desperate things. We knew a lot about each other. Too much, as it turned out. But it was impossible to foresee what was coming.

There was a Sacred Heart Hospice not far from my hotel which the Germans had turned into a hospital for their wounded. I was able to get bottles of chloroform, which I sent along the line. Chloroform was used sometimes to render Germans unconscious when arms and uniforms were wanted.

Another thing I did was to help in finding airmen who'd been shot down. One night we were out searching for the crew of a Fairy Battle fighter bomber which had been shot down. We'd found two of the crew, and they told us they were sure the other member had got out safely. They'd seen his parachute coming down into some trees. It was coming daylight before we found him. He was unconscious up in the fork of a tree. He had broken a leg. It was too late to try to get him down and shift him. The Germans were already on the move. We cut away his parachute and the ropes which would have drawn attention to him. They put me up in the tree to stay with him until night came again. He needed someone with him in case he regained consciousness and called out or tried to get down. I had some morphine to give him if it was needed. He did rouse and begin to moan, so I put him off to sleep again. It was dark when they came back. They came on a motorbike and sidecar and wearing German uniforms. When I saw them come to my tree and stop, I thought I was finished.

They'd waited on a rise on a quiet road where the German patrols regularly went. Two of them had tied a stout wire to a tree and stayed there. The others had gone, one each way, about a kilometre along the road with their torches. When a motorbike patrol on its own had passed them, they'd signalled to the men on the rise, who had quickly tied the other end of their wire round a tree on the opposite side, stretching it tight across the road. The patrol had been thrown off. They'd been killed, and their clothes, weapons, and motorbike taken. Such things were always wanted. We put the airman into the sidecar, and they took him away.

The Germans were beginning to tire in their efforts to make the people of the Zone collaborate. Some were genuinely puzzled by the hate they caused. Now the French found themselves up against the terrors of forced labour. The barbarous cruelties of hostages punished for the so-called misdeeds of the city; curfews; meatless weeks; the confiscation of warm clothing and boots; the endless variety of mean tricks which the Nazis thought so clever. I used to wonder how they thought up some of their tricks. On one occasion, the entire population was ordered to go to the Mairie to have their ration books checked, in the evening. On their way home, German soldiers stopped every passerby and confiscated his or her torch on the grounds that it was not properly dimmed. It was just another way of getting five thousand torches which the Nazis needed.

Another night, they handed out 400 tickets to music lovers for an opera at the Grande Theatre.

When the members of the audience got home, it was to find German officers in possession of their houses, roaring with laughter and saying, 'We had to get good billets. So we decided to take over those houses that had no tenants. You'll find plenty of deserted buildings on the outskirts of the town.'

In the midst of plenty, the people of the Zone were given rations which barely kept body and soul together, while the Germans gorged.

Here were the standard rations for the month:

1 kg potatoes
25g meat
25g sugar

2 kg bread
½ bottle of olive oil

And that's when we could get them.

Every day, Nazi inspectors supervised the market arrangements.

If the potatoes looked good, they would put up red flags. This meant that no French could be served until the Germans had had their choice.

We often had to wait for hours in bitter cold and then see everything vanish. This led to rioting.

Once, the women of Lille were so enraged they rushed the stalls, seized the potatoes, and literally drove the Nazis out of the square. After that, guards were placed there with loaded rifles.

As for milk, butter, eggs, they weren't to be found on the open market.

Sick children could get an allowance of milk—but only with a certificate signed by a German doctor.

'What? A certificate from your own doctor?' I heard a Nazi tell a distressed mother. 'That's no good. You must bring the child here to be examined. She's too ill to be moved! That's just too bad! You don't think we're going to run after you, do you?'

How the people lived at all was a marvel.

They scrounged, they pilfered, and they sold up their belongings to buy on the black market, which was just another Nazi ramp, whereby officers sold stuff at three and four times its value and pocketed fortunes.

I wasn't so badly off as some, for a wealthy friend used to pass me slabs of chocolate which I could eat or barter for other things. Even so, I grew thin as a lath.

To me, nothing could compare with the merciless cruelty of deliberate starvation. Day after day, I returned home with an empty shopping bag, except perhaps for a loaf of bread which had to last a week. My bag was full of meat coupons, but I never even saw meat at the butcher's. I took home some very odd-looking offal one morning. Marie-Louise tried to cook the thin flat slices, but they curled up and was as tough as rubber.

'What on earth was it, Marie-Louise? I've never seen anything like it before.'

'Neither have I,' said the old woman. 'Ask the butcher.'

I did and felt sick at his reply.

'It was cow's udder. Of course, you couldn't eat it if you cooked it. The only way to get your teeth into it is to eat it raw.'

On one occasion, while out searching for food, I noticed a crowd of people struggling with Germans in front of the town hall.

'What's all the excitement?' I asked, nudging another woman with a shopping basket, who stood by looking on.

'It's those filthy Nazis again,' she replied. 'They have stuck up notices all over the town which reads, ALL PEOPLE OF LILLE WHO ARE UNEMPLOYED CAN REPORT TO THE MAIRIE, FOR THREE DAYS' WORK AT HIGH WAGES. There are so many unemployed here I can't imagine how they live,' she went on. 'Well, they applied for jobs, and now just look at the result. At least four hundred men, women, and girls have been split up and are being shipped to Germany. Those poor girls, they don't even know the fate that awaits them.'

I watched them all as they fought and struggled and screamed, but the Nazis had soon overpowered them. Once the lorries had been filled up and moved off, all was quiet once more.

After that, no one in the Zone dared apply for a job, and terrible stories trickled through of what had happened to many of those who had been taken away.

The most dreadful part of the whole business was that one never knew what to expect next. It didn't seem safe to go anywhere anymore. Like so many wretched people who found consolation in prayer for lost friends or relatives, I wanted to go to church, as I'd always done since I came to France years before. But I didn't dare to go. On the previous Sunday, Nazi troops had been marching up and down singing their Nazi songs outside the church. I'd crept into a doorway to watch them. I'd had a feeling that it wouldn't be safe to enter the church. I waited. Suddenly, I saw five lorries draw up in front of it. Military police had cordoned off the street. Then, as the worshippers had come out from the service, the Nazis seized all the men between the ages of seventeen and twenty-five. I felt as if my heart was breaking as I watched them tearing husbands from wives, sons from mothers, beating up those who resisted, and refusing to let any of the victims go for any of their belongings. Rumour had it that they'd gone to Poland to build underground fortifications, and that several who had tried to escape had been shot out of hand.

On the night of Black Sunday, all Lille was in mourning.

Old Madame Mousson, whose seventeen-year-old son had been taken away, came to my house. 'He has gone off without a pullover, without a heavy overcoat, without his heavy boots,' she moaned.

She never heard from her boy again.

She was not alone. In particular, the Nazi search for Jews never let up. While I was waiting at the station to meet Paul one cold and miserable day, I was shattered to see a number of Jews—young, old, sick—stripped of all their dignity, being packed into cattle trucks, trucks with planks of wood on the windows so that little air could enter or leave. I counted seventy to a truck, no toilets, no doctors, no medications, no room to stand, and no room to breathe. It would even offend death. It was hard to imagine, while looking on in horror, that there was once humanity and dignity among the Germans. But I tried to rationalise these were not the peacetime Germans I'd known; these were the Nazi Youth, the fanatics, the horrendous SS.

With a power that emanated not from the body but from the spirit, one truckload of prisoners charged toward the door as the SS were bolting it, and the struggle for survival began. How many would come out of that hellhole alive at the other end? I was quite sure that those who survived could never again walk, talk, or feel like human beings. The German's bible was death, humiliation, and dehumanisation. There did not seem to be anything anyone could do about it. Man's inhumanity to man exploded at that railway station. Most of us were born to live, and to die—but to live first! The train, with its cargo of misery, moved off quickly. The Germans always seemed to be in a hurry. Death was always urgent with them. Jewish death. In their eyes, there was no place on this earth for Jews.

*   *   *

ANNE ANGELO

CHAPTER 21

The Luftwaffe Is Mauled

I N SUCH CONDITIONS, hatred of the Germans was bound to grow. After the first shock of defeat, the Zone led the way in bitter resistance.

The 'V' campaign began. The first 'V' was chalked up in full view of General Keitel's window, and the idea caught on like anything, with the Germans making frantic efforts to arrest the culprits.

Later on, photos of Hitler had to be withdrawn from the whole Zone because they were altered so comically.

Students led the Resistance campaigns, and not a day passed without them being up to something new.

At the cinema, we booed newsreels showing pictures of German triumphs. Arrests couldn't stop this practice.

Then German HQ solemnly issued an order that in future, the lights must go up during the showing of newsreels and anyone caught demonstrating would be court-martialled.

'Everyone to bring a newspaper to the cinema,' came the underground order.

I went that night. It was a packed house. German soldiers standing all along the sides. The newsreel came on, and the lights went up.

Germans watched tensely to catch any demonstrators. Instead, a newspaper went up before each face—a forest of paper shutting out any view of German victories on the screen.

Some of the Nazis lost their heads and dashed among the people, striking the papers away.

The carrying of newspapers into cinemas was next forbidden. People sat bolt upright, eyes closed!

So it went on.

But all this was trifling compared to the success of the De Gaullist movement.

Except for a few factory owners who did not mind who gave them contracts, and dance hostesses who would take money from anyone, the Zone was 100 percent for de Gaulle.

They spat on Darlan and Laval, they respected Petain for trying his best in an impossible position, but de Gaulle was their hero.

In spite of the most severe punishments, the men refused to give up wearing rings with the Croix de Lorraine sign. Women still wore the brooches.

And these de Gaullists did not stop at wearing rings.

Ceaselessly they collected arms and uniforms, went out at night to burn German aircraft, set fires going when RAF raids were on.

Every young man had one ambition—to break through the ring of steel round the Zone and get to England and de Gaulle.

Scores of them had been shot down trying to cross the heavily guarded Somme.

It was no secret that the best chance lay in going through in the uniform of an officer or an SS man. The German guards feared these two types and were slow to challenge in case they got something more than a ticking off.

It was because uniforms were so precious that many naked Germans were fished out of canals and rivers. But this led to reprisals on hostages, so something better had to be devised.

Germans simply disappeared. A number of skeletons were found in a deserted cellar. Germans for sure. But it couldn't be proved. There was nothing left to identify them.

Sabotage grew in the Zone.

At first, everything was so closely guarded by the hundreds of thousands of German troops that the people got very few opportunities.

They cut military telephones every night. Lorries were often put out of action.

But little could be done along the coastal area from which all civilians were cleared right out.

Sabotage was more successful in the mining area of Lens and Seclin.

There the Nazis had to contend with flooding, small explosions, thefts of explosives which were stored away for the day of vengeance.

After the fall of France, Hitler offered the miners splendid wages to go to the Ruhr and promised extra allowances and rations for their families at home. A few hundred went. It was either that or starvation.

The first month, they drew half the wages promised. They kicked up a row. Wages were then reduced to pocket money. There was more trouble. The ringleaders were sent to prison, and it was slavery for the rest.

Meanwhile, their families and their old workmates at home were callously ignored by the Germans. This led to strikes in the Forbidden Zone and more shootings.

In the big mills around Lille, the Nazis were more cunning. They gave their word of honour that orders were only for Vichy France.

One day, however, they grew impatient at the slow delivery. Troops, rushed to the factory to collect all they could, let the cat out of the bag that everything was going to Germany.

That night, the mill caught fire.

A parachute factory was set, going after much trouble. Workers were apparently indifferent. But soon military courts were trying people for sabotage, furiously admitting that many of the parachutes had failed to open.

Taken by and large, however, sabotage had never really got under way on a big scale.

This was solely due to the fact that the Zone was so heavily garrisoned with thousands of picked troops.

I wondered what was causing this sudden wave of brutality. I knew from experience that as long as things were going right for them, the Germans could behave fairly decently. Could this sudden change in their behaviour mean that all was not well with the master race?

I wasn't kept long in doubt. The battered town was swarming with invaders. Infantry men, pioneers, engineers, labour units, youth battalions, and the rest. Up until now, all had been drunk with victory. The lords of creation were getting ready to wipe out Britain, the last little obstacle in their path. In dreadful contrast to the swaggering Nazis were the wretched survivors of the civil population. They were still stunned by defeat and continually deafened by the loudspeakers telling them how the British had betrayed them. It had broken my heart to see the poor French being trampled in the mud by those brutes who gorged and goose-stepped and sang the song, 'We're marching to England'.

Then suddenly the scene changed. The Nazis had no time to spare for amusement. There was no more trickery for the time being. They no longer tried to be friends with the civilians. Anybody who got in their way was ruthlessly dealt with.

The town crackled with invasion preparations. Marching columns, tanks, lorries piled high with timber, all private cars requisitioned, bicycles heaped up on the barges which were collected in the canals for removal to the coast, troops exercising, and aircraft assembled on every possible field for kilometres around.

The young fanatical Nazis were exultant. 'The hour is about to strike,' they boasted. German pilots and air crews, several hundred of them, were billeted in nearly all the houses around my hotel. Word swept through the town that Goering was going to give them a pep talk. He came. But the civil population did not see him. Whole streets were cordoned off. Closed cars arrived. Pilots and staff officers assembled at the Carlton Hotel.

It was an open secret that the battle of the skies would begin the next day. That night the pilots got blind drunk on champagne.

The next day, from my balcony, I could see them being whirled off in cars to the emergency airfields on the outskirts of the town. Several hundred planes set off in the direction of England.

Meanwhile, German soldiers gathered in every cafe listening to a kind of running commentary on the battles in the air. They drank toasts to their pilots as the radio announcements came through that scores of British machines had been brought down for almost no cost to the Germans. The cafes rang with the exultant shouts of 'Heil Hitler' and 'Seig Heil'.

So it went on for a day or two until the French, who might almost have been sleepwalking, suddenly woke up, and the whisper went the rounds. 'Count the machines going out. Count them coming home.'

They did. And they realised that the Luftwaffe must be getting a terrible mauling. One hundred and ten planes left Lille one morning, eighty-eight returned. The following day, seventy came back out of ninety-five.

That night the word was spread from house to house, from cafe to cafe. 'Be at the marketplace at eight o'clock tomorrow morning. The Boches are going to get a surprise.'

The next morning, the marketplace was packed as once again, the Luftwaffe circled overhead before heading for England.

Very carefully, the great crowd counted the German machines. One hundred and twenty. And a thousand people chalked this number on the pavements. Then they waited patiently for the ragged survivors to return. Time dragged on, but eventually, the first German planes came back. Then more and more. But only ninety-two returned in all. For each 120 was substituted 92. Then the crowd melted away.

The Nazis were white with rage, as they saw the pavement everywhere covered with the telltale figures. At teatime, the Luftwaffe set out once more. The people tried the dodge again, but troops drove them away, threatening to shoot.

Just the same, the correct figures were chalked on walls, hoardings, and even on the backs of German sentries. One could almost see the cocky Nazis wilting as the truth at last filtered into their stupid brains. The RAF had the measure of the Luftwaffe.

Next day, again, one hundred and twenty planes were counted going out. A squadron of twenty came roaring back, then another, and another until exactly one hundred and twenty had returned. French faces fell, and it was the Nazis' turn to triumph.

It wasn't until the following day that the French realised that they had been tricked as the Luftwaffe repeated its performance and gave the show away. As the first squadron of twenty came roaring over the rooftops, it flew rather low. Just behind the leader on its right was a plane belching black smoke from the exhaust. The squadron disappeared. Then a few minutes later, another squadron came into view, and again the machine behind the leader was belching black smoke. That same machine was there the third time the planes passed over, and the fourth and fifth.

But long before that, the people were laughing at the discomfiture of the Germans. For it was the same squadron going round and round the town.

It was not only to hoodwink the French people that this bluff was staged. The Nazis realised that their great army in the forbidden zone, on tiptoe for the invasion, was being seriously demoralised by the sight of the maimed Luftwaffe limping home each day.

That demoralisation had to be stopped. They went to extraordinary lengths to fool their own men.

But the damage had been done. Spirits began to sink. Word filtered through of the RAF bombing the Rhineland. The German soldiers realised that they were up against real resistance. Then when the Battle of Britain was nearly at an end, the Nazi pilots began to lose their nerve.

I had my ear to the window nearest to the house next door. It was a requisitioned house overflowing with German pilots and aircrews.

Whistles blew. Armed men dashed up in lorries and rushed the house. One pilot, struggling desperately, was dragged out, his head streaming blood. The rest, sixty or seventy of them, went quietly. The arrested airmen were chained in pairs by the wrists, bundled into lorries covered with tarpaulins, and driven off to the Rouchin barracks. They never returned. They had mutinied. Wild rumours swept the town. I spoke to a corporal in the house next door. He was extremely informative.

'Those fellows', he said, 'bore the brunt of it, in Norway, Holland, Belgium, and France. Now they have to face up to the RAF. They are not cowards, but to keep it up against the Spitfires is more than flesh and blood can stand. They only asked for three days' rest.'

Tension grew and grew. A student who laid a wreath on a monument erected to the memory of the citizens who were shot by the Boches in the 1914–1918 war was shot dead on the spot. Guards drove back the people who tried to lift him. The Nazis then lost their heads completely. In front of the crowd which had gathered, they blew the sacred monument to pieces. From then on, the tension was greater than ever. Doubts and fears made the Germans so jumpy that it was fatal to open one's mouth in their hearing.

I was as jumpy as they were, but for a different reason. I was so miserably hungry I couldn't control my temper.

'Isn't there anything at all in the house to eat, Marie-Louise? Can't you even make some soup?' I asked one morning. I had breakfasted on one cup of ersatz coffee, which had no connection whatsoever with coffee beans. Actually, the Germans made it from acorns.

'Unless you can manage to find something, mademoiselle, there is not even a crust of bread,' she replied. I went off with an aching heart and an empty stomach to the market. The butcher had rabbits. I stood patiently in the queue, and my eyes lit up at the sight of a meal at last. An hour later, I walked off with my precious parcel, licking my lips with anticipation. A German noticed my apparent joy and viciously knocked the parcel out of my hands. The contents rolled in the gutter, where he promptly started to tramp it into the mud. My rage knew no bounds. I threw myself at him, shrieking, 'Schweinhund, schweinhund'. That infuriated him. He blew his whistle, and in a matter of seconds, I was being pushed and shoved into a lorry and was once more driven to the prison of Loos.

* * *

CHAPTER 22

The Kindly Wardress

T HE SAME WARDRESS was there, looking as plump as ever. 'Aren't you becoming quite a regular visitor, Mademoiselle Angelo?' she said, a twinkle in her eye. Apparently, the more one went to prison, the more one was respected and admired by the French population. I was fast becoming a heroine.

'As a regular visitor to your famous establishment, I expect a great deal of consideration. To begin with', I said lightly, 'I want a meal fit for a king, sheets on my bed, and some juicy novels to read to take my mind off the Nazis.'

'It will be an honour to provide you with all you mention,' the wardress replied, bowing low. I thought she was being funny as she let herself out, locking the door behind her.

About an hour later, the jingling of keys made me look up from my bed, where I'd flung myself down. I knew it wasn't a German, I was so accustomed to the noise of their heavy boots on the stone corridors. The door opened, and the wardress appeared with a tray covered by a serviette. Under her arm, she had two sheets. I stared in amazement. Surely, I was dreaming. Surely, that tray was a mirage. I had starved so long that my brain was going soft. But no, the wardress lifted the serviette off the tray. In the middle of the tray was a plate piled high with pork chops, peas, roast potatoes, and sausages, beautiful golden-brown sausages. On an equally huge plate sat an apple pie big enough for six ordinary people. There were six large slices of German bread, and, joys of joys, lying down on the tray, half a bottle of white wine. I seized her arm and shook her.

'Is that food real? How did you get it? Is it all for me?'

'Calm yourself. It's quite real. You may eat it all if you can. Actually, a friend of mine works in the staff officers' quarters. They won't miss it, but if you do hear them come along, hide it all under your mattress. I don't think they'll come. They have their hands full.'

I grabbed the chops and proceeded to tear them with my teeth. I felt like a lion at the zoo, but I didn't care. They tasted so good. As the juice trickled down my chin, I pushed it back into my mouth with my grubby fingers. What did it matter? This was real food at last. If it killed me, I would eat the lot.

The wardress was talking to me, but I listened without turning round. I could not waste a minute in conversation, even with my benefactress. I had a horrible suspicion that unless I hurried and ate the lot, it might be taken away from me.

'I'll hide these sheets under your blankets. You can put them on your bed when you're ready. I daren't stay to do it. I might be missed.'

I mumbled something which was meant to be thanks, and the wardress left. Except for the bread which I intended to keep for a lean day, I ate up the entire meal and then lay down on my bed to digest it.

I felt dreadfully uncomfortable. I knew the only way to get peace from my stomach, which kept turning over and over, was to be sick. But the thought of wasting such a precious meal was sacrilege. How I wished I were a cow and able to keep chewing it over and over again.

The wardress came back for the empties, bringing a pile of books with her. She stared in astonishment at the empty plates. Not even a crumb remained. Then she turned her eyes to my green face. 'I expected this,' she said, holding out a packet of bicarbonate of soda. I took it and gave her a look full of gratitude. Once I was alone again, I staggered to the washbasin, and filling up the mug which was chained to the wall, emptied the entire contents of the packet into it. After that, I felt at peace with the world.

For three days, I lived like a king, I slept like a log. Home was never like this. Nobody ever came near me except the wardress, and there were no search parties ringing the doorbell two or three times a night as in my own home. This really was heavenly.

I nearly broke my heart when, at the end of third day, I was brought before that same hulking officer.

'Mademoiselle Angelo', he barked, 'I am warning you. Unless you can keep a civil tongue in your head, you will come back here to prison. I think eventually, we could teach you to treat our soldiers with respect. We will not tolerate insolence. Now you may go home, but remember what I have said.'

I went home very reluctantly. During the next month, I managed to pay three short visits to my newly found paradise. It was so much more than a home away from home.

During my spells of liberty, I was preparing to make a hasty exit should the Germans carry out their threat to send me to Germany. It could happen anytime now. I had obtained an identity card in the name of Lucienne Suin. The original holder of this card had been born in Lille about the same time as I'd been born in Scotland. She had dark-brown eyes as I had, and we were the same height. Only, the original Lucienne had red hair. I had arranged for my hairdresser to make me a wig. I also arranged with a Frenchwoman to say that Lucienne had been working for her for years and that she herself had sent her to the hotel in Lille for the duration, as she was going to Paris in the near future and didn't need her. Providing I wasn't caught in the streets, Marie-Louise, Jacques, and Uncle knew what to do to give me warning that the Germans had come to collect me. Then, of course, I would use the hiding place behind the drawers until it was safe to come out as Lucienne Suin.

I was rather intrigued by the whole affair, except for one thing. I could no longer pay a visit to my beloved prison of Loos. I considered that in itself sufficient punishment for anyone. The Nazis didn't need to pile it on by sending me to Germany.

I spent the time looking out of my window at the grim-faced troops marching in endless columns towards the coast. To feed these troops, the Germans had looted all the farms for kilometres around, carrying away pigs in closed vans. But they couldn't stop the pigs squealing. Stories reached the people of colossal invasion exercises on the beaches. I could hear the RAF pounding away day and night in a nonstop attack on the ports. The crisis was near.

But what happened was something very different from what the people had expected, or what the Nazis had planned. I was startled by the sound of whistle alarms. German troops hurried to their quarters. Motorcyclists dashed along the roads, clearing the way. Staff officers dashed around in huge cars looking very grim.

Soon detachments of soldiers marched off through the streets requisitioning all big houses and turning the occupants out without ceremony. Other soldiers rushed about collecting bedding which they took to the requisitioned houses. When my doorbell rang, I and my companions stayed put. No one attempted to open it. The Germans rang and rang and hammered on the door, kicked it, and shouted and swore; but the door remained shut. Short of driving a tank through it, they could do nothing about it; and fortunately for the occupants, the Germans were in a tearing hurry. They soon moved off to other houses.

Then came a procession of vans from the coast, all closed. I could hear a dreadful groaning.

'Can you hear the pigs squealing?' asked Marie-Louise, who had come up for her view of the procession. The casualties were taken into the makeshift hospitals, hundreds and hundreds of them. And rumour went round that they were not merely wounded but horribly burned. To curb the French people's curiosity, the Germans ordered all civilians to stay indoors. But even then, they couldn't prevent them from learning the truth.

All night, casualties flowed into the town. There must have been thousands. The town was full of stories. German soldiers, if there were no Gestapo men near, discussed the matter all day long. It seemed clear that something had gone badly wrong with the big invasion exercises. The RAF had been on a bombing raid. A German tanker had caught fire and exploded. The troops had jumped into the water to escape the shower of burning spirit. But even then, there was no escape, for patches of oil on the water had still burned, and those who could not swim were trapped. 'It was as if the sea were alight', declared the German soldiers again and again. And they were scared—dead scared. If this could happen on an exercise, what would be their fate when they put to sea with the RAF overhead, to say nothing of the British fleet all round them? Invasion would be hell, and they knew it.

During the next few days, the French people noticed that the morale of the German troops had gone down to zero. All their plans had been laid. The tanks and guns and the barges were ready, but the men had no heart for the job. A wave of suicides followed. There was more mutiny. One unit in Lille issued with oilskins and ordered to the coast, locked themselves in the Ronchin barracks and refused to parade. The German Army had been disillusioned. It was afraid. How all this revived the spirits of the conquered people. But the Nazis were not resigned to defeat. Not a bit of it. They still maintained that they could 'eat' the British Army, if only they could get to grips with it. They had terrific faith in the Panzers. But they just could not see how they could cross that strip of water without the majority of them being massacred. The young fanatics still declared that Hitler would find a way to overcome their obstacle, but the older soldiers only shook their heads.

Much as I hated the Germans, the screaming and groaning of the wounded in the houses across the street was like a knife turning in my heart. Killing men outright was one thing, but to leave them writhing in agony was the height of brutality. I spoke to the talkative corporal next door.

'Why are they screaming so much? Can't the doctors do anything to help them?' I asked him.

'They are not allowed to,' he replied, his face twisting with pain as he listened. 'Hitler's orders are that no drugs or dressings are to be wasted on the too badly wounded. Only those who can make a quick recovery must be treated. He will not tolerate any long-term cures. Those who are too badly wounded must be shot.'

I stared at him in horror. 'It can't be,' I cried. 'Surely, not even Hitler would do such a thing to his own men? They are his fellow countrymen. What kind of a monster is he?'

'Mademoiselle, for your own sake, don't let the Gestapo hear you talk of our beloved Fuhrer in such derogatory terms. We would never dare to say what we think. We keep up the stupid pretence of hero

ANNE ANGELO

worship. Heil Hitler.' He raised his arm. I felt sorry for him and the thousands of others who had to obey blindly or perish.

'Tell me something,' I asked him, 'why are all the dead carried out in pairs tied back to back?'

He looked at me as if trying to decide whether or not it would be safe to tell me. Apparently, he decided that it was, for he said, 'It's that Gestapo swine at the Kommandatur. He gets an allowance for coffins to bury the men. He puts two bodies in each. He must be making a nice fat income for his old age.'

'Good God,' I exclaimed, horrified. 'Do they miss any opportunity for being mean and brutal?'

I woke next morning with a feeling of impending doom. I couldn't explain it, but for no reason, I was trembling with fear. Marie-Louise came up to my room, her eyes red as if she'd been crying.

'What's wrong, Marie-Louise?' I asked, almost afraid of the answer I would receive.

'The lorry driver was shot yesterday.'

'Oh no, Marie-Louise. We can't do without him, especially at this time. We're bound to be flooded out with RAF men. What can we do?'

'That's not the most serious part of it. He was betrayed by one of our own countrymen. I suppose this traitor was tempted by the huge rewards offered for the capture of any member of the Resistance,' she said slowly. 'But what we are all afraid of is, did they make him talk? Did they torture him sufficiently to make him give us all away?'

I just stared at the old woman. My heart was pounding, and I could not find a word to say. I hoped none of the pilots would be sent to me just in case the net was being dragged tighter. But what was the use of hoping?

That night, five RAF men arrived. The following night, three more arrived. As long as they remained in the hiding place, they were quite safe. Nobody knew of it except Jacques, Marie-Louise, and Uncle. I realised why it was safer not to know the other members of the organisation and how they worked.

How I pitied those men lying in hiding with only wine to drink. If only I could get them some food. Anything, but how. It was really too risky to go back to prison, but I had no alternative. I'd made myself a petticoat, the hem of which I turned up and buttoned round my waist. Each time I went to prison, I had saved all I couldn't eat and filled up this pocket with my spoils. Nobody noticed how much my figure had changed for the worse by the time I walked out, but it kept the household alive for a week.

I decided to go in again, risk or no risk. I went to a cafe for a drink and stretched my legs out in front of me, just as a Nazi officer passed by. He tripped and went sprawling. I laughed. He whistled. The usual lorry, always handy, drove up. Once more, I was on my way to Loos.

I felt quite happy about it, until I got there. My old enemy, the hulking officer, was there. He sat bolt upright when he saw who was being brought in.

'Mademoiselle,' he yelled. 'I warned you I would teach you a lesson if you persisted in your attitude towards the German Army. You will be locked in the cachot for three days.' I was terrified. I had not bargained for this.

'You can't do that. I only laughed. Haven't you a sense of humour either?'

He leaned back in his chair. 'I am going to laugh each time I think of you in that place,' he replied brutally.

'Why can't I go into a cell as usual?' I asked.

'For the simple reason that there is no wardress to look after you. I have no doubt, like many others who come here, you were on exceedingly good terms with your wardress. Maybe you would like to know that she was shot yesterday for breaking prison rules. I thought that would give you something to think about while you rot in your cage.' He almost spat the last few words at me. 'Take her away!' he yelled. Screaming and fighting, I was locked up in the dreaded cachot.

All night I squatted in that cold, damp, horrible hole that stank like the vilest sewer. The next morning, I was half dragged and half carried out to the courtyard. I was incapable of standing, the light burnt my eyes, and I could not repress vomiting—all the worse on an empty stomach.

ANNE ANGELO

There were about a hundred others in the courtyard by the time the Nazis had finished. Two Gestapo officers stood on a small dais.

Their English was perfect. We had to form two lines when our names were called. This exercise went on for quite a while, yet we had no idea what it all meant. With drizzling rain falling from the leaden skies, we were feeling very miserable and uncertain.

The Gestapo men yelled at the SS soldiers to take the line I was in back to an adjacent hall and to leave the Jews outside. The reason for two lines became clear, they had separated the Jews from all the others, and how I pitied them. I recognised quite a few of them. I'd shopped at their stores for years, but I never knew they were Jews. Once more, the usual question: how did the Germans know?

Within minutes, the air outside was rent with piercing screams from some of those unfortunate people. We couldn't see what was happening, but I had a very good idea, as one of our proteges, a young Jewish man whom we kept hidden with friends, had told us of the horrific brutalities meted out to the Jews. He had managed to escape during an air raid while in transit from one camp to another. Between the brutal treatment in the camps and the hellish conditions on the trains, many had lost the last surviving members of their families and were robbed of all shreds of individuality. When I last saw him, he was a lonely, emaciated shadow of himself, functioning in limbo. The horrors he spoke of in those camps made the inmates question their belief in God. From the screaming which we heard coming from the courtyard, we were sure that there would not be many left to transport to a camp. One of the men in our line clambered onto the shoulders of another and was able to see through a small high window. What he saw and described was sickening. One by one, the SS men would lift a finger and point at one of the prisoners standing pale faced and terrified. The poor unfortunate selected was then attacked with rubber truncheons and iron prods. The guards kicked, beat, and tortured each innocent victim; and when the tortured body no longer moved, they used their revolvers. The brutal random selection went on for hours, and when the Nazi angels of death departed, they left behind dozens of twisted and tortured bodies of men and women and youths. Babies were crying everywhere. Even the depraved Hun had not the courage to massacre little children, not yet anyway. Certainly, it would come later. After all, as we had discovered, their orders were complete extermination of the Jews.

We were taken outside to see what could happen to us should we even try to disobey their slightest command. We stared in horror; most women fainted. I felt as if the earth beneath my feet was trembling. A strange silence descended on the crowd, broken only by the children crying, but who among us would have the courage to pick up any of those human morsels, motherless and alone? None of us. As we were herded off, we saw a truck arrive, and within minutes, all the surviving children were bundled into it, some screaming; others, who probably did not understand what was going on, were crying for their mothers or just from hunger. Two enormous women in German uniform got in with them. We knew they were going somewhere and could only guess at their fate.

*   *   *

ANNE ANGELO

Looking along rue Solferino – The Halles Centrales (Markets),
with the Sacre Coeur Church on the corner of rue Nationale.

CHAPTER 23

Christmas 1940

BY THE TIME I was let out, I was incapable of walking, sitting, or even thinking. I was sore all over. I was stunned. How I managed to get home was something I never knew. Marie-Louise had managed to make some soup. I didn't know where she had got the vegetables, but I had a shrewd suspicion that the old woman had started going round the German dustbins. The soup was quite good and very hot. They got me to bed, and I slept for twenty-four hours. By that time, I was my old self once more. Youth had the most amazing powers of recovery. I turned my attention to the matter at hand.

Jacques was frantically searching for a means of breaking through the ring of steel round the zone.

Scores of people had been shot trying to cross the heavily guarded Somme. Somehow or other, Jacques had managed to slip through the cordon at the gates of the town. This hadn't been too difficult. His papers stated that he worked outside the town and lived inside it. He went to a farm, borrowed a bicycle, and reached the Somme. He started to explore the surrounding countryside for future reference. An old woman at a farm told him after a long chat that if he wanted to cross the Somme, he should talk to her son, who was at a café in a nearby village. Jacques went. In the café, a funeral party had assembled. He had never in his life seen such an odd assortment of mourners. They were mostly young men, looking anything but unhappy.

Up came the hearse. The mourners piled into four coaches, about seven in each one. By this time, they were all looking very solemn. Down the road went the procession. The cemetery lay beyond the line guarded by a company of SS men who stopped the coaches, examined passes, waved the mourners on.

After the burial service, the mourners got into the coaches and drove out by another gate to come back by a bridge three hundred metres away. For a matter of seconds, the coaches passed behind a belt of trees, and in that time, out leapt a dozen of the youngest men who scattered unseen. The coaches on the return journey over the line were challenged by a different party of guards. As there were still four men in each, they suspected nothing. The timing of the funeral always coincided with the changing of the SS guards.

What celebrations there were on the return to the café.

Jacques had discussed the plan with the others on his return. It was a brilliant idea, except that it was much more difficult than their other methods had been.

It took Jacques a week to contact another lorry driver, but the driver refused to take two British pilots across the Somme. He would take them out of the forbidden zone, but not across the Somme. That suited Jacques quite well, and in no time the men were being 'briefed' as mourners. Two days later, they were in Paris, where the underground movement was working much more smoothly than in the forbidden zone. They were fortunate enough to be outside the Nazi headquarters and free to plan and carry out escapes.

Some weeks later, we heard that the trick of 'mourners' had been seen through, and several of the organisers had been shot.

The Nazis were at their wits' end to know how so many British pilots were vanishing into thin air. They actually saw them come down but caught very few of them. Once more, the old cry went up. 'We must exterminate the British agents.'

Just before Christmas 1940, when Gestapo agents had me under the closest watch, a woman carrying a Peke came to my house in the rue Nationale.

'Are you the English girl known as the Angel?' she asked. She spoke French with a definite British accent.

I had grown suspicious of strangers. Was this a trap? Was she just another fake agent?

'Who are you?'

'Oh, I'm Mrs Wodehouse, from Le Touquet. My husband is the author. Perhaps you'll be able to help me.'

She looked ill and pathetic. I invited her in. I asked her who had sent her.

'I'm living at Hesdin', she explained, 'and my neuritis has got very bad. I came to Lille to see the doctor. I met Suzanne, the hairdresser, this morning, and she gave me your address.'

My private hotel was full of refugees, but I was sorry for Mrs Wodehouse, and I willingly agreed to let her have a room.

She went back to Hesdin that night, but three days later, she returned with two cases of personal belongings and 'Wonder', the Peke.

There was trouble at once.

Round came the Germans, demanding to know why she had removed from Hesdin without permission, accusing her of coming to Lille to spy on army secrets.

They threatened her with imprisonment, but she held her ground.

One morning, at 8 am, Gestapo officers came thundering at the door.

'Where is Mrs Wodehouse's room?'

I took them to the first floor, saying I would waken her, but one of them flung me brutally aside.

'We can announce ourselves,' he said.

'You won't. If you do, I'll report you for improper behaviour towards respectable women,' I flashed indignantly.

I happened to have been tipped off that an order had been issued calling on these agents to stop bursting into bedrooms in the middle of the night unless they had very good reason to believe that fugitives were hidden there.

Sure enough, my remark brought them to a halt. They cursed and swore. But they stood by till I roused Mrs Wodehouse.

From what they said while they were waiting, I gathered they had some fantastic idea that Mrs Wodehouse went out at night contacting British sympathisers and saboteurs!

When she came out in her dressing gown, they cross-examined her

ANNE ANGELO

about her activities and, finally, insisted that she put on all her clothes and accompany them to Gestapo headquarters.

There, for fully twenty-four hours, they put her through a form of third degree, denying her even food, until she was exhausted.

They suspected her because she had been seen to give money to beggars!

Gifts to beggars were things the Nazis couldn't understand.

'It's money for military secrets. They are not beggars, they are British agents.' That was the kind of ridiculous accusation they made.

Finally, she was allowed to come back to my house, but she was warned that she had her liberty only as a hostage. If there was any trouble, she would be clapped into prison or into a camp.

Indignantly, she wrote to friends in unoccupied France and to her daughter in Kent—only to have the letters returned by the German censor with a further warning about her behaviour.

No one who lived in Lille will forget Christmas Day 1940.

It was announced that Hitler was coming to the city to visit his victorious troops, and that there were to be great celebrations.

Swiftly an order followed, fining Lille a million francs because of some sabotage or other, and ordering a meatless Christmas week, with curfew at 4.30 p.m.

The thermometer was down to sixteen degrees of frost. We had no heating. It was awful.

But did the Germans worry?

Not likely.

They went ahead with preparations for their Fuhrer on a magnificent scale.

In the street around the German headquarters were placed huge Christmas trees, twenty feet high, festooned with coloured lights.

Shops were plundered to provide presents to tie on the trees.

Nazi troopers went round the houses and took away valuable pictures for the same purpose.

Even dolls and toys were stolen, to be sent to the little Fritzes and Berthas in Germany.

As a special privilege, it was announced that the French would be allowed to file past the brilliant scene on Christmas Eve.

But there was nothing for the children of Lille—no food, no toys, no celebrations.

On Christmas Day, the Huns sat down to the biggest gorge they'd ever had.

One big fellow came along the street munching on a bunch of big sausages, and a French child looked at the food with pleading eyes.

The Boche must have been touched. He was about to hand over a sausage when a plainclothes Gestapo man ran across the road.

'None of that,' he ordered sharply. 'This is a meatless week for the French. Do you want to disobey orders?'

Afterwards, the Nazis gleefully told us how the whole Zone had been fined and put on a meatless week on one excuse or another so that the conquerors needn't go short.

If Hitler reached Lille, none of us knew about it. I never met anyone who saw him anywhere in the Zone that week.

*   *   *

ANNE ANGELO

CHAPTER 24

The Net Tightens

THE WORD WAS out that the Germans were about to take action on their threats to send all persons holding British passports to concentration camps in Germany.

I was all ready to vanish into thin air. I never left the house. Each time the doorbell rang, I got into the hiding place. I'd had no idea that the men who'd been hiding there could get such a perfect view of any Germans who entered the house. As I looked through the air vents, I could see four men blustering in the hall. Marie-Louise kept telling them that mademoiselle had gone to Paris.

'Tell us the truth, or it will be worse for you.' The poor old woman was visibly trembling with fear. I could see her so plainly standing in the hall plucking at her apron with shaking fingers.

'But it is the truth,' she replied. 'She went to Paris with a German officer. He had a few days' leave. They are great friends.' I nearly burst out laughing at Marie-Louise's expression, which was meant to imply, 'They are so much in love'. Unfortunately, I couldn't see whether she was blushing.

'We will search the house,' he replied, no longer shouting.

It was quite half an hour before I again saw them standing in the hall. They were actually saluting Marie-Louise. The old woman was filled with embarrassment.

Once they had gone, I crept down to the kitchen.

'Did they believe you?' I asked breathlessly.

'I think they did, but they will return next week. They said they were taking a very serious view of your breaking your parole and leaving the zone. They also said that all British subjects are leaving for Germany in the morning at six.'

I heaved a sigh of relief. 'Thank God I've missed that at least.'

Jacques and Uncle came in as usual by the back door on the side of the garden.

'Jacques', I said, 'don't bring any more pilots here for the time being. It's my turn to use the hiding place.'

'So it has come at last,' he said. 'Still, there's room for all of you in there.'

'Oh, Jacques', I protested, 'think of me a little sometimes. You can't possibly expect me to lie on my back for days surrounded by pilots also lying on their backs. That's asking for trouble. We have plenty already without asking for more.'

'Well', he replied, shrugging his shoulders, 'it may not happen.'

The following week, the Germans were back again. Once more, the house was searched. 'She should have returned by this time,' said one of the Nazis.

Marie-Louise took a letter out of her pocket and handed it to him. He read it aloud so that his fellow officers would hear.

Dear Marie-Louise,

I have had such a wonderful time with Fritz. Unfortunately, he had to return to the Forbidden Zone as his leave was up, but he introduced me to a friend of his, a Gestapo chief here in Paris. I have promised to stay with him as long as he wishes me to, and he has arranged to make everything all right for me with the authorities in the zone. I feel proud to be his friend, he has such powers in Paris.

I shall let you know if I ever intend to return to the zone. In the meantime, this is heaven.

Kindest regards,
Anne Angelo

The four officers looked at each other, blank amazement on their faces. 'I think we are wasting our time,' said one of them. He handed the letter back to Marie-Louise, and, clicking their heels and saluting her, they left. I laughed till my sides ached.

A few weeks later, I took my place among the people as Lucienne Suin. I tried my disguise on the shrewdest person in the house— Jacques. He was fooled completely. I took a look at myself in the mirror and was almost terrified of my own reflection. I had a bronzy haircut with a fringe and as straight as a poker. I'd taken out my five false teeth, which made me look like a perfect idiot each time I smiled. I wore glasses, which gave me an everlasting tic, and my badly cut skirt was nearly down to my ankles. In my own words, I looked like a 'ruddy awful mess'.

'Not even my own mother would know me,' I cried excitedly.

'Your own mother would disown you if she saw you now,' said Marie-Louise.

'Before I forget, in case I have to get away in a hurry. If ever you get the chance to commit a really good murder, would you do me a favour and polish off that swine up at the prison. Apart from the fact that he shut me up in the cachot, I would like to make him pay for shooting that lovely wardress. Anytime you need anything belonging to a German, pick him. It shouldn't be difficult. His car could have an accident, or you can try to lure him here on some pretext or other. Do what you like, but get him before the war is over.'

'Sure', said Jacques, 'it will be a pleasure.'

During the next few weeks, I actually began to feel like Lucienne Suin. It was marvellous to be able to talk to the officers, and even help them search for me. They were very persistent in spite of several other letters from Paris in which I wrote of the wonderful time I was having with my friend Hans. Each time they left after searching the house, I roared with laughter at the thought that they had only to reach out and they would have their prey.

A dozen times, I worked out schemes to get out of the Zone to the comparative sanctuary of Paris, or any other big town.

Each time I had to reject the idea. There seemed no way of getting through the cordon of bayonets that cut us off from the rest of France.

Then came the crisis, when I had to act—and act quickly.

Olga Morrison was the trouble. She was a white Russian and hated Stalin and his government. Everybody had trusted her. She knew everybody in our area and went and informed on us. Nobody had dreamed she'd do that. It caused chaos initially because no one knew where the leak was. The Germans put out a reward of 5,000 francs for information leading to the capture of the woman known as the Angel. Olga went and tried to collect it.

To be caught meant the concentration camp—or worse.

It was the afternoon of Friday, 28 February 1941. Bitterly cold, I was huddled up on the second floor of my house.

One of our people working in the German Headquarters in the Old Bourse passed the word out. I got an urgent message telling me to get out immediately; the Gestapo knew who I was. I was told later too that Olga had come to a nasty end. She'd been found pinned to the door of a brothel in rue Nationale by a bayonet through her chest.

*   *   *

**Anne escaped from the Forbidden Zone wearing
old clothes and clogs, posing as Lucienne Suin,
servant girl.**

From Anne Angelo's story
published in *The Weekly News*
Dundee, September 1941.

CHAPTER 25

Escape From The Forbidden Zone

CHOOSING TIMES WHEN things were quiet, I stowed everything I could carry into the cavity under the wardrobe floor in the Blue Room, where I'd been hiding the escapees. I thought there was a chance it might all be safe there in case I could ever get back again. It was at least better than leaving them where they were. All my best things I packed into boxes and suitcases and got them away to the Villeneuves at Moretz, Bonne-maman's people near the Swiss border. I sent them a note telling them how things were with me and asking them to look after them for me.

It was the third day. I'd done all I could and thought it was time to be going.

We settled at Bonne-maman's villa at Fecamp as being the best place to wait for a chance to cross the Channel to England. It was where the Channel narrowed, but not where the Germans had their heaviest defences.

Stefan and Jacqueline, where Uncle took me, were a young French couple. He said I could trust them implicitly. It would probably be a couple of days. I was to stay in the house and keep out of sight. He asked if I still had any petrol for my motor car. I told him the Buick was in the garage and there was benzene there too. He took my keys and left. It was an emotional farewell; we both knew it could well be the last time we'd ever see each other.

It was natural that he'd have to be careful what he told anybody. But it would have been better if he'd given me some idea of what to expect. I nearly wrecked everything.

It was the second evening. Just after dark, I was sitting in the front parlour with the light out, keeping watch out through the corner of the curtains. It was unmistakably my Buick. It stopped, and two SS men got out. They were in full uniform and had machine-pistols hanging from their shoulders. They came and banged on the door. Naturally, I thought something had gone wrong. I grabbed my things and got down behind the armchair in the corner.

Stefan came through, and after some talk, I heard them all go through to the kitchen. It seemed that the best thing for me was to grab the chance while it was there. If I could get out and away, there'd be nothing to show I'd ever been there. It would leave Stefan and Jacqueline in the clear. With a bit of luck, the keys might even be in the Buick and I could get away with it—just as I had done with the Packard from outside the Old Bourse.

I'd got out from behind my armchair with my things without a sound, got the parlour door opened, and was working on the lock on the front door. Another moment, and I'd have been gone. But Stefan came out and caught me. He said everything was all right. I had nothing to worry about. They were friends. He took me through and introduced me to Gerry and Mack. They were English, but both had faultless German. They'd come to take me to Fecamp. And that's what they did. We sailed through everything, me in between them as their prisoner. They were impressive-looking men. One was a sergeant and the other a korporal. Their automatic weapons plainly in sight across their knees.

At the villa, they waited until they saw everything was all right and then drove away. I never saw my Buick again.

I was a little over a week at Fecamp. It was lovely. All the pressure was gone, and I was able to relax. There were Germans going about in lorries, but they didn't bother us. The caretaker and his wife were over sixty and treated me as a daughter.

They came for me at dark. I'll never forget that night. They looked like fishermen in dark clothes. They were both French in their early twenties. They'd had to wait for a night with not too much wind. They said this was going to be good; there were a lot of patches of fog. They gave me some stuff to blacken my face and hands. They used it too. I'd only be able to take my shoulder bag and wear dark clothes. One of them had a roll of corrugated cardboard about two metres long.

We went about two kilometres along towards Yport before turning towards the sea. They told me that if anything went wrong, I was to drop flat and lie perfectly still. If I got caught, that was just too bad. I'd be on my own. But if I didn't, and we got separated, I was to keep still until everything was quiet again and then make my way back to the villa. Someone would be in touch. They cautioned me not to make any sound. There were microphones that could pick up anything. And then we started in.

I soon saw what the roll of cardboard was for. It was smooth on the outside and corrugated on the inside. They pushed it through the coils of barbed wire, end first, and then opened it out so that it became a stiff tunnel for us to wriggle through. One of them first, then me, and then the other one. When he was through, he re-rolled it tightly and pulled it through after him. There wasn't a sound. And there was nothing to show that anybody'd been through. We had to hurry to be within the shelter of some bushes before the sentry came along. They knew the times. The fog was perfect. He must have passed within three metres of us. And then we had to hurry to be clear before he came round again. There were tripwires and mines. I had to put my feet exactly where they put theirs. Then more barbed wire. And then we were through and heading for the rocks.

In their shelter, a torch flicked its message out seawards. At certain intervals, it was repeated. Silently, a little dory with two men in it appeared. Not a word was said. My two companions held it while I got in. They pushed us off and merged back into the fog and rocks. There was no sound from our oars. The sea was like heaving glass. But even so, the little rippled under our bows sounded awfully loud to me. We were about a hundred metres out when the fog parted and left us fully exposed under a bright moon. I expected every minute to hear a shout and gunfire. But there wasn't. And then we were across it, and I was clambering up the side of a small fishing boat.

It could have been the *Saucy Shrimp* again for all I could tell. There were four men on board, and none of them was either Etienne or Pierre.

But that didn't mean a thing. They could have been shanghaied into the German Navy, and she could have been sold. The little dory went round to be tied under our stern, the sails tightened up, and we slid silently away. After a while, progress was poor, so they started the engine.

They told me they were taking me to Folkestone. There'd be no trouble there. They knew the challenge signals and the responses. We'd go straight in. We'd heard fast motorboats moving about around us but hadn't seen anything. Suddenly there was a huge explosion and a great glare of fire. They let me look through their night binoculars. A big ship was on fire and sinking. There were a lot of ships, I couldn't see how many, there were too many fog patches, although it was getting thinner. The whole Channel ahead of us was full of ships. Another one exploded in fire. They told me it was torpedoes or mines. We stopped and lay there rolling gently on the swell. There were fast motorboats rushing about, firing off guns at everybody. We started up again and turned and crept along closer to the French coast. We couldn't go too close; the shore batteries would be on the alert with all the fuss going on. It would take only one shell to sink us.

A little while afterwards, they came and said they were sorry but they couldn't take me across. It was too risky. The ships were still coming.

There were warships amongst them; there wasn't a chance of getting through them, and it was impossible to know how long it would go on for. (I learned later that this was a British convoy. Sixteen ships, escorted by destroyers and motor-torpedo-boats going from Chatham to Portsmouth, were attacked by mine-laying German E-boats whose mines got two ships.) It was well after daylight before the battle ended and the Channel was clear. It just wasn't a night for any crossing such as we'd had in mind. The circumstances were undeniably against me. It was only a couple of hours before it would be getting light. They'd have to put me back in France again. I couldn't argue. I was in their hands. They headed for a place they knew. Two of them took me in the dory. One stayed in it while the other took me through the defences. And there he left me. He said the road to St Valery-sur-Somme and Abbeyville was straight ahead of me. Or, if I wanted to, I could go the other way, and it would take me back to Fecamp. I think that was about the worst pickle I was ever in.

I was so utterly exposed and helpless. I didn't know the area. Oh yes, I'd driven along it a few times with Bonne-maman. But going in the luxurious opulence of a chauffeur-driven Packard with everybody hoping for your patronage, and going along with a shabby shoulder bag and a price on your head are very different things. Whichever way I went, the first German patrol would grab me. They'd certainly want to know what I was doing out on the road so early. I'd be taken in for questioning, and that would be fatal.

But which way to go? I figured Fecamp was a good hundred kilometres away. There were some big towns to get through, Dieppe among them, where I knew there was a lot of German activity. I'd need to be lucky. And if I did get through, it could be a dead end. I had no contacts there, and no way of making any.

St Valery, Abbeyville, and Lille were more dangerous; the checks were very strict, but I knew there'd be help waiting for me. And that's what I needed—help to get back to Scotland. I decided to stay on the road. Across the fields, I'd be much more conspicuous and get filthy.

I must've been going for about three hours, in broad daylight, about six thirty, before anybody came along. It was a farmer. Going my way with a couple of big strong horses and a cart piled high with farm produce. He stopped alongside me, and we exchanged 'Good mornings' in French and agreed about the weather. He was about forty-five, with deep-set thoughtful eyes. I saw them take in my hat, clothes, and shoes. I thanked heaven I'd washed the black off my hands and face when they'd told me, on the boat, we'd sail straight in to Folkestone. Otherwise, he'd likely have thought I was some sort of a loony and driven on.

He asked me how far I was going. I told him I was going to St Valery. He said he was too. He cleared the seat beside him and offered me a lift. He had a good face and was so obviously what he appeared to be that I didn't hesitate. I clambered up, and away we went. It was the smartest thing I ever did. He turned out to be an absolute godsend. He took to me and treated me like his own daughter.

He said he'd been born and had grown up in the area and knew practically everybody. Where had I stayed last night? I told him I was only passing through. He tried me with some German. My German had never been good. About all I had was things the girls at the I de la Paix called the German officers behind their backs. Then he asked me, in clear English, if I'd had any breakfast. I knew he'd seen I'd understood the question, so I answered in English and said no, I hadn't.

Instantly, he changed. He took his pipe from his mouth and smiled.

'Ah so!' he said. 'It is what I thought, no? You have troubles with le Boche? Never mind. They make troubles for me too. I, Emile, I will help you.'

He said he had to deliver some cheeses at St Valery, and we would have breakfast there. Then he was going on to the markets in Abbeyville. I could go with him if I liked. I told him I had no pass. He said it didn't matter. He was well known; he'd been going to the markets there for about twenty years. He'd get me through as his niece. So then I told him that actually, I wanted to get to Lille. He became very serious.

'Lille? But that is dangerous,' he said. 'The Germans there are bad. You are English. If they catch you, you will not live long. You must be a very brave girl. But do not tell me anymore. I do not want to know. But if you want to go to Lille, maybe I can help you there too. We will see.'

At St Valery, we had breakfast at the café where he delivered his cheeses. He was obviously well known. He wouldn't let me pay for anything. At the Abbeyville checkpoint, he didn't even get down. There was some talk in German which made them smile. He handed them a dozen duck eggs, and they waved us through.

He had to go to different places in the markets to unload, and I saw him talking with men and knew they were talking about me. I took off my hat and put it in my shoulder bag. And I ruffled my hair a bit so I'd look more like a country girl.

He came back with a man whom he introduced as Francois. After we'd talked a while, Francois said, 'Yes, all right. I'll take her.' He was the lorry driver who'd come through from Lille to pick up a load for the markets there. He'd take me back with him. I think he'd been summing me up. He patted me on the knee; I was still sitting up on the seat of the farmer's cart. 'So now you have a new Uncle, mam'selle. But do not worry. We will get you to Lille. Have you been there before? Do you know it?'

I told him yes, I'd been there and knew it well.

'C'est bien,' he said. 'So there is no problem there. I go first to les Halles Centrales on rue Solferino. Then I go to . . .'

'But that will do fine,' I butted in. 'If you can get me to les Halles Centrales, that will be lovely. My friends live not far from there. It couldn't be better.' I didn't tell them that rue Solferino ran past the side of my hotel where I'd have to call in for a few minutes. Nor that it would take me straight to safety in the house in Place Philippe le Bon. It pays not to say more than you have to.

I stayed with Emile while Francois got his load. When he was ready to go, he came and got me. Emile and I were more than uncle and niece by that time; we were like father and daughter. He was marvellous. Before we parted, I got his address and full name. He wasn't entirely happy about it. He said it was risky. But I wrote it in such a way that it wouldn't make any sense to anyone else. I felt I had to. I hoped that someday I'd be able to repay him for all he'd done.

At the Lille gate, it was much the same as it had been at Abbeyville. There was a bit of talk in German; he handed them something in a bag; they had a brief glance at my Lucienne Suin identity card, and through we went. It was just before dark when we got to the Halles, and within five minutes, I was in the shrubbery of 241 heading for the back steps. I had no idea of what I was going to find.

But it was all okay. Marie-Louise and old Jacques were naturally horrified to see me. Almost in tears, they begged and pleaded with me to go. 'They are going to kill you, mademoiselle. And they say they will kill us if they find you have been back and we have not told them. Please go, mademoiselle. Have no worries. We will not tell them you have been. But please go now.'

They said the Germans, stormtroopers, and Gestapo had burst in from the back and front not five minutes after I'd gone. They'd searched the whole house. Everybody had been questioned. It was the same each time they'd come. I guessed things must have been pretty rough. I had

ANNE ANGELO

to go up to the bureau to get a few things to replace what I'd had to leave behind at Fecamp. Everything was in a mess. The drawers had all been emptied out onto the floor. All the things had been thrown out of the wardrobe. I grabbed what I needed and ran. It was dark as I walked along Solferino to Place Philippe le Bon and safety.

*   *   *

CHAPTER 26

To Safety In An Orange Case

I WAS FIVE DAYS at Philippe le Bon, waiting until they could get me away. Those five days, hiding and waiting for a loud banging on the door, showed me how helpless we were. We'd made our plans. They'd been good plans; everything had gone smoothly. Until there was all that fuss and bother in the Channel. Nobody could have foreseen that. But here I was, back where I'd have been over a week ago.

They found me a lorry driver who was going through with a load of oranges from the Kommandant Lille to the Kommandant, Paris. He was a bright little bird of a man. He said he'd put me in a box in the middle of his load. In view of who they were for he didn't think we'd have any bother. He didn't want any money for it. He said it would be a pleasure on account of the way the Germans had treated his wife.

I was early at the markets, but he was already loaded up with a cover on and tied down. He put me up on the seat beside him. I reminded him I hadn't got a White Pass, but he said not to worry.

At the barrier, he showed them the papers saying who the load was for. They had a brief glance at me and my papers. He held out a bag of oranges he'd had on the seat between us. 'Here, how about these? A gift from the Lille Kommandant. Can you use them?'

They were taken and we went through.

We made good time. There was no trouble at Arras, Bapaume, and Albert. Next ahead of us was Amiens. It was the danger point. It was on the Somme which they'd made the boundary of the Forbidden Zone. Even the smallest bridges were manned, and they had savage Alsatian dogs on both sides of the river to prevent people from swimming across.

He stuck to the main road. He said to do anything else would be suspicious.

On the outskirts, he turned off and went a fair way along a side road and stopped. He undid his load right down to the bottom where he had a case with only a few loose oranges in it. He took them out, put me in, and scattered them all on top of me. Then he nailed the lid on and fixed his load again.

He got back onto the highway and headed for the checkpoint.

I wasn't very happy in there. I was cramped, with the oranges pressing down on me. I couldn't move, and I couldn't get enough air. We stopped three or four times before I knew we were there. And then I heard him take off his cover and let down his sides and tailgate. They got up and shifted everything. They smashed cases open. They worked right down to the floor. At one stage, there was a uniformed leg within centimetres of my face. If he'd bent down, he might have seen me. My case was right at the bottom, against the back of the cabin. Suddenly they all went, taking him with them. I nearly panicked. I thought they'd found something and taken him away. I'd be left to suffocate. I was just on the point of calling out when he came back.

He was humming a little tune. He got up and re-stacked his load. He wriggled a couple of fingers through and touched my shoulder. I knew then that we'd done it. They didn't let him finish. They told him he was blocking the line, to get out, and finish it somewhere else. And that was fine. He drove along to the first side road and stopped and let me out. It was as well they had told him to move along and do his work somewhere else. I couldn't have lasted much longer. I remembered him starting to open my case. And the next thing I knew, he was leaning over me and holding a small flask of cognac to my lips. 'Come on,' he was, urging me. 'Just a little drop. It'll do you good.'

And it did too. It and the fresh air worked wonders. We got his load all fixed and covered again, but before we got back in, we danced a little jig together there on the roadway. He was a lovely little man. At the Paris checkpoint, I stayed up on the seat beside him; he used the bag of oranges trick again, and within half an hour, I was safe in a café.

The proprietor's wife took me into a room beyond the cafe, where I managed to freshen up and rest a little.

'You'll be quite safe here,' said the friendly little woman. 'We know you've done so much in the war effort. We'll take great care to see that nothing happens to you.' She brought out some cold bacon and boiled eggs and real coffee, a drink which I had not tasted for months. After the meal, I felt very much better.

'Where's the driver?' I asked.

'He's gone,' the woman replied calmly.

'But I didn't even thank him,' I cried, bitterly ashamed.

'Don't worry, mademoiselle. We're waiting for you and the British to help us one day. You're our only hope.'

I would have liked to stay there all day, but it was impossible.

'A "passeur" is expecting you tonight at Chalons to take you across the demarcation line. There's no time to waste. You must leave within the next hour,' said the kind old lady.

'But how do I get there?' I asked, wondering who really were the master race in France.

'By lorry.'

'Oh no,' I said. 'Not again. I couldn't get into another box. The way I feel, I should scream.'

'There, there, my dear,' the woman replied, patting my shoulder. 'You don't need to go in a box. You can sit with the driver, and I'll give you a cushion to sit on. How's that?'

I hugged her. 'But will it be quite safe?' I asked quickly.

'Of course, my dear. Nobody is looking for poor little Lucienne Suin. They are looking for mademoiselle. Angelo.'

If I hadn't been feeling so dreadful physically, I would have enjoyed my drive to Chalons. It was spring. The country looked beautiful. Outside Paris, with only an occasional German here and there on a bicycle, the air smelt clean and pure. My driver, Robert, spent the time telling me funny stories till I roared with laughter. We stopped at a café in Chalons, where the proprietor brought me their speciality. A huge plate of snails. I had never acquired the taste for snails in spite of the years I'd spent in France, but these were delicious.

ANNE ANGELO

About midnight, my 'passeur' came along. We were introduced, and then we went into the back room, where he explained that he had to bribe the sentry on duty in the early hours of the morning.

'How much?' I asked.

'About one thousand francs,' he replied.

'All right,' I said. 'Turn your back while I dig it out of my corsets.' I gave him the money. 'Now what do we do?'

'Well, I'll take you somewhere to sleep and pick you up at dawn. Don't hide anything on yourself, give it to me. I am never searched, but you might be.'

'How do you manage to escape search?' I asked him.

'Well, I live here and work across the line. I'm back and forth every day. I sometimes come home for my lunch too,' he replied, shrugging. 'They all know me, and you don't search a generous friend of long standing.'

We went back to the café, where there was much hand shaking and good wishes. 'Tell the British we are waiting for them,' they shouted.

'I will,' I promised as I set off with my 'passeur'.

I was led into a house. It was very dark. We mounted the stairs and stopped before a door. 'There's a bed in there. You can have a good night's sleep till I come for you in the morning,' he said, pushing me in. I entered and tripped over something hard. I passed my hand over it but couldn't make out what it was. I clambered over it, feeling for a bed. I found one and flopped into it. Groans filled the air and the bed, and I realised that I wasn't alone.

'Move over,' I whispered to the form on the edge of the bed. It moved. I squeezed in, and in no time was fast asleep.

A knock at the door woke me up. It was dawn. In the early morning light, I could see where I had spent the night. It was quite a small bedroom, but it held a bed which stretched from one side of the room to the other. It was quite the biggest bed I'd ever seen. On it were a dozen people of both sexes. The thing I had tripped over was a motorbike.

My 'passeur' was waiting for me. We walked right up to the sentry, who asked for our identity cards. We produced them. He handed mine back first and nodded for me to pass on. I went. I couldn't go fast enough. I presumed that my 'passeur' was handing over the bribe.

I knew I had to walk to the next village, where I would meet my 'passeur', who would hand me back my papers, including my British passport, which I had given him before leaving.

I saw two German officers riding along towards me on bicycles. I felt terrified. I didn't quite know why. I hadn't been warned about meeting stray Germans. I didn't know what I was supposed to say or do. They stopped me, and one asked for my papers.

'What papers?' I said, trying to play the innocent.

He was a match for me. He simply took my bag, emptied everything out, scanned my Lucienne Suin identity card, and said sharply, 'You're from Lille. From the Forbidden Zone. Where's your special pass to get out?'

I protested I had come from Paris, not Lille. I had not been in Lille since the evacuation.

'Liar.'

I was shaken almost out of my wits, but I stuck to my story—that I had lost my father in the invasion, had combed Paris for him in vain, and knew he must be somewhere in unoccupied France.

Then suddenly I broke down. For weeks my nerves had been on edge. Now I sobbed as if I could never stop.

After half an hour of this, I saw they were baffled. I had started crying because I couldn't help it. But I kept on crying. I saw it was my only hope.

After searching my clothing, they threatened me with prison for trying to get over the line illegally. I began to scream—and that did it!

'Shut up! You're driving us crazy,' one of them said. 'Now find your father. But I'm sorry for him if you catch up on him.'

*   *   *

CHAPTER 27

Monte Carlo

I WAS TERRIBLY RELIEVED to meet my 'passeur' in the next town.

A few hours later, I was in a train heading for Marseilles. From there I left once more by train for Nice. From Nice I took a 'bus' to Monte Carlo. It was a most peculiar bus. Apparently, they had no petrol down here, so they had rigged up a contraption which burnt coke at the back. For the life of me, I could not see how those cinders could make the thing move, but it did, though not very fast. Every now and then, it stopped and the driver got down to rake out the ashes. I wondered if he found any clinkers. All passengers had to alight each time we came to a hill and walk up. The poor bus could hardly pull itself up, but it was really funny going downhill, especially if one had a back seat. The old bus scattered ashes behind it all the way down the hill. As it was night, those cinders made a fascinating pattern on the road. Of course, the noise was deafening, but we got there just the same.

I woke up the caretaker of Bonne-maman's apartment, who handed me the keys. My joy knew no bounds as I entered the hall and found four suitcases which I had sent off months before, never expecting them to reach Monte Carlo at all. At the time, I'd realised that it would be quite impossible for me to take the cases with me when the time came for me to make a dash for it. I also knew that it wasn't safe to send luggage by rail as it got lost or pilfered in nine cases out of ten. I had taken a chance, however, and addressed them to Bonne-maman, and here they were ahead of me. They were all intact; everything was as I had packed it. I made some tea, real tea, and went to bed.

Next day, after a bath, I got into the first decent clothes I had worn for ages. It felt good to be a human being again instead of a rat in a hole. It was good to be alive on the Riviera in spring.

Outwardly, Monte Carlo hadn't changed. Apart from the lack of food, it looked its usual glittering self. There was the usual abundance of flowers and fruit, but unfortunately, one could not eat flowers. Still, one could pass the time very pleasantly sitting outside the Café de Paris facing the Casino and spend pence drinking aperitifs.

Most English and American people had left, their villas abandoned, but there were still a few who lived there permanently. Unfortunately, the place was alive with Czechs, Austrians, and Germans. They seemed to be there in their hundreds, some even in uniform. How nice it was to sit at a table next to a crowd of Germans knowing they had neither the power nor the inclination to touch me. I wondered what they were doing there. Had they fled from their own countries? Were they deserters? How did they manage to live down here? I had no intention, however, of satisfying my curiosity by speaking to one of them.

After a few weeks of peaceful laziness, I thought it was time to make some plans to get somewhere I could make some money. It was hopeless trying to get a job in Monte Carlo. Most of the shops were empty. No food arrived. Apparently, the Germans, with or without consent of the Vichy government, had installed themselves in Marseilles. From there they directed all the merchandise which arrived from all over the world to the occupied zone.

I went to the British consul in Monte Carlo, who was unable to help me to find work. He advised me to go to the various consuls in Nice for papers to leave the country through Spain and Portugal. In the meantime, I'd made friends with the secretary of the consul in Monte Carlo. She was a large well-built girl of twenty-eight or so with a passion for swimming and sunbathing.

Every day we met at three o'clock for a cocktail at the Cafe de Paris, where we exchanged news of the war. Her friend Jess Simmons loved to hear my stories of life in the forbidden zone. We chattered on for hours. On one occasion, as we were laughing over some incident or other, we heard a camera click at the next table. A good-looking young man arose, bowed to us, and walked away.

'I wonder what that man can see in us to make him take a photo,' I said, a little puzzled.

'Maybe he's going to stick us above his bed and make pinup girls of us,' laughed Jess.

'Crazy coon,' I muttered and promptly forgot all about it.

A few days later, I met Jess as usual, but my friend couldn't stay. The consul had asked her to find me and bring me immediately to his office. She looked very upset. She was so confused that I couldn't make head or tail of her story. As we entered, the consul spread out a newspaper in front of me. I stared. It was a picture of myself and Jess laughing outside the café, and underneath were these words:

ENGLISH GIRLS AMUSED AT THE IDEA OF BRITAIN WINNING THE WAR. GIRL ON RIGHT HAS JUST TOLD HER FRIEND OF THE WONDERFUL BEHAVIOUR OF THE GERMANS IN THE FORBIDDEN ZONE WHICH SHE HAS JUST LEFT. SHE HAS GREAT RESPECT FOR THEM. SHE WISHES TO LEAVE FOR AMERICA IF POSSIBLE, IF NOT, ANY OTHER COUNTRY BUT BRITAIN. SHE SWEARS SHE WILL NOT RETURN TO A COUNTRY WHERE PEOPLE ARE SO STUPID AND COWARDLY.

My face was purple with rage as I read it. I had never said anything like these words which stared at me from the paper. The British consul was equally livid.

'This is a peaceful community, and I will not tolerate such impudence from you,' he said furiously. 'The sooner you go, the better.'

'How dare you insult me like this?' I stormed. 'Those are lies. You do not need to believe me, but surely, you can believe your own secretary. She has been with you for years.'

'I believe neither of you,' he thundered. 'I believe what I see in black and white.'

*   *   *

CHAPTER 28

The Last Leg

THAT MADE UP my mind. I must move on, go back to England. And how to find Gerald?

That night, I packed one suitcase, selecting only the most practical items. Months of fleeing had taught me well in the art of packing for survival. The next morning, the eleventh of June 1941, I caught another homemade bus to Nice, where I first went to see Mr Basil MacGowan, the American vice consul in charge of British interests. He made me out a visa valid for travel in Spain and Portugal. Just to be doubly sure, I went around to the Portuguese Consulate and received a '30 day visa while in transit to England'.

Five days later, I'd reached Marseilles, where I saw the Spanish Consul and secured another visa for 'transit through Spain, good in Portugal'.

On the eighteenth of June, I crossed the frontier into Spain at Port Bau. My finances had been depleted. Whilst the British and American consulates had given me a few pounds or dollars to get to the next city, this had more than been expended on food, transport, accommodation, and visa fees. I had in my possession fifty dollars in American notes, a cheque for fifty-two pounds, plus fifty French francs.

Everybody seemed to be stamping my passport and counting my money. The customs people were the worst. For the first time in my entire life, and having travelled all over Europe for years, they asked me to strip and be searched.

The next stop was Madrid, by which time I was heartily sick of teeming masses of humanity smelling of sweat and garlic crammed into those hideous creaking trains with wooden seats. The fight for survival must have been very strong to endure so much and still continue on. Madrid seemed a more civilised place. I sat down at a cafe and asked for a drink. While I sipped whatever it was, I couldn't understand why there were no women around. The waiter spoke a little English and told me that Spanish women were not allowed out alone except during certain hours when they were taking their children to or from school. The only women one saw were 'ladies of the night' as he put it. I understood why I was getting such looks from the sweaty males who passed me by.

In Spain there had been an abundance of food, but hungry as I had been, the peculiar taste of the food made me feel sick. There had been one train a day out of Madrid, and I had received orders to be on it. The Spanish authorities wanted no English people to stay in their towns for more than twenty-four hours. No sane English person would have wanted to stay.

The Spanish had not even bothered to clean up their country since the revolution. There was chaos everywhere. Lampposts still lay across the streets, holes in the roads had never been repaired. Judging by the overflow, dustbins were emptied once a year. And everywhere, masses of filthy children trailed after people who strolled lazily along the pavements.

On the twenty-second of June, I crossed the border into Portugal at a place called Beria-Mari, and within a few hours, I was in Lisbon, to wait for a ship. Three days later, I picked up a 30 day visa at the British Consulate.

But Lisbon. This was paradise. I had always imagined that Portugal was just a smaller replica of Spain. But this was the most Americanised country I'd seen. In great contrast to the poverty of Spain, this country was prosperous. Everybody seemed well off, every second person seemed to have a huge American car. The restaurants and cafés were packed with people eating the most enormous meals. Everybody looked happy.

I met other English people who'd been living in Lisbon for months. They were all waiting for a ship. I hoped a ship would take many months to arrive before tearing me away from this paradise. But I was unlucky. Within a week of arriving, a Portuguese coal boat had agreed to take off all the British people and land them at Gibraltar. I just couldn't win, and to make matters worse, my suitcases, which I had sent to Lisbon from Monaco, hadn't arrived when it was time to leave. There was nothing I could do but board this filthy coal boat with about forty other refugees and hope that our destination, Gibraltar, would be pleasant and somehow we'd all get home one day. I'd even lost track of the date, but it didn't matter anyway.

It wasn't a case of the Portuguese disliking the English, far from it. I had never met with such generosity in my whole life. But they didn't want to be brought into the War on the pretext that they were harbouring British subjects or on any other pretext the Germans might think up. I tearfully left Lisbon. Friends I had made in the hotel threw bouquets of flowers up to me on the deck. Others bought me sweets for the journey. I adored them all, and with an aching heart, I sailed away from the only really peaceful country in Europe.

Everything we ate tasted of coal, and our faces were black. There weren't enough bathrooms, so we just stayed dirty. There weren't enough bunks; they never carried passengers. We were told to listen for alarms, and the crew explained to us that certain alarms meant aircraft overhead and we'd have to go down to the hold and stay there until the all-clear. A different signal meant submarines in the area and we'd have to go on deck till the danger was over. It was all so unfair, but there was nothing fair about this whole damned war. It had become survival of the craftiest. We were in territorial waters within the three-mile limit of a neutral country, yet we were bombed or chased by submarines for three days and nights. I'd walked around that boat during the entire trip with a small mattress tied to my back so that I could get a little sleep wherever I happened to be at the time of the all-clear. It didn't matter where I slept, on the piles of coal or on the deck—it just didn't matter.

We steamed slowly down the coast, keeping within the territorial waters where we hoped we were safe from attack. Even though, my companions and I spent the whole of each night and day on the upper deck just in case we were torpedoed. It was such a change to see the coastline lit up during the entire journey. By mid-morning on the last day, we were entering Gibraltar.

The first sight which met our eyes was HMS *Ark Royal* in all its splendour, plus several destroyers. We looked a sorry mess, especially in contrast to the wonderful-looking sailors and officers. They looked so clean and fit—a sight which none of us had encountered for a very long time.

My companions and I were the only women in the area. The women and children had been evacuated a few months earlier. I went ashore with a new girlfriend I had met in Lisbon.

We found a small hotel—with a real bed and a real bath. For half a day, we washed ourselves and our clothes. It was a glorious day, and just perfect for drying. Finally feeling half human again, we turned our thoughts to eating and set off down the street.

As we entered a bar for a drink, we were surrounded by a number of officers from the *Ark Royal*. They were wonderful-looking men in their white suits and gold braid. They all drank like fish.

'You know', said one named Terry, 'we haven't seen a woman for ninety days. We must celebrate.'

And celebrate we did. For nearly six days. If we weren't all drinking and dancing, we were swimming. Our last evening arrived only too soon. I turned my charm on the captain of the troopship and asked for permission for the officers of the *Ark Royal* to come aboard on our last evening. Orders had been given that no civilian would be allowed ashore that evening. I wasn't a bit surprised at the order, as the night before, Judy and I had returned two hours late and much too merry even to find our cabin, which we shared with four others. The captain refused, but I still persisted. But he went on refusing. I gave in and settled down to play bridge with some other women.

We had no sooner started our game than in walked the officers from the aircraft carrier. The captain had relented. The game stopped, and Judy and I went up on deck with the men, who miraculously produced bottles of gin, lime, and whisky. We had a merry little party of our own. It was pitch dark, not a light anywhere, and then we all started playing postman's knock

I had no idea how long the game lasted. I had no idea how I got back to my cabin. I had no idea who had undressed me and put me to bed. All I knew was that I had tripped on a coil of rope, and that was all I could remember.

'Who put me to bed last night?' I asked Judy next morning as I sat up on my bunk, holding my aching head.

'Don't talk to me, Anne. You make me sick,' Judy replied.

I asked the others, but no one would tell me, not even the captain. The officers looked at me sideways when I met them, but not one of them would tell me what I had done. I decided to leave well alone. I was quite sure I had made a perfect spectacle of myself, but as no one wanted to tell me about it, it was much wiser to give them a chance to forget it.

It was so comforting to look out of the porthole every morning and see our escorts always in the same positions. The *Ark Royal* and several destroyers all lined up. It gave one a feeling of safety to be convoyed night and day. The ships looked like watchdogs ready to pounce on anyone who dared to touch their charges. Our ship was the *Cythea*, crammed with soldiers and civilians.

I played deck tennis or sunbathed most of the day between alerts. My favourite partner for tennis was a Canadian seaman who had been torpedoed four times.

'You're not lucky, Tim,' I said one afternoon as we sunbathed. 'You're probably a magnet for torpedoes. For the sake of the other people on this ship I ought to push you overboard before something hits us.'

'Don't be crazy,' he laughed. 'In any case, you stick to me, honey. I always get picked up.'

'Tell me about the sinkings, Tim.'

'I guess there ain't much to tell,' he replied. 'It's all luck, or fate if you like it that way. To start with, I was torpedoed by a German U-boat, which picked me up. I had a piece of shrapnel in my foot. They made me walk to a table, operated on it, and I stood up afterwards and walked away. They sure treated me well, I must say that. A few days later, we were sunk by a British destroyer, and again I was among the survivors picked up. But this time, of course, I wasn't a prisoner. Within a week, we were bombed by German aircraft and later picked up by a German destroyer, and then, believe it or not, in less than forty-eight hours, I was

ANNE ANGELO

in the drink again. I was finally rescued by a British ship which dropped me at Gib. Holy jeez, I've had enough cold water to last me a lifetime.'

'Fantastic,' I said. 'You must be a ruddy cat with five more lives to go. I'll accept your offer and stick close to you. They seem to have made a marvellous job of your foot, judging by the way you always beat me at deck tennis.'

'Oh, it's okay now, I guess.'

On waking up one morning several days later, I was disappointed to notice the absence of our escort. There was no *Ark Royal* in its usual position. There were no destroyers. The convoy was on its own.

The weather was terribly hot. I wondered where we were going. It surely must be to a hot country, judging by the terrific heat. Rumours were afloat that we were bound for South Africa. I was thrilled at the idea. All day, there were alerts. I couldn't see anything in the sky. There were probably German subs around, but there was no excitement.

About three days later, the weather suddenly changed. Everybody rushed around looking for warm clothes and rugs. The skies were grey, the sea had lost its smooth blue surface, and now it was choppy and forbidding looking.

'I say, Judy', I said, waking up that morning, 'it's perishing cold. We can't be going to South Africa after all. We've changed course. Just look at that sky. If that isn't an English sky, I'll eat my hat.'

Judy shivered as she looked out of the porthole.

'Just our ruddy luck. They shouldn't do these things to us. They roast us in sunshine and then transfer us to the Artic Circle. Who wanted to go to England anyway?' I went on furiously. Judy was a wanderer and had been practically all round the world. I'd learnt that Judy had a very angry husband in England just waiting for her to return, and here she was, being practically dropped in his lap.

The following morning, I looked out of my porthole again. My worst fears were realised. If there was one country in the entire world which I never wanted to see again, it was Scotland. To make matters worse, it was the thirteenth of July. I was superstitious about the thirteenth.

Maybe it was just as well that we did land there, however. It made me feel that I really should go home to see Mother. Not that I loved mother any less during my prolonged absence.

As I passed through the security people, they informed me that I would not be able to go home, as home happened to be in a protected area. It would take two or three weeks to get a pass for me.

'If you think I have travelled thousands of miles to get home just to sleep on a doorstep, then you can think again,' I told them.

'Well, if you prefer to go as far as Inverness, you can—only they won't let you go beyond it without a pass.'

'I will take a chance,' I replied. 'If you like, I will make a bet with you that I shall be home within twenty-four hours. If I could get through the German lines, you don't think this one is more difficult, do you?'

He laughed. 'I don't think I'll bet. Good luck.'

Early next morning, I was in Inverness. I had my ticket and went to pass the Scots soldiers at the barrier.

'Your pass please,' asked one of them.

'I haven't got a pass. I'm just back from France, and my home is only thirty miles away. Now get out of my way,' I said, trying to brush past him. It was no use. He and his companion barred the way, and no matter how hard I pushed them, they didn't budge an inch. It was like pushing a wall over.

'Ye canna' go in there,' they chorused.

'Get out of the way. I want to go home,' I replied, kicking one of them.

'I woudna' dee that if I were ye,' replied my victim broadly, taking no notice of the kick. I'll go and fetch my officer.'

Left alone with only one of them, I thought it would be easy, but not a bit of it. I might just as well have tried to push the Rock of Gibraltar over. 'Get out of my way before I push you under a train,' I hissed, but he just stood there till his companion returned with an officer.

I explained my circumstances. He explained the law. I got mad. He gave in.

'If I let you go, you must report to the police until we've checked up on you. In the meantime, I'll have your pass sent on to you, and if

ANNE ANGELO

you want to leave the area, ask for a pass well in advance. These things take time.'

Within an hour, I was at home. As I entered the house, Mother gave one scream and fell in a dead faint. I rushed to help her.

'What's the matter, Mother darling? It's me, don't you remember me?'

'But you're dead,' wailed Mother. 'You died months ago, the Red Cross sent me a telegram. I have carried it in my pocket ever since.' She gave it to me, and I tore it up into small pieces.

'It's all a mistake. During that evacuation, so many were lost or killed they could never get the exact figures. Anyway, I'm home now, so why bother about it?'

'You'll never go away again, will you, dear?' pleaded Mother, drying her tears.

'Don't let's think about going away when I've only just got here,' I replied, kissing the old lady affectionately.

We spent a good hour asking about each other over and over.

'I don't suppose there's any mail for me?' I asked, hoping that maybe, just maybe, Gerald had dropped a note.

'Only one from the War Office,' she said.

I jumped to my feet, made a grab for it on the mantlepiece, and tore it open. I wanted to scream! 'Can you believe this, Mother? A bill for the small amounts I got from the various consuls to get from one place to another on my way home, after giving thousands of francs of my own money to all the pilots and soldiers I sent home from France! I can't believe it. It is *they* who owe me a small fortune!' I was really fuming, but I'd attend to that matter later.

The most important matter to be dealt with first was to find Gerald, but how?

*   *   *

CHAPTER 29

Invergordon

I'D BEEN HOME a couple of weeks when I got the perfect way to settle it. The Dundee *Weekly News* approached me to write some articles on my experiences in France under the Nazi heel. It was an ideal way of letting people know I was home and safe and sound. I did a series from 20 September to 25 October. They gave me front-page rating with my name and photograph bold and clear. There could be no mistaking who it was and where I was. I garbled critical details sufficiently to protect the people still in France. Perhaps Gerald would see them. It was my only hope. I couldn't stay in Invergordon. Father made it clear that it was time for me to move on. In any case, it would be much easier for me to look for Gerald from London than from the Highlands.

Our parting had been a frantic few moments clouded by fear and haste. He'd said, 'You have to get out. Go back to Scotland. You should be safe enough there, and I'll know where to find you. When I can, I'll be in touch.'

I'd got away safely, but I had no way of knowing if he had. He'd have been a much greater prize. I was pretty sure he was in military intelligence although he'd never said so. It was the only thing that could explain his odd comings and goings.

He'd been a major when we'd first met in the early days of the War.

If he hadn't got away, he'd certainly have been questioned, and they'd have shot what was left.

I couldn't write anywhere to find out if he was safe. I didn't know his full name. I'd asked him often enough, but he'd never told me. All I had was his Christian name—Gerald. At first, during those days of the phoney war, curiosity had made me go round asking anyone I could, trying to find out. I'd had French and British Army officers billeted with me in the hotel. I'd asked them, but I'd had to stop it. I'd been cautioned by no less a person than HRH the Duke of Gloucester who'd come to a conference.

'You just stop it, young miss,' he'd said after he'd satisfied himself as to my identity. 'If he didn't tell you his name, you can be jolly sure he had good reason not to. We're not over here for a picnic, you know. This is war. And remember, what you don't know, you can't be made to tell. Do I make myself clear?'

He had. He'd made himself so clear that I never asked again. And his words about 'can't be made to tell' made lots of things clear when the Germans came.

But as I said in the beginning, waiting isn't easy. For women like me in wartime, waiting for word of their men, waiting becomes a soul-destroying purgatory. Days crawl into nights, and nights drag on into yet another dreary day. It's like sitting alone in a slow train being taken through an interminable succession of tunnels not knowing what's going to be at the end.

It was about a fortnight later. In the month I'd been home, I'd hardly set foot out of the house. It certainly wasn't easy. I was in the parlour reading *Hamlet*. It had rained all night, and I had a good fire on. I'd just read the tragic duel scene and was sitting there thinking about it and feeling sorry for poor Hamlet.

It seemed to me we had lots in common. He'd never had the chance of a proper life either. He'd had the intrigues of his uncle. I'd had my father and now the War. My thoughts were broken by Mother coming in. It surprised me; she seldom did.

'I hope I'm not wrong, dear,' she said, putting her hands on my shoulders from behind. 'But I think your man's here. There's an Army officer at the door asking for you. Will you go, or shall I bring him in here?'

'There's a what? Oh, there's not, is there? Oh heavens! No, it's all right. I'll go.' And with a quick dab at my hair in the sideboard mirror, I went.

But as soon as I saw him there, framed against the light, it all went cold. It wasn't him. He wasn't tall enough, and he wasn't big enough. My Gerald stood a good six feet two and big with it. This fellow was no bigger than I was. He was a major. He had a briefcase in his hand.

'Yes, Major. Do you want to see me?'

'Miss Angelo? Miss Anne Angelo?' He was about thirty-five with a small moustache.

'Yes.' I wondered what on earth he could want with me. I hadn't had very good experiences with Army officers, except with my Gerald, of course, but he was one in a million—and with majors especially. I'd found that British, French, or German, they all had scant regard for the rights and welfare of civilians.

'Major J. H. Hughes, from the War Office, London.' He took an identity card from his top-left pocket, opened it, and held it for me to see. 'Could you spare me a few minutes? I'd like to have a talk with you.'

'Yes, Major. Go ahead. What's it about?'

'Well, er, would it be all right if I came in? It's not very convenient here, and it's perishing cold.'

I realised it was cold. His words floated away in little white puffs.

I didn't want to let him in. I couldn't think of any business he could have with me. But he'd said he'd come up from London to see me, so there had to be something.

'All right, Major. Come in.' And I stood aside to let him. 'Go straight ahead. The first door on the left there.'

I was closing the door when suddenly, it came to me that it must be Gerald. That's what he'd come about. Something must have happened. I had a feeling of cold dread as I went in.

But he'd put his cap and briefcase on the table and was standing with his back to the fire and with my Shakespeare open in his hand.

It jarred me. It didn't fit. I hadn't let him in to read my Shakespeare. He'd had no right to touch it. His words made it worse.

'*Hamlet* eh? Great stuff. Know it well myself. Marvellous fellow, old Shakespeare. All the finer philosophies of life, what? Good reading, every word of it.'

'Oh, you think so, do you? But that's enough of that. Suppose you get on with it. Tell me what you've come for. If you've got bad news for me, let me have it. I've had bad news before.'

I knew it was wrong as soon as I'd said it. He was so taken aback.

'I'm very sorry', he said, 'if I've offended you. I certainly didn't intend to. And you're wrong about me having bad news for you. I haven't. I don't know why you should think I have. I've come up here because we think you might be able to help us.'

He took his briefcase from the table and went across to the settee under the window.

'Is it all right if I sit here?' he said, sitting there as he said it. It was done so casually that I didn't see the reason for it then. From his case he took a file which he opened on his knee and studied.

'Yes,' he said after a minute or two. 'Well, there's just a couple of questions first, if you don't mind. But I think you'll see why.'

I took a chair from the table and turned it so I could sit with my arms on its back, facing him.

'Well, what are they?'

'Have you ever been in Europe?'

It was so silly it made me suspicious. Surely, they must have seen at least some of my articles down in London. I realised why he'd sat where he had. His face was in shadow while mine was in the light. The Germans and French had used the same trick.

'Could I see that identity card again, please, Major?'

This time I took it. The photo was unmistakably him. And the rest seemed authentic enough. But so did the ones that I'd personally faked. The uniform looked genuine, but that didn't mean anything either. Our men had worn German uniforms. I gave it back to him and resolved to go carefully.

'Yes, I have.'

'Could you tell me what parts exactly?'

'Yes. I was in France, Monaco, and Switzerland. Italy, Algeria, and Spain.'

'Good. We're interested in France. What parts of it do you know?'

Well. I've been to most of it. Pretty well from Dunkerque to Marseille. I spent many holidays along the centre coast.'

'Ah, yes. That's what we're interested in. The centre coast. What areas do you know?'

'Oh, St Lunaire, St Nazaire, St Malo, Avranches, Bayeux, and Le Fecamp. I know them fairly well. Is that enough?'

'Yes, indeed. Very good. And you said you were on holidays. How did you travel? By train or car?'

'Always by car. I had good ones, and I like driving.'

'Then you'd know the roads, wouldn't you? And how did you find the French standards of driving? Have any accidents?'

'Yes, as a matter of fact, I did. I had two. But they weren't with the French. They were both with members of your own Army. One was with a dispatch rider and caused me no end of bother. But the other was the happiest thing that ever happened to me. Through it I met the most wonderful man in the world. But it was the driver's fault, not mine.'

'I see.' And I thought there was a smile in his eyes. 'And I think you said you were based in Paris. Is that right?'

'No, it's not. I didn't say anything of the kind. I was based in Lille. But what's this all about, Major? I think I've been patient enough.'

'Yes, you have. But there's just one more. What do you know about white heather? Does it grow anywhere else but in Scotland?'

That did it. Like the sun bursting through the clouds, it made everything clear. He was okay. He was only checking me. But the mention of white heather sent a great surge of joy through me. It proved at least that Gerald had known I was over there. So he must've been alive. And he probably still was. His hand could have written these questions. My face must have shown my feelings for he came over and shook my hand warmly.

'I'm very pleased to meet you, Miss Angelo. Very pleased indeed. You've had quite some experiences, haven't you?'

'But tell me. What have you really come up here to see me about?'

'Yes. Well, I suppose that's a fair question. But as I said in the first place, we think you might be able to help us. And now that I've spoken to you, I'm pretty sure you can. But I had to make sure of you before letting you know what it was.'

The clock on the sideboard broke in with its musical chimes of twelve.

'By Jove, is it really that?' he asked, looking at his watch. 'So it is. Oh good heavens! My poor driver! He must be frozen stiff out there. I say, would it be all right if he came in? Maybe he could wait in the kitchen or somewhere. We're going to be a while yet. And do you think there'd be any chance of a cup of tea? We had to get away early, and it was a long drive.'

He went out and got his driver, and I took him into the kitchen and left him with Mother.

We talked for about an hour, and I pointed out many details on the maps he had brought.

'Another cup, Major?' I asked as he drained it and set it down.

'No thanks. I've done fine, thank you very much. And do tell your mother her cake was much appreciated. So don't you think it's a good idea for you to go back to France?'

'No, I don't. Not for me. I'm too well known. I was plain lucky with that last thing. To go back again would be asking for trouble. No, there must be others better than me.'

'Yes, but you know the whole area so well. And we'd look after you. You'd have an entirely new identity. We'd air-drop you in, and you'd have all the assistance you need. I think you'd be able to do a lot.'

'I don't think so. I don't think I'd be any good to you at all. They'd simply watch everywhere I went, note all my contacts, and then move in and clean up the lot.'

'Yes, all right, if that's the way you feel. And by the way, those articles you wrote were seen in Germany. They caused quite a stir. Anyway, thanks for all this.' And he tapped the file he was holding. 'It's just what we're looking for.'

'Is there any real chance of making a landing? In the face of what they've got massed along those beaches?'

'I'm afraid I can't discuss that with you. But tell me, what happened at Facamp? They got you off all right, didn't they? But you didn't turn up on the other side. What happened?'

'Oh yes. They got me off all right. Everything was going fine. But some English and German motor-torpedo-boats started having a go at each other right ahead of us by the English coast. We had to turn back. They put me ashore again in France. I had to get back to Lille and then go right through France to Marseille and then to Spain. I got to Gibraltar and came home on a coal boat.'

'Oh, so that's where you got to. And how long did that take you?'

'A couple of months. I got here in September.'

He opened the file, turned a couple of pages, and made some notes.

'Yes. Well, I think that tidies everything up.' And he closed it. 'Would you mind getting my driver for me, please?' He put the file into his briefcase and picked up his cap.

'Oh, but just a moment. I have something for you. You have to sign for it.' From a side pocket, he took a small packet wrapped in brown paper and gave it to me. It had a typewritten note attached 'To be handed to Miss Angelo—PERSONALLY. In no circumstances to any other person. Obtain her signature.'

As soon as I took it, I knew what it was. I flexed it in my hand to make sure. There was no doubt about it. It was Mother's soft-backed copy of Robbie Burns Poems which I'd given to Gerald. He'd asked me for it. He'd said he'd always carry it in his top-left pocket. 'You never know, it might turn a bullet,' he'd said. I'd known what he meant and loved him for it. Now he'd sent it back like this.

'Where did you get this, Major?'

'It was with the file, Miss. Why? Is there anything wrong?'

'Was there any message with it? Did you have to tell me anything?'

'No, miss. Just what it says there. To get your signature.'

His face told me nothing. He was Army again. I signed his receipt and gave it to him.

'You'll find your driver in the kitchen, straight across the hall. My mother will let you out. Good day to you, Major.' And I left him there and went up to my room. From my window, I watched them go out, carefully shut the gate, and drive away.

They were so typically Army. They'd come, for their own purposes, and having got what they'd wanted, they'd gone. There'd never be a thought for me. But they'd broken the one link I'd had. They'd put an emptiness where I'd had a small warmth of satisfaction. And they'd left me more doubts. Doubts I couldn't find answers for.

Why could he have sent it back? And why in that way? Why no explanation? If I'd done something, or if Father had said something about me, didn't I have the right to be told? Could all the happy times we'd had, all the things we'd been through together, be forgotten so easily? I could find no answers.

Or did it mean he was dead? Had they found it in his effects and sent it to me? But if that was it, would they have wanted a receipt? I didn't think so. Nor would they have worried about it not being given to anyone else. They'd have simply sent it with a covering letter and been done with it.

Those things suggested his hand. And that meant he was still alive. But I couldn't be sure. I was even less sure than I'd been before.

I tore the end of the wrapping away. It was my Burns, all right. The sprig of white heather Mother had put in it showed plainly between the ends of the pages. I tossed the thing into my drawer and closed it.

Far out to the east, where grey of sky met grey of sea, a faint gleam showed and vanished as Cromarty Light blinked its message out into the gathering gloom. At my window there, alone, I felt like that. I too was waiting for a ship that might, or might not, come. There was nothing for me to do but wait.

*   *   *

CHAPTER 30

In Search Of Gerald

MY MIND WAS made up. I decided to go down to London. It would be easier to find Gerald there than waiting in Scotland.

A week later, I was on a train from London to St Albans, ready to start work as a café manageress. I had no knowledge of cafés or MDF regulations, but was quite convinced I could muddle through somehow. This would be my base for the time being.

On arriving, my hopes of muddling through sank right down to zero. I might have managed a small one, but this huge place, beautifully equipped and arranged, needed experience. As I entered and looked round, my first impulse was to run away, but the supervisor had seen me and came over to greet me. He showed me around, saying, 'Of course everything is in an awful mess, but I'm quite sure you'll straighten it out in no time.'

Strangely enough, I did straighten it out in spite of my ignorance, but my biggest nightmare was staff. The contrast between English staff and the staff I was used to in France was unbelievable. All I had were three teenagers for waitresses, one old cook, and one washing-up woman. To expect to serve three hundred lunches and the same number of dinners in the evening was too ludicrous for words, but with the help of the Army boyfriends of my waitresses, whom I called in, or rather bribed, we succeeded in keeping going.

There was no time to look for Gerald during the day, and by bedtime around midnight, or later, I was too tired to think. So for a short time, at least the pain of missing him eased. But there were always Sundays when we were closed. By ten, my mind would start its usual merry-go-round. I had to find him. Whether or not we ever managed to get married was unimportant. I thought of all the married people I knew. The best marriages never lasted; the rest just limped unattractively along towards the cemetery gates. But I also knew that Gerald did not believe in living together. I was still trying to get my world into focus, still looking for a way of life that would enable me to wake up every morning with pleasure, instead of dread and apathy. Self-pity would get me nowhere, and the War Office would tell me nothing. Once or twice, I started crying, but I controlled my tears and forced myself to keep calm. I just waited and waited, longing only for the opportunity to tell him that nothing was more important to me than his belief that I loved him enough to prevent anyone keeping us apart. Was his wife alive? How could I ever find out? The bombings in London had been so horrific. So many people had died, but then again, she didn't live there. She lived safely in Ireland. Gerald may have been in London!

Mondays were busy days, and one such day, as usual, I was helping with the tables. Then the strangest feeling came over me that someone was watching. Months under the German occupation had had the effect of giving me almost a sixth sense, of being on edge and aware of anyone closely watching me from behind. Before even seeing him, I felt that Gerald was standing there. I felt like shivering, but I moved as smoothly as if I had seen him only yesterday. He smiled in an attempt to dispel the awkwardness between us, and I searched without success for the words which would enable us to relax. I felt so outrageously happy I could imagine everybody taking one look at me in disgust and turning away.

The sight of him filled my life with a kind of radiance it didn't have before. It was only a few seconds, but it seemed much longer before we reached each other, and I was caught in a fierce embrace and could hardly breathe. It didn't matter; somehow I knew that everything was all right in his world. He had the air of a young man who suddenly found himself completely and helplessly in love for the first time. I knew his problems had been solved, but I had no intention at that particular moment of asking him how.

He asked me if I still loved him, and I told him I had room In my heart for only one person, and that was him, and no matter what happened, I would love him all my life. How I silently thanked God for bringing him safely home. As I held him close, I was aware of his warm body throbbing with life as he bent to whisper in my ear, 'I'm free. We can be married tomorrow.'

To me, marriage was not important, but to him, I knew it was the only way we could be together, and I was ecstatic for him. Somehow I knew we could make a success of it, sticking to proprieties. We were so right for each other, and I would believe in the sanctity of those vows and make up for all the unhappiness he'd had in his life. Whether or not our time together would be long or short, I would make every minute count. I closed my eyes and sat down and leaned back, surrendering myself to an emotion at last, quite commonplace—happiness.

*　　*　　*

Printed in Great Britain
by Amazon

35271884R00137